THE PATHS
SYMBOLIC KNOWLEDGE

CULTURAL STUDIES AND THE SYMBOLIC, 2

International Editorial Advisory Board

Professor Cyrus Hamlin (Yale)
Professor John Krois (Hamboldt-Universität, Berlin)
Professor Dr Barbara Naumann (Zurich)
Professor Dr Detlev Pätzold (Groningen)
Professor Dr Birgit Recki (Hamburg)

Previously published

Cultural Studies and the Symbolic, 1. Edited by Paul Bishop and R. H. Stephenson. Leeds: Northern Universities Press, 2003. ISBN: 1 904350 03 8

THE PATHS OF SYMBOLIC KNOWLEDGE

OCCASIONAL PAPERS IN CASSIRER AND CULTURAL-THEORY STUDIES, PRESENTED AT THE UNIVERSITY OF GLASGOW'S CENTRE FOR INTERCULTURAL STUDIES

Edited by

PAUL BISHOP AND R. H. STEPHENSON

MANEY

2006

All rights reserved: no part of this publication may be reproduced, stored in a retrieval system, or transmitted in any form or by any means, electronic, mechanical, photocopying or otherwise, without the written consent of the copyright holder.

Published by Maney Publishing, Suite 1C, Joseph's Well, Hanover Walk, Leeds LS3 1AB, UK; www.maney.co.uk

Maney Publishing is the trading name of W. S. Maney & Son Ltd
Typeset and printed by The Charlesworth Group, Wakefield, UK.

© The Centre for Intercultural Studies, University of Glasgow, 2006

ISBN 1-904350-27-5 (978-1-904350-27-9)

Front cover: Raphael, An Allegory ('Vision of a Knight'), about 1504; The National Gallery, London.

CONTENTS

		PAGE
Foreword by Paul Bishop and R. H. Stephenson		vii
Acknowledgements		xv
Contributors		xvii

1. Metabasis and Translation: Ernst Cassirer and Walter Benjamin on Language Theory
    by Barbara Naumann (Zurich) ... 1

2. Myth and Religion in Cassirer's Philosophy of Symbolic Forms
    by Louis Dupré (Yale) ... 15

3. Ernst Cassirer and Oswald Spengler: Two Philosophies of Culture in the Light of a Political Polemic
    by Dina Gusejnova (Cambridge) ... 28

4. Cassirer, Warburg, and the Irrational
    by Edward Skidelsky (Oxford) ... 42

5. 'Eine geistige Urform der geschichtlichen Erkenntnis'? Cassirer and Bachofen on the Symbol
    by Paul Bishop (Glasgow) ... 51

6. The Symbolization of Culture: Nietzsche in the Footsteps of Goethe, Schiller, Schopenhauer, and Wagner
    by Martine Prange (Groningen) ... 70

7. Schiller's 'Concrete' Theory of Culture: Reflections on the 200th Anniversary of his Death
    by R. H. Stephenson (Glasgow) ... 92

Index ... 118

FOREWORD

The famous story of the choice of Hercules is attributed to the Sophist thinker of the fifth century BC, Prodicos. In his *Memorabilia* (*Reminiscences of Socrates*), Xenophon relates how Socrates, in conversation with Aristippus, retells Prodicos' story of Hercules' encounter at the crossroads:

> When Hercules was passing from boyhood to youth's estate, wherein the young, now becoming their own masters, show whether they will approach life by the path of virtue or the path of vice, he went out into a quiet place, and sat pondering which road to take. And there appeared two women of great stature making towards him. The one was fair to see and of high bearing; and her limbs were adorned with purity, her eyes with modesty; sober was her figure, and her robe was white. The other was plump and soft, with high feeding. Her face was made up to heighten its natural white and pink, her figure to exaggerate her height. Open-eyed was she; and dressed so as to disclose all her charms. [. . .] When they drew nigh to Hercules, the first pursued the even tenor of her way: but the other, all eager to outdo her, ran to meet him, crying: 'Hercules, I see that you are in doubt which path to take towards life. Make me your friend; follow me, and I will lead you along the pleasantest and easiest road. You shall taste all the sweets of life; and hardship you shall never know [. . .].' Now when Hercules heard this, he asked, 'Lady, pray, what is your name?' 'My friends call me Happiness,' she said, 'but among those that hate me I am nicknamed Vice.' Meantime the other had drawn near, and she said, 'I, too, am come to you, Hercules: I know your parents and I have taken note of your character during the time of your education. Therefore I hope that, if you take the road that leads to me, you will turn out a right doer of high and noble deeds, and I shall be yet more highly honoured and more illustrious for the blessings I bestow. But I will not deceive you by a pleasant prelude: I will rather tell you truly the things that are, as the gods have ordained them. For of all things good and fair, the gods give nothing to man without toil and effort [. . .].' And Vice [. . .] answered and said, 'Hercules, mark you how hard and long is that road of joy, of which this woman tells? but I will lead you by a short and easy road to happiness.' And Virtue said, 'What good thing is thine, poor wretch, or what pleasant thing dost thou know, if thou wilt do nought to win them? [. . .] O Hercules, thou son of goodly parents, if thou wilt labour earnestly on this wise, thou mayest have for thine own the most blessed happiness.'[1]

The theme of the choice of Hercules became one frequently depicted in Western art, particularly in painting of the Renaissance and Baroque periods.[2] The story has been depicted by artists as diverse as Cranach the Elder, Benvenuto, Dürer, Rubens, Veronese, and Poussin. From the very beginning when it was first told by Prodicos, the story has been used to illustrate a fundamental philosophical choice. For this reason, a version by Paolo de Matteis was commissioned in 1712 by Shaftesbury as an illustration for *An Inquiry Concerning Virtue, or Merit* (1699), as emblematic of all moral decisions.[3] As Lawrence E. Klein has suggested, Shaftesbury turned the opposition of pleasure and virtue into a personal signature through his use of the story of the choice of Hercules in 'Moralists' [in his *Characteristicks of Men, Manners, Opinions, Times*] and in *A Notion of the Historical Draught or Tabulature of the Judgement of Hercules*.[4]

In a variant of the story, the figure of Hercules is replaced by the Roman hero Scipio Africanus, who has a dream in which Virtue and Pleasure contend for his allegiance.[5] The treatment of this theme by Raphael adorns the front cover of our own volume.[6] Within the Christian tradition, the motif could, stripped of its Classical, pagan associations, be transformed to represent the choice of the believer, as in the case of the vision of Catharine of Sienna.[7] Indeed, the Christian version of the choice of Hercules can be found in Christ's words in the Bible: 'Enter ye in at the strait gate: for wide is the gate, and broad is the way, that leadeth to destruction, and many there be which go in thereat: Because strait is the gate and narrow is the way, which leadeth it unto life, and few there be that find it.'[8] For the biocentric philosopher, Ludwig Klages, the story of the choice of Hercules as told by Prodicos was a perfect anticipation of the essence of Christianity.[9]

The motif surfaces both directly and indirectly in all kinds of different texts, in different ways. Bach's cantata BWV 213, composed in 1733, set to music a text by Christian Friedrich Henrici (known as Picander), in which the voices of Virtue and Vice vie for the attention of the hero. Then again, in the poems of Schiller (the 200th anniversary of whose death is being remembered in the year in which we are editing this volume), the motif of the choice of Hercules underlies several texts, most directly in 'Die idealische Freiheit' ['Ideal Freedom'] —

> *Aus dem Leben heraus sind der Wege zwei dir geöffnet:*
>   *Zum Ideale führt einer, der andre zum Tod.*
> *Siehe, daß du bei Zeiten noch frei auf dem ersten entspringest,*
>   *Ehe die Parze mit Zwang dich auf dem andern entführt.*

> Two high-ways before thee lie from realms of mortal breath;
>   One to the ideal land — the other leads to Death.
> Look that thou spring forth betimes on that ætherial way,
>   Ere on the downward road the Fates thy struggling soul convey.[10]

— and, more indirectly, in 'Die zwei Tugendwege' ['The Two Paths of Virtue'], in which the Virtuous path itself is divided into the twin ways of Striving and Endurance:

Zwei sind der Pfade, auf welchen der Mensch zur Tugend emporstrebt.
  Schließt sich der eine dir zu, tut sich der andre dir auf.
Handelnd erringt der Glückliche sie, der Leidende duldend.
  Wohl dem, den sein Geschick liebend auf beiden geführt!

Two are the paths by which Man may ascend to the summit of Virtue.
  Clos'd be the one, to his feet open the other is found.
Striving, the Fortunate Man attains her — the Suff'rer enduring.
  Happy! whose favouring Fate leads him by both to the goal.[11]

In fact, it is no exaggeration to describe the choice of Hercules as an icon, and as such it attracted the attention of one of the foremost members of the circle associated with the Warburg Circle, Erwin Panofsky (1892–1968); his monograph, *Hercules am Scheidwege* (1930), constitutes a major treatment of the theme and its significance in Western art from Antiquity to the Renaissance.[12] As Panofsky's analysis shows, the various treatments of the choice of Hercules demonstrate the significance of cultural continuity through the centuries. This point was made more generally by Goethe when, in his *West-östlicher Divan*, he wrote:

> *Wer nicht von dreitausend Jahren*
> *Sich weiß Rechenschaft zu geben,*
> *Bleib im Dunkeln unerfahren,*
> *Mag von Tag zu Tage leben.*
>
> Those who cannot draw conclusions
> From three thousand years of learning
> Stay naïve in dark confusions,
> Day to day live undiscerning.[13]

At the same time, the choice of Hercules, as well as embodying this cultural continuity, presents us with a challenge to our theoretical approach to culture. We can either take the easy path and accept the current hermeneutic orthodoxies of popular cultural studies, or we can, following Rilke's maxim that 'for a thing to be difficult is yet another reason for us to do it' (*daß etwas schwer ist, muß uns ein Grund mehr sein, es zu tun*),[14] and seek a more challenging, but potentially more enriching, account of culture and its significance. If we engage upon what Hegel called 'the labour of the concept' (*die Arbeit des Begriffs*),[15] then we undoubtedly choose the harder path; but we also choose what is, ultimately, the more rewarding one.

Such an account, and such a path, we find in the philosophy of culture articulated by Ernst Cassirer, particularly in its systematic presentation in *The Philosophy of Symbolic Forms* (1923–1929). For Cassirer, as the English art critic Herbert Read explained, it is 'only in so far as the mind uses the sensuous forms of word and image to express the realm of pure feeling' that it can maintain 'a complete hold on reality'.[16] Later philosophers, such as Susanne K.

Langer, developed Cassirer's philosophy of symbolic forms, applying it to the world of art as a whole in *Philosophy in a New Key* (1946), *Feeling and Form* (1953), and the three-volume work *Mind: An Essay on Human Feeling* (1967–1982).[17] In Read's words, the significance that 'these non-verbal, non-discursive forms of thought have for the development of human intelligence' is 'enormous', and 'to neglect them in favour of purely conceptual and discursive modes of thought is to leave the world of feeling unarticulated, unexpressed, with consequences that are individually neurotic and socially disastrous'.[18]

Through the work of the Centre for Intercultural Studies at the University of Glasgow and, in particular, through the AHRC-funded research project 'Conceptions of Cultural Studies in Cassirer's Theory of Symbolic Forms', we have made the choice and undertaken the task — truly Herculean! — of seeking to deepen our understanding of Cassirer's philosophy of culture and to promote interest in it among colleagues in the academic world and beyond. Forming part of this ongoing task, this volume brings together a collection of papers which reflect the broad sweep, both historical and theoretical, of Ernst Cassirer's philosophy of symbolic forms. For they range from language-theory to myth and religion; and all are set, with varying degrees of emphasis, in a comparative context. Cassirer's arguments are examined in relation to Walter Benjamin, Oswald Spengler, Aby Warburg, and Martin Heidegger, amongst other twentieth-century figures; while three of the major sources of Cassirer's ideas are studied from the perspective of cultural history: Goethe, Schiller, and Nietzsche.

Professor Barbara Naumann's paper (delivered as the fourth Ernst Cassirer Annual Lecture in the University of Glasgow in November 2003) examines the question of transition from symbolic form to symbolic form within Cassirer's overall schema. In 'Metabasis and Translation: Ernst Cassirer and Walter Benjamin on Language Theory', Naumann uncovers the fact that, although Cassirer operates with the concept of 'transformation' and not that of 'translation', language on his account may, broadly speaking, be understood as a form of translation from symbolic level to symbolic level. Comparison with Benjamin's apparently very different theory of translation reveals that (in both theories) translation is a universal factor in cultural life, even at the level of what at first sight may seem to be naïve, unmediated, experience.

In December 2004 Professor Louis Dupré delivered the University of Glasgow's fifth Ernst Cassirer Annual Lecture. Entitled 'Myth and Religion in Cassirer's Philosophy of Symbolic Forms', the lecture takes as its point of departure the question, raised by Heidegger, of whether in seeking to ground his scheme in myth Cassirer is not hampered by the epistemological constraints of Marburg neo-Kantianism. Rejecting the lack of empirical data in Schelling's (otherwise admirable) theory of myth, Cassirer also objects to nineteenth-century interpretations of myth as a kind of primitive science. He argues in his own account that the distinctive feature of myth lies in its distinctive symbolic *function*. But in stressing that myth justifies sacred time, in that the transient signifies what is eternal, Cassirer moves into the specifically religious sphere; and, at this point, the epistemological question hanging over Cassirer's thought takes on a different tincture: is Cassirer really in a position to distinguish adequately (immanent) myth from (transcendent) religion?

Three further contributions to this volume were first delivered in the context of the international conference entitled 'Cassirers Philosophie der Natur- und Geisteswissenschaften und der Moderne', held under the auspices of the Institute for Philosophy in Moscow in 2004. These papers have been substantially revised for publication in this volume. In Dina Gusejnova's contribution, 'Ernst Cassirer and Oswald Spengler: Two Philosophies of Culture in the Light of a Political Polemic', the comparison of Oswald Spengler's and Cassirer's cultural theories brings out a fruitful ambivalence on Cassirer's part. On the one hand, Cassirer is critical of Spengler's irrationalist and fatalistic tendencies; on the other, he admires the reach of Spengler's mystically tinged style. Cassirer's understanding of his own work as a positive *political* contribution is revealed in the context of Spengler's political stance, especially with regard to their respective reception of Goethe and reactions to the First World War. Within the widespread contemporary debate on 'culture' versus 'civilization', Cassirer seeks to expose Spengler's outlook as a modern form of (recurrent) myth-making, a stance that has obscured some important affinities between the two.

The affinity between Cassirer and the great art-historian Aby Warburg was very strong indeed. As Edward Skidelsky demonstrates in his paper, 'Cassirer, Warburg, and the Irrational', each man derived a great deal from the other in their common pursuit, that of understanding symbolic thought. Though both shared a view of culture as divided into various modes, Cassirer sought conciliation where Warburg discerned disparity. Yet both saw myth as the dynamic, disturbing element in the system of culture; and both saw the new barbarism of fascism as the culmination of a distinctively modern tendency, thus anticipating some central aspects of the Frankfurt School.

Paul Bishop's paper, '"Eine geistige Urform der geschichtlichen Erkenntnis?" Cassirer and Bachofen on the Symbol' provides an overview of the different approaches to myth or 'schools' in the twentieth century, as the context of Cassirer's engagement with this problem in his philosophy. Bishop points to the revival of myth as part of the Romantic project, which continued into the twentieth century in the form of the renaissance — and radicalization — of philology in Germany. The central figure in these developments, and a figure to whom Cassirer paid attention in his notes for the fourth volume of the *Philosophy of Symbolic Forms*, is Johann Jakob Bachofen, and Bishop's paper explores the affinities, and the differences, between Bachofen and Cassirer in their conceptions of the symbol and of symbolic form.

The remaining two papers introduce two other major figures to the debate on Cassirer: Nietzsche, and Schiller. The roots of the Apollonian-Dionysian tension are traced in some detail in Martine Prange's paper. Nietzsche, in coming to terms with versions of cultural symbolization in the works of Goethe, Schiller, Schopenhauer, and Wagner, presents the symbolizing power of art, on her account, as the great antidote, along with myth, to the bloodless Apollonianism of 'Socratic' culture.

Finally, Roger Stephenson's reflections on Schiller seek to bring out the apparent paradox that Schiller's thought, despite its demonstrable relevance to today's cultural theorizing, is almost universally neglected (except in those writings that are, wittingly or unwittingly, indebted to Cassirer's mediation of Weimar Classicism). As mentioned above, the year 2005 has seen many commemorative events on the occasion of the 200th anniversary of Schiller's death in 1805. As we had occasion to note in our 'Foreword' to the first collection in this series, a volume containing papers from a colloquium held at the University of Glasgow in 1999, the 200th anniversary of Goethe's birth in 1749 saw reports in the international press concerning the body of the poet. According to these reports, in November 1970 GDR scientists had unlocked Goethe's tomb in the royal vault in Weimar, exhumed the body from the sarcophagus, and removed it for cleaning and inspection.[19] This time, the international press carried a story surrounding the identity of the skull inside Schiller's coffin in the Weimar crypt. According to the report in the *Observer* newspaper, not everyone is sure that, when Schiller's body was moved from a mass grave in the cemetery in Weimar, the correct skull was identified.[20] Could Goethe, who temporarily kept Schiller's skull in his house when writing the poem known as 'Schillers Reliquien' ['Schiller's Remains'] (1826), which includes the lines —

> *Geheim Gefäß! Orakelsprüche spendend,*
> *Wie bin ich wert, dich in der Hand zu halten?*
> *Dich höchsten Schatz aus Moder fromm entwendend*
> *Und in die freie Luft, zu freiem Sinnen,*
> *Zum Sonnenlicht andächtig hin mich wendend.*
>
> Mysterious vessel, oracles declaring!
> Let fittingly me breach your dank immuring;
> In humble hand you, treasured prize, now bearing
> To open air, to sense in contemplation,
> I turn with reverence to the sunlight flaring.[21]

— could he have been looking at the wrong skull? Far removed from such journalistic speculation, Stephenson's historico-analytic survey of some of

Schiller's representative texts, poetic and theoretical, demonstrates, particularly by reference to the newly fashionable topic of identity-and-violence, that Schiller's cultural theory, like Cassirer's, can handle, with immense subtlety, precisely the same issues that animate our contemporary, 'postmodern' world of discourse.

In a recent introduction to contemporary cultural study, Ernst Cassirer's influence is unmistakable, although his *name* is never mentioned, not least in the definition of culture that the joint authors offer as 'referring to that entire range of institutions, artefacts and practices that make up our *symbolic universe*'.[22] The omission here of an explicit coming-to-terms with Cassirer is also surprising, because the German tradition of *Kulturwissenschaft* (from Herder to Habermas) is, for once, given respectful attention in the context of discussing versions of cultural theory available to the practitioners of cultural studies.[23] An opportunity has been missed to bring home Cassirer's conviction that all humanistic study is essentially intercultural, and that, if it is to progress, this fact needs to be raised to consciousness by the entertainment of the most adequate theory available. That Cassirer's own theory bids fare to help fulfil this vital task in our own day is the underlying message of all the contributions to this volume.

PAUL BISHOP

R. H. STEPHENSON

Notes

[1] Xenophon, *Memorabilia (Reminiscences of Socrates)*, Book II, 1, 21–34; in Xenophon, *Memorabilia and Oeconomicus; Symposium and Apology*, trans. by E. C. Marchant; and by O. J. Todd (Cambridge, MA; London: Harvard University Press; William Heinemann, 1968), pp. 95–103; translation adapted.

[2] Lucia Impelluso, *Gods and Heroes in Art*, ed. by Stefano Zuffi, trans. by Thomas Michael Hartmann (Los Angeles: The Paul J. Getty Museum, 2003), p. 108.

[3] Julia Annas, *Ancient Philosophy* (Oxford: Oxford University Press, 2000), pp. 37–38 and 41–43.

[4] Lawrence E. Klein, *Shaftesbury and the Culture of Politeness: Moral Discourse and Cultural Politics in Early Eighteenth-Century England* (Cambridge: Cambridge University Press, 1994), p. 62.

[5] See Silius Italicus, *Punica*, Book 15, 18–128; in Silius Italica, *Punica*, trans. by J. D. Duff, 2 vols (London; Cambridge, MA: William Heinemann; Harvard University Press, 1934), vol. 2, 327–35.

[6] Raphael's painting 'An Allegory ("Vision of a Knight")' (c. 1504) is in the National Gallery, London.

[7] According to one account, St Catharine had a vision in which Christ 'presented her with two crowns, one of gold and the other of thorns, bidding her choose which of the two she pleased. She answered, "I desire, O Lord, to live here always conformed to your passion, and to find pain and suffering my repose and delight". Then eagerly taking up the crown of thorns, she forcibly pressed it upon her head' (Alban Butler, *The Lives of the Fathers, Martyrs and other principal Saints, edited for Daily Use*, ed. by Bernard Kelly, 7th edn, 6 vols (London and Dublin: Virtue and Company, 1954), vol. 1, 434).

[8] Gospel according to St Matthew, 7: 13–14; cf. Gospel according to St Luke, 13: 24.

[9] Ludwig Klages, *Der Geist als Widersacher der Seele*, 6th edn (Bonn: Bouvier Verlag Herbert Grundmann, 1981), pp. 752–53.

[10] Friedrich Schiller, *Sämtliche Gedichte*, ed. by Jochen Golz (Frankfurt am Main and Leipzig: Insel, 1991), p. 283; *The Minor Poems of Schiller*, ed. and trans. by John Herman Merivale (London: William Pickering, 1844), p. 161.

[11] Schiller, *Sämtliche Gedichte*, p. 230; *The Minor Poems of Schiller*, p. 113.

[12] For further discussion, see Erwin Panofsky, *Hercules am Scheidewege und andere antike Bildstoffe in der neueren Kunst* [*Studien der Bibliothek Warburg*, vol. 18] (Leipzig and Berlin: B. G. Teubner, 1930; reprinted Berlin: Gebr. Mann Verlag [Edition Logos], 1997).

[13] Goethe, *Gedichte in zeitlicher Folge*, ed. by Heinz Nicolai (Frankfurt am Main: Insel Verlag, 1982), p. 855; J. W. von Goethe, *Poems of the West and East: West-Eastern Divan — West-Östlicher Divan: Bi-Lingual Edition of the Complete Poems*, trans. by John Whaley (Berne, Berlin, Frankfurt am Main: Peter Lang, 1998), p. 189.

[14] *Briefe an einen jungen Dichter*, letter to Franz Xaver Kappus of 14 May 1904 (Rainer Maria Rilke, *Werke: Kommentierte Ausgabe in vier Bänden*, ed. by Manfred Engel, Ulrich Fülleborn, Horst Nalewski, August Stahl (Frankfurt am Main: Insel Verlag, 1996), vol. 4, 534).

[15] *Phänomenologie des Geistes*, 'Vorrede' (G. W. F. Hegel, *Werke*, ed. by Eva Moldenhauer and Karl Markus Michel, 20 vols (Frankfurt am Main: Suhrkamp, 1986), vol. 3, 65).

[16] Herbert Read, 'Education Through Art' (1963), in *Selected Writings: Poetry and Criticism* (London: Faber and Faber, 1963), pp. 361–75 (p. 372).

[17] See Susanne K. Langer, *Philosophy in a New Key: A Study in the Symbolism of Reason, Rite, and Art* (Cambridge, MA, and London: Harvard University Press, 1942); *Feeling and Form: A Theory of Art developed from 'Philosophy in a New Key'* (London: Routledge and Kegan Paul, 1953); and *Mind: An Essay on Human Feeling*, 3 vols (Baltimore: Johns Hopkins Press, 1967–1982). For further discussion of Langer's work and its significance, see Peter A. Bertocci, 'Susanne K. Langer's Theory of Feeling and Mind', *Review of Metaphysics*, 23 (1970), 527–51; and Arthur C. Danto, 'Mind as Feeling; Form as Presence: Langer as Philosopher', *The Journal of Philosophy*, 81, no. 11 (November 1984), 641–47.

[18] Read, 'Education Through Art', p. 372.

[19] *Goethe 2000: Intercultural Readings of his Work* (Leeds: Northern Universities Press, 2000), 'Foreword', p. x.

[20] See Luke Harding, 'Tale of two skulls divides Germany', *The Observer*, 8 May 2005.

[21] Goethe, *Gedichte in zeitlicher Folge*, p.1071; Goethe, *Selected Poems*, trans. by John Whaley (London: J. M. Dent, 1998), p. 147.

[22] Andrew Milner and Jeff Browitt, *Contemporary Cultural Theory: An Introduction* [1991] (London: Routledge, 2002), p. 5 (our emphasis).

[23] Milner and Browitt, *Contemporary Cultural Theory*, pp. 22–25.

ACKNOWLEDGEMENTS

We should like to thank the speakers who accepted our invitation to address the Centre for Intercultural Studies and have offered their papers for publication. Our special thanks go to Meta Jamison for her kind assistance with technical matters in the preparation of this volume.

It is a pleasure to acknowledge that both our editorial work and our individual contributions were made possible by the award to the Centre by the Arts and Humanities Research Council (AHRC) of a Large Research-Grant for a five-year project (2002–2007) on 'Conceptions of Cultural Studies in Cassirer's Theory of Symbolic Forms'.

PB
RHS

CONTRIBUTORS

PAUL BISHOP is Professor of German at the University of Glasgow. He recently edited *Nietzsche and Antiquity: His Reaction and Response to the Classical Tradition* (2004) and he is the co-author (with R. H. Stephenson) of *Friedrich Nietzsche and Weimar Classicism* (2005). He is currently working on a monograph examining the relationship between analytical psychology and Weimar classicism.

LOUIS DUPRÉ was T. Lawrason Riggs Professor of the philosophy of religion at Yale University. He is a foreign member of the Belgian Royal Academy of Letters, Arts and Sciences, and a member of the American Academy of Arts and Sciences. In addition to having written fifteen books, four collective works, and some two hundred articles, he has received numerous honorary degrees. He has just completed a long study on the Enlightenment that will appear with Yale University Press, and at present he is working on a study of religion and Romanticism.

DINA GUSEJNOVA is currently a doctoral student at Cambridge working on interwar German intellectual circles, with a particular interest in the Stefan George circle and the network of Count Harry Kessler. Her present paper in this volume is based on her earlier work as part of the MPhil programme in political thought and intellectual history at Cambridge, the focus of which was Ernst Cassirer.

BARBARA NAUMANN is Professor of German and Comparative Literature in the Deutsches Seminar of Zurich University. Her research fields include German and European literature of the eighteenth to twentieth centuries, literature and the arts, and cultural and gender studies; she is currently engaged on a research project into mediality and transference in literature. The author of *Musikalisches Ideen-Instrument: Das Musikalische in Poetik und Sprachtheorie der Frühromantik* (1990) and *Philosophie und Poetik des Symbols: Cassirer und Goethe* (1998), her most recent publications include *Bilder — Denken: Bildlichkeit und Argumentation* (2004) (edited with Edgar Pankow), *Rhythmus — Spuren eines Wechselspiels in Künsten und Wissenschaften* (2005), and editing volume 10 of the Ernst-Cassirer-Nachlaßausgabe, *Kleine Schriften zur Goethe und zur Geistesgeschichte* (2005).

MARTINE PRANGE lectures at the Institute for Philosophy at the University of Groningen (The Netherlands), where she is working on a dissertation entitled 'Nietzsche's Ideal Europe', a study of the development of Nietzsche's cultural ideals for Europe in relation to his musical aesthetics. Her book on Nietzsche's *The Gay Science* has recently been published under the title *Lof der Méditerranée: Nietzsches vrolijke wetenschap tussen noord en zuid* (2005). Forthcoming publications will examine Schillerian aesthetics in Nietzsche's early work and Nietzsche's relation to Italy.

EDWARD SKIDELSKY is a writer living in Sussex. He has recently completed, as a doctoral thesis at Oxford, an intellectual biography of Cassirer, entitled *Ernst Cassirer: Between Myth and Reason*. He is also a regular contributor to the *TLS*, *Prospect*, *New Statesman*, and the *Telegraph*, on subjects including philosophy, religion, and German and Russian history.

R. H. STEPHENSON is William Jacks Professor of German at the University of Glasgow, and Director of its Centre for Intercultural Studies. He has published widely on various aspects of German and comparative literature and thought, including monographs on Goethe's wisdom literature, his conception of science, and (with Paul Bishop) on *Friedrich Nietzsche and Weimar Classicism* (2005).

METABASIS AND TRANSLATION: ERNST CASSIRER AND WALTER BENJAMIN ON LANGUAGE THEORY

By BARBARA NAUMANN

In Ernst Cassirer's works the word 'translation' cannot be found. Particularly in *The Philosophy of Symbolic Forms,* but also in other essays concerning the problem of symbols, Cassirer traced and retraced the development of myth, language, technology and science, and with the analysis and phenomenology of these forms he formulated the core of his philosophical work. Although in Cassirer's works one does indeed find a continuous discussion of an inner connection between the symbolic forms, after a second reading one can only conclude that he never mentions the translation of the various symbolic forms. Even where Cassirer discusses language in the narrower sense of the term, he describes the transformation processes of various linguistic forms without using the word 'translation'. Can we conclude from this that, for Cassirer, the theme of translation did not belong to the field of philosophically interesting questions? Or is this an indication that in the context of symbolic philosophy he developed a different terminology in order to treat what in linguistic theory is referred to as translation and translatability?

In this paper, these questions will be discussed with reference to Cassirer's remarks on language, symbol and representation. And here we can draw an obvious comparison with that contemporary of Cassirer's who developed the theme of translation as a key to a general theory of language: Walter Benjamin. Particularly Benjamin's early essay 'On Language in General and on the Human Language' ['Über Sprache überhaupt und die Sprache des Menschen'] (1916) as well as his famous study 'The Task of the Translator' ['Die Aufgabe des Übersetzers'] (1923) develop the perspectives of translation continually transpiring in language and in art, a translation that nevertheless must always fail. These appear to be perspectives that stand in complete contradiction to Cassirer's conception of linguistic transformation.

I should like to begin my reflections on the relationship between translation and symbolic transformation with a short poem. It was written by an author Ernst Cassirer could not have known, and it deals with a lyric moment that has no direct correlative in Cassirer's theory of language and philosophy of symbols. Nevertheless, this small lyric text clearly illustrates what I would like to discuss in the field of linguistic theory: a 'symbolic approach to the world',[1] a technique and process that reflects a fundamental transformability of symbolic forms that can be understood as a result of translation. The poem, written by the Danish poetess Inger Christensen, describes someone looking up at the heavens and the process of linguistic cognition that takes place as this person is looking:

> I see the light clouds
> I see the light sun
> I see how they lightly
> Depict an endless path
>
> As if they felt trust
> In me, standing on the earth,
> As if they knew that I
> Am their words.[2]

In the course of this poem the observation of the clouds and the sun inspires an intention that finds expression in poetic language. At the same time, the observation contains a process that is unforeseeable, since the conjunctional phrase 'as if they knew' marks an uncertainty related to the result expressed in language. The 'seeing' described in the poem could be referred to as a translation of natural observation into poetic language, if only there were not that small irritation. It lies in the verb 'to be'. For the poem tells us that 'I am their words', and not 'I mean' or 'express' their words. Here we recognize a paradoxically constructed subjectivity that, although it thinks of itself as 'small and insignificant', nevertheless 'admits it can correspond to the world, even if it cannot create the world'.[3] This is the poem's real achievement: in language it creates a correspondence with the world, a worldly structure. I would like to take this structure as my point of departure in order to reflect upon a characteristic of Ernst Cassirer's linguistic theory.

Cassirer also interprets the symbolic approach to the world as the only possible manifestation of the world itself, although in Cassirer's texts it is not a matter of poetic representations in the narrower sense of the word. An ellipsis like the one in Inger Christensen's poem that introduces the lyric subjectivity with the self-being of language can also be found in Cassirer's works: his theory of language also dispenses with a sketch of translation from one symbolic sphere to another. On closer examination Cassirer's evasion or concealment of the term 'translation' is curious. For there is scarcely another philosophical œuvre of the twentieth century that is as concerned with the relationship between the individual cultural forms, their dynamics and their interaction, as Cassirer's. No other theory appears to place the transformation processes of language and culture as firmly at the centre of attention. Indeed, in his theory of the development of language Cassirer formulates the basic characteristics of a relationally and processually developing philosophy of symbols. It appears that translation processes are an integral part of the development of symbolic forms. In the following I shall characterize in more detail the manner in which Cassirer regards this problem.

At the beginning of his linguistic theory, Cassirer poses the question of the genesis of 'expression', 'representation', and 'meaning'. These three terms construct a sequence of stages in both the linguistic-historical sense as well as in regard to an increasing abstraction, which at its highest level is referred to as 'pure meaning'. The three symbolic steps of the mimetic, the analogical, and the purely symbolic function of language correspond to the sequential stages leading to abstraction. In still other works, Cassirer continually applied the sequential model in order to illustrate the indirect and mediate modus of the symbol in the varying contexts of pre-scientific (mythic) and scientific cognition.[4] Cassirer reconstructs the process of the increasing abstraction of the symbolic as the path of the sign from fetish to scientific formula and he thus chooses the increasing abstraction as his central thread in the historical development of the process of cognition. In its course, the step from one level to the next, the transformation from one symbolic approach to the world to the next, is a particular problem. The question of the dynamic motivating this step, and in what form it transpires, can be understood as a question of translation. Symbolic processes of transformation or transposition in language take place, according to Cassirer, already at the first level, the pure phonetic expression of, for example, pain, joy, fear, etc. Cassirer's philosophical position in linguistic theory can be characterized by the fact that neither the object itself nor its perception is connected with the original application of language, but rather a human *activity*: the activity of a first articulation that he understands as an activity of transformation. In this first transformation Cassirer recognizes not only the representation of things or relations, but already a certain form of 'knowledge', and thus a certain form of abstraction, however it may be constructed. For that reason he referred to the process of the first articulation as a change of levels, or more precisely, as a transition to another form or genre of knowledge: 'The mere space of activity becomes a space of sight; the field of action becomes a field of vision. And in this very transition, this *metabasis eis allo genos*, language plays an essential role.'[5]

The phrase *metabasis eis allo genos*, literally a 'transition' into another genre, is one of the most often-used philosophical terms in Cassirer's works, and it appears in argumentative contexts in which linguistic processes of translation or transition in the sphere of language are being described. *Metabasis* is Cassirer's key term for the process of symbolic translation.[6] It is noteworthy that this expression carried negative connotations in ancient philosophy (for example, in Aristotle's works); it was used to classify an inadmissible movement of thought, a leap in categories, and thus a logical error. Cassirer almost always uses this term positively. He applies the term in order to underscore a processual modus. The *metabasis* is an activity of thought and cognition, in a certain sense an unforeseen course of perception that is transposed into another symbolic form.[7] It is obvious that with the use of this term Cassirer indicates not only the change between categories, but also a blank space, a lacuna, since the word *metabasis* itself contains the sense of transition in movement, a leap through or passing over. In this leaping movement Cassirer senses an insatiable moment in the symbolic process, and thus also a lacuna on the level of the temporality and causality of language development that must be continually reflected upon.

In reference to the 'transition from nature to culture' in his collection of essays *On the Logic of Cultural Sciences* (1942) Cassirer wrote that this transition

> offers us in this respect a new puzzle. It only confirms what natural observation teaches us: that every genuine development is basically a *metabasis eis allo genos* that we can designate, but we can no longer explain causally. Experience and thought, empiricism and philosophy are all in the same position here. They both have no other way to define the 'suchness', the 'an-sich' of man than to illustrate it in its manifestations. The only way they can gain knowledge of the 'essence' of man is to view man in culture and in the mirror of culture; but they cannot turn around the mirror of culture in order to see what is behind it.[8]

Man's linguistic activity obtains from the world of things its articulations without being mimetically bound to it. On a number of occasions in his works Cassirer criticizes the notion that linguistic development is guided first and foremost by mimetic moments; he points out that in linguistic activity itself there is already a construction of a certain approach to the world that distinguishes the givenness of things and differentiates their specific contours and position in a symbolic system.[9] The accentuation of symbolic relations is one of the consequences Cassirer draws from Kant's critical insight into the constitution and construction of human experience. In reference to the development of a child's language, Cassirer documents the first phase of man's use and creation of language with the phrase 'a hunger for names'.[10] The child's hunger for names or the 'obsession with giving names' to things represents a sort of Adamitic naming using a system of sounds that at the same time serves the development 'and fixation of certain objective notions'.[11] Even this first step in language transpires, according to Cassirer, in an atmosphere of freedom, since for Cassirer, there lies in the childlike — as well as the mythic — naming of things an opening to the world, an expression of independence that allows man to 'intervene in the world and rebuild it for himself independently'.[12] The quasi Adamitic name-giving does not know of any division between 'word' and 'thing', but it is characterized by the fact that 'the word is rather an objective component of the thing, indeed it comprises its actual essence'.[13] On this level one could say that expression and meaning coincide, since all sensual aspects of pronunciation can potentially become carriers of meaning. And yet neither in this first linguistic process nor in the more abstract linguistic processes on the level of representation or pure meaning do we find mimetic or mirroring processes. With this consequential rejection of theories of imitation Cassirer is following the linguist Wilhelm von Humboldt. Cassirer notes, for example: 'In each of the signs it creates, the mind comprehends the object while at the same time comprehending itself and the rules of its own creativity' (PsF, 1, 26). Cassirer attributes the expression of human freedom in this self-reflexive act to every original mental activity. Even the ability, already in the act of name-giving, to find a language, to take an active approach to the world and to structure the world symbolically is in a sense an expression of a free self-reflexive act. The origin, also the origin of language in Cassirer's philosophy, is thus neither related to existential force, nor to metaphysical uncertainty, but is rather related to an *Urphänomen*, an inexplicable original manifestation of symbolic pregnance which things can obtain for the human.

Although there is an unflagging post-Kantian cognitive optimism in this conception, still another, more far-reaching impulse can be found in the term 'symbolic pregnance'. Cassirer's critique is aimed at an instrumental and medial conception of language. Language, in Cassirer's view, is a living form of ubiquitously transpiring processes of transformation. And these processes are thus also processes of translation that obtain a positive character through the creation of meaning. Only when we begin to understand language as a system of references creating meaning, a system of symbolic references, can we do justice to its constructive and, in Cassirer's sense, abstract character.

The question of the origin of the transformational function of language, or in other words, the ubiquitous translation of language, is always implied in Cassirer's symbolic philosophy. When we read Cassirer's statement that '[a]long with the purely cognitive function of language, the function of linguistic thought and the function of artistic observation must be considered in a manner that reveals how together they complete not only a very specific construction *of* the world, but also and moreover a very specific approach *to* the world, to an objective complex of meaning and to an objective contemplative whole' (PsF, 1, 11), we find that herein lies a continuous reference to the central role of the Kantian critique of the impossibility of a conception of a thing in itself, a 'Ding an sich'. It is only the insight into the fact that things not in themselves, but rather in their appearances for humans, are given, that allows the concept of cognition to take on fixed contours. This implies a process leading to a contemplative manifestation of things, and thus also to the thought that a thing in itself is not available to direct contemplation. Since this thing in itself is unapproachable and cannot be directly translated, translation itself must always transport the unnamable point of departure of language that makes all speech appear as symbolic. For this reason Cassirer speaks of symbolic transformations and not of translations. If a structuring act leading to the world and thus to the creation of meaning comprises the central symbolic function of language, then one could equally understand language in the broad sense as a form of translation. The line quoted from Inger Christensen's poem about the clouds — 'that I am their language' — could, in this context, be read as a translation that is at the same time a symbolic linguistic construction and an approach to the world.

Cassirer's linguistic theory, like his theory of symbols, is a doctrine of meaning, a theory of the 'sense' that sensual forms obtain on various levels of abstraction. The peculiarity of a linguistic construction of the world is comprehended here in relation to its coherence. In the always-specific manner of inner coherence lies the character of every symbolic form. Between the developmental stages of languages as between language and non-linguistic methods of comprehending experience one must always assume that there are continual processes of translation. Cassirer refers to these processes of *metabasis* as discontinuities. One can fairly assume that for Cassirer traditional theories of translation were too strongly bound to conceptions of similarity and continuity and that they thus were of no interest to him. By contrast, the *metabasis* accentuates via discontinuity a moment within inexplicable and undifferentiatable processes in the course of obtaining a symbolic approach to the world. In another passage in the third volume of *The Philosophy of Symbolic Forms*, entitled *The Phenomenology of Symbolic Forms*, Cassirer gave to this discontinuous and indeterminable point of departure in the symbolic process the name 'symbolic pregnance' (PsF, 3, 235). That things themselves can obtain a symbolic pregnance and thus turn from being mute, expressionless, and — as far as the individual is concerned — meaningless objects of one's surroundings into sensual and ultimately meaningful things is in itself another *metabasis*. The *metabasis* lies in the differential character of symbolic pregnance. It marks the place where symbolic philosophy raises the question of the origin of language.

A Comparison with Walter Benjamin

Here at last we can take a comparative look at Walter Benjamin's theory of language and translation. As we know, Benjamin developed his theory of translation in the so-called 'Translator essay' from his experience with his translations of Baudelaire, particularly the 'Tableaux parisiens'. Thus Benjamin's point of departure is different from Cassirer's, for whom the philological task and practice of translating between various languages plays no particular role at all. But it is still apparent that Benjamin's theory of translation also implies a fundamental theory of language, and in this sense it bears a certain relationship to the critique of cognition Cassirer offers us.[14] It is impossible to reduce Benjamin's theory of translation to a commentary on the difficulties that result from translating an œuvre from one national language to another. Already in his early essay 'On Language in General and on Human Language' Benjamin focuses upon a general and, at this stage, theologically informed theory that is developed by using the term 'translation' in reference to a translation from the language of God to the mute language of things and from there to a human semiotic language.

Like Cassirer, Benjamin works with a transformational model. But Benjamin begins by differentiating between various languages and their problematical relationships to each other. When, in his early text on translation, Benjamin establishes a differentiation by using the theological or linguistic-magical image of the loss of a unified, singular, *divine* and 'cognitive language',[15] he draws a conclusion that is astonishingly similar to Cassirer in one point. Namely: in the practice of giving names, in the original act of pronouncing a name, Benjamin sees the most significant aspect of human expression: 'The translation of the language of things into the language of humans is not only a translation of the mute into that of the phonetic, it is also a translation of the nameless into the named' (GS, 2.1, 151). Where, however, Cassirer recognizes here the opening of a linguistic movement departing from symbolic pregnance, from symbolic cognition and a symbolic construction as an approach to the world, Benjamin's early translation theory is more concerned with the loss: first, the lost of a metaphysical perfection, the loss of the divine language due to the passage into an inner-worldly linguistic differentiation, and then, as a result of this, the loss of the immanence of cognition *in* and *as* language.

Benjamin's Adamitic concept of language is articulated in the critical linguistic tradition of Jewish thought which — following the Jewish enlightenment, the Haskala — once again studied the rabbinical discussions from the age preceding this enlightenment. The background of the theory concerning the origin of language led to the question: in which language did God create the world and the things inhabiting it? By returning to the problem of translation in the framework of language in general, '*Sprache überhaupt*', Benjamin adds to the problem of translation a linguistic-critical transformation. It becomes a determination of the general modus in which language is thought and exists. Although he is not able to offer an answer to the question of the origin of language, Benjamin manages to find in the Adamitic naming of things a shorthand formula that leaves open the linguistically and historically precarious question, and makes it a point of departure for a modern theory of meaning. The confrontation with the Adamitic naming of things evokes the problem of finding a language that envisages the intention to mean as motivated by the loss of a unified meaning.

For Cassirer, by contrast, the symbolic activity is not characterized by a loss, but rather it becomes first and foremost an expression of human freedom leading to an abstract understanding of the world. The symbolic activity is based upon an 'act of freedom, upon a "point of view which reason gives to itself". [. . .] But here, again, as everywhere else, true freedom is not a contradiction to a bond or obligation; it is rather its beginning and origin' (PsF, 3, 492). Thus Cassirer's theory in his *Phenomenology of Symbolic Forms*. Already in the voracious appetite of children for giving names Cassirer recognizes such aspects of freedom. By contrast, Benjamin's Adamitic name-giving, the first act of translation of a 'language of things' into a not yet arbitrary human language,[16] is characterized by a spontaneously given but nevertheless at the same time *necessary* naming.

With the use of human language as a form of cognition, history enters into Benjamin's conception of language. Language must now be thought of as a plethora of various languages in a continuous historical process. This gives rise to the relationship of arbitrariness and semioticity which was for Benjamin an indication of the fall from the divine and unified language of names.[17] Benjamin associates historicity with the notion of the catastrophic discontinuity of languages. In the rise of the differentiation of languages and their search for a no longer immediately available meaning, abstraction and cognition begin, but also the necessity for translation, which is thus an indication of the absence of original meaning.[18] A network of correspondences and disfigured similarities characterizes the linguistic world Benjamin sketches for us.[19] The activity of the translator is, in the context of this network of correspondences and disfigurations, unavoidably confronted with difficulties, since reliable relational similarities have disappeared and a seamless act of transformation, or rather an act of transformation without loss, can no longer occur. The unavoidable failure of the translator, or in other words, the task of the translator, is for Benjamin an expression of the deficient relationship of the individual languages to each other, and an indication of the fundamental metaphysical lack existing in the relationship between language, expression, the 'type of intending' something, and meaning. In the 'Translator essay' Benjamin writes:

> In order to comprehend the real relationship between original and translation, one has to contemplate a consideration whose intention is certainly analogous to the paths of thought in which the critique of cognition traverses in order to prove the impossibility of a theory of reflection. Where it shows that in cognition no objectivity is possible, not even the claim to objectivity, if it consisted in reflections of reality, here it can be proven that no translation would be possible if it attempted to be essentially a similarity with the original. (GS, 4.1, 12)[20]

Translation in the naïve sense of a precise correspondence between the original and the translation — the often discussed faithfulness to form and/or content — is, according to this theory, categorically impossible, since already the original has no ahistorical sense that could be transposed into any number of linguistic forms. Added to the historical change to which every work is subjected throughout its reception is another complication facing the translation: in the linguistic form of every work, in what Benjamin refers to as the 'type of intending', a specific untranslatable core is contained. Benjamin's term 'pure language' is aimed at this non-transformable 'magical' aspect of language. The task of the translator consists in the struggle against losing sight of that unattainable 'pure language' and in finding a 'type of intending' in another language and another manner of writing which, although necessarily different, ought to have a relationship of similarity with the type of intending in the original text. But here Benjamin shifts the aim of his reflections on translation from a metaphysical and theologically informed linguistic theory in his early essay to a theory of the necessary losses and necessary disfigurations characteristic of every linguistic translation and (since every language is translation) of every linguistic application. Benjamin replies to the disjunction between the 'intended' and the 'type of intending', the disjunction between word and sentence (GS, 4.1, 14) that proves that all faithful translation is impossible, with a symbolic term:

> There remains in all languages and in all their structures not only that which is communicated, but also that which cannot be communicated, something symbolizing or symbolized that varies according to the context. That which is symbolizing lies only in the limited structures of the language; but that which is symbolized lies in the development of the language itself. And that which is striving to represent itself, or even to create, in the development of languages — that is the core of pure language itself. (GS 4.1, 19)

The symbolic in language thus indicates that there can no longer be a unified and original language, a totality of pure language. In the passage I have just quoted, the theological and melancholic motif of the lost unity of language remains the contextual background, even if here it is bereft of its messianic promise of deliverance.[21]

The basic characteristics of Benjamin's theory of translation have been discussed in detail in various studies. So I will not continue to present it here; instead, let us place in perspective the correspondences and differences between a melancholic theory of translation that appeals to a unifying but nevertheless lost linguistic and metaphysical background, and Cassirer's theory of language and transformation, which is obviously rooted in the cultural context and in cultural differentiations. Benjamin's concept of symbol is a reaction to the theologically informed figure of loss. And especially here, even in the secular theory of the 'Translator essay', Benjamin retains a melancholic relationship to metaphysics. Cassirer's model of the symbol, which begins with the notion of symbolic pregnance, would appear at first glance to be more positive, cognitively more optimistic, even more naïve. But it is possible to demonstrate that this model also has an irreducible negativity. For it develops the formation of the symbolic approach to the world not only in the direction of pregnance, but also as a path of increasing abstraction. In Cassirer's linguistic pluriversum the individual is oriented not so much in an existing, an already created world, but rather in a world that he alone creates for himself, however inadequate it may be. Herein lies a significant similarity to Benjamin's thought on language, which takes its point of departure from the Adamitic language of names. In both theories, in Benjamin's and in Cassirer's, the task of the translator is thus, if not in name, than in deed, a ubiquitous task. Benjamin interprets it as a reaction to a concealed meaning, whereas Cassirer describes it as a transformational product, as a construction of meaning in a non-linear transformation (*metabasis*) from one form to another.

Symbol Theory as Translation Theory

One could say that, for Cassirer, symbol theory has always been a theory of translation, but a theory of translation in which no other concept of translation can be formulated, since his theory does not presuppose the existence of different spheres of language that could be projected into one another. Transitions, transpositions, transformations and constructions build in a general way the constant motifs and forms of movement of symbolic philosophy. That symbolic constructions can always be thought of as translatable into each other is obvious in the omniscience of the term *metabasis*.

Cassirer attributes a function and a dignity to the term 'symbol' that historically for years has been absorbed only by semiotic theory. But the historical and linguistic volume of the *Philosophy of Symbolic Forms* does not do justice to his claim. For Cassirer offers only an abbreviated historical assessment of the change from the pre-linguistic sign to linguistic meaning, the process of signification. Instead of a precise historical description of the origin of signification we find an analysis of a general symbol-generating principle, namely 'symbolic pregnance'.

It is of particular significance for the history of philosophy that Cassirer also liberated the symbol from its Platonic or transcendental context.[22] Through the association of the symbolic with an immanent cultural and historical context Cassirer not only manages to develop a newly defined cultural and historical concept of the symbol, he also opens fundamentally new paths for *critical* symbolic thought. It was obviously Cassirer's intention to understand the process of abstraction inherent in symbol-genesis, not as a belated process that lies on a different level by comparison with 'original' or primitive thought, which would thus have a different quality. In the narrow relation of symbol and thought that describes symbolic forms as a condition for the possibility of thought, the term 'translation' has no place of its own, although a process of translation is implied in it. Even the problem of the plurality of languages — for Benjamin a point of departure in his own reflections upon language — is entirely passed over in Cassirer's generalizing manner of explanation, since from the symbol theory point of view languages, as symbolic approaches to the world, must appear as essentially identical in their symbolic essence. Cassirer is thus interested in a theory of language *per se*; he is interested in the symbolic and linguistic 'being in the world' that thinks of the world as always already linguistically comprehended, although on different abstract levels of development.

Inger Christensen's poem offers us another indication of the translation theory inherent in the concept of the symbol, again a theory of translation which appears to have been subsumed in Cassirer's concept of the symbol. Christensen's poem not only shows us, as I mentioned, a subjective image of the universe. It also shows how the lyric subject as well as what it sees are both constituted in the act of contemplation of a symbolic — a linguistic — pregnance: in this case, the clouds and the heavens. The poem describes a transformational process in the symbolic potential of language, an approach to the world. In the symbolic form of the poem, the language of the clouds manifests itself as an 'as if' in speech. One could interpret the poem as a translation of the clouds into a human language: a human language that imagines the world and the clouds as 'knowing'. The clouds and the world become clouds and world in the symbolic act of lyric representation, 'as if they knew that I am their words'. As soon as the lyric moment presents us with a rich linguistic version of a subject, a process of linguistic structuring also sets in. It would be senseless to separate vision and expression, cognition and formulation, into an 'earlier' and 'later', into a temporal chain or into aspects of a causal relationship. Rather, the process of poetic structuring in language appears to mean all of this at one and the same time.

Cassirer studied just such a relationship of translation in his symbolic philosophy. He investigated the relation of literature and science, particularly with reference to Goethe. The manner in which Goethe develops a symbolic relationship between poetry and science brought Cassirer to recognize the necessary inner referentiality of symbolic forms. In this instance one could speak of a process of translation, and indeed Cassirer translated Goethe's comments on science into the logic of his own philosophical and cultural symbol theory. Cassirer's discussion of Goethe's comments on the relationship of poetry and science is a product of the fact that, in Goethe's works, Cassirer found that this relation had not only been reflected upon, but also treated in detail as a symbolic art form.[23] In this context it is also clear that in the modus of a symbolic structuring 'to' the world a process of translation is always implied, and it begins at a point of departure — a text as source, or the 'world' — that it cannot possess and cannot immediately know. Instead, the point of departure, like the symbolic process itself, is created in the act of translation. In the third volume of the *Philosophy of Symbolic Forms* Cassirer used the term 'symbolic pregnance' to refer to the possibility of initiating this process, and he uses this phrase to qualify an indefinable mobile foundation of the symbolic process as a sort of '*Ur*-phenomenon', a first phenomenon.[24]

The temporal coincidence of origin and movement, of the development of a point of departure or a text and its translation, is a fundamental characteristic of symbol-philosophy. Consequentially, symbol-philosophy does not differentiate thematically the notion of translation, although it does describe a movement of translation between the various symbolic forms. A translation as *metabasis* is a ubiquitous component, an aspect contributing to every symbolic form. For that reason we find ourselves confronted with the strange fact that translation itself is never referred to in Cassirer's works. But since things, or objects, do obtain a symbolic pregnance, Inger Christensen can also let them speak, so that they sketch 'an endless path,/As if they felt trust/In me, standing on the earth'.

Translation by BRIAN POOLE

Notes

[1] The German passage reads: 'Neben der reinen Erkenntnisfunktion gilt es, die Funktion des sprachlichen Denkens und die Funktion der künstlerischen Anschauung derart zu begreifen, daß daraus ersichtlich wird, wie in ihnen allen eine ganz bestimmte Gestaltung nicht sowohl *der* Welt, als vielmehr *zur* Welt, zu einem objektiven Sinnzusammenhang und einem objektiven Anschauungsganzen sich vollzieht' (Ernst Cassirer, *Philosophie der symbolischen Formen*, vol. 1, *Die Sprache* [1923] (Darmstadt: Wissenschaftliche Buchgesellschaft, 1988), 11). In this paper I also refer to *Philosophie der symbolischen Formen*, vol. 2, *Das mythische Denken* [1925] (Darmstadt: Primus Verlag, 1997), and *Philosophie der symbolischen Formen: Dritter Teil: Phänomenologie der Erkenntnis* (Darmstadt: Primus Verlag, 1997). Henceforth abbreviated as PsF, followed by volume number and page reference).

[2] For a commentary on this poem, see Harald Hartung, *Masken und Stimmen. Figuren der modernen Lyrik* (Munich: Hanser, 1996), p. 66. The original Danish poem reads: 'Jeg ser de 'lette skyer/Jeg ser den lette sol/Jeg ser hvor let de tegner/Et endeløst forløb/Som om de føler tillid/Til mig der står på jorden/Som om de ved at jeg / Er deres ord' (Inger Christensen, *Samlede digte* (Copenhagen: Gyldendal, 1991), poem no. 8 from the cycle 'Det' [1969], p. 331).

[3] Hartung, *Masken und Stimmen*, p. 266.

[4] In his essay 'Der Begriff der symbolischen Form im Aufbau der Geisteswissenschaften' (1923), Cassirer developed, even before the publication of the philosophy of symbolic forms, the basic three-step model, thereby referring to Goethe's famous essay on mimesis, mannerism, and style, 'Einfache Nachahmung der Natur, Manier, Stil' (see Cassirer, *Wesen und Wirkung des Symbolbegriffs* (Darmstadt: Wissenschaftliche Buchgesellschaft, 1983),

pp. 169–200 (especially pp. 181–82); and Goethe, *Werke* [Hamburger Ausgabe], ed. Erich Trunz, 12th edn, 14 vols (Munich: Beck, 1981), vol. 12, pp. 30–34).

[5] Ernst Cassirer, *Symbol, Technik, Sprache*, ed. by Ernst Wolfgang Orth and John Michael Krois (Hamburg: Meiner, 1985), p. 128.

[6] Cassirer's concept of metabasis as translation has proved fruitful also in other disciplines, for example, with the art historian and member of the Warburg circle Edgar Wind, who had started as a student of Cassirer's. In his book *Das Experiment und die Metaphysik*, Wind talks about how 'die Art des Eingehens [der Idee in die Welt, durch ihre künstlerische Realisierung — BN], die Form der Verkörperung, in den verschiedenen Gebieten des Geistes' is 'verschieden', but that 'allen gemeinsam ist aber die Tatsache, daß im Akt der Verkörperung eine μεταβασισ εισ αλλο γενοσ stattfindet, eine Selbsttranszendenz, die im Verlauf der sogenannten "Empirie" ihre metaphysische Bestätigung oder Verwerfung findet' (Edgar Wind, *Das Experiment und die Metaphysik: Zur Auflösung der kosmologischen Antinomien* (Tübingen: Mohr, 1934), p. 33). According to Wind, a work of art can only be conceived of as a translation into the formal language of art — and therefore as symbolic in a Cassirerian sense. Wind interprets the process of art-creation analogous to the way in which Cassirer generally outlines the transfer from one symbolic level to another. There is, however, one decisive difference between the two: Wind, as a critic of Renaissance art, does not adhere to the idea of increasing abstraction as the development of symbolic forms. For further discussion, see Bernhard Buschendorf's commentary on Wind, in Edgar Wind, *Heidnische Mysterien in der Renaissance* (Frankfurt am Main: Suhrkamp, 1987), pp. 396–415 (embodiment as metabasis is discussed in particular on p. 400).

[7] See Cassirer, *Symbol, Technik, Sprache*, p. 35, note 5.

[8] Ernst Cassirer, 'Formproblem und Kausalproblem', in *Zur Logik der Kulturwissenschaften: Fünf Studien* [1942] 5th edn (Darmstadt: Wissenschaftliche Buchgesellschaft, 1989), p. 62.

[9] Compare with Cassirer's comment: 'Der Gegenstand läßt sich nicht als ein nacktes Ansich unabhängig von den wesentlichen Kategorien der Naturerkenntnis, die seine eigene Form erst konstituieren, zur Darstellung bringen' (PsF, 1, 6). From this, the sciences have to draw the conclusion that the 'Anspruch auf eine "unmittelbare" Erfassung und Wiedergabe des Wirklichen' will have to be abandoned (ibid.).

[10] Cassirer here follows a work on language psychology by Clara and William Stern, *Die Kindersprache: Eine psychologische und sprachtheoretische Untersuchung* (Leipzig: J. A. Barth, 1928), p. 190; see Cassirer, *Symbol, Technik, Sprache*, p. 128.

[11] Cassirer, *Symbol, Technik, Sprache*, p. 129.

[12] Cassirer, *Symbol, Technik, Sprache*, p. 129.

[13] Cassirer, *Symbol, Technik, Sprache*, p. 129.

[14] Compare with Winfried Menninghaus, who explains the universalisation of the concept of translation, the 'Universalisierung des Übersetzungsbegriffs' in Benjamin's early essay on language (*Walter Benjamins Theorie der Sprachmagie* (Frankfurt am Main: Suhrkamp, 1980), p. 52.)

[15] Walter Benjamin, *Gesammelte Schriften*, ed. by Rolf Tiedemann and Hermann Schweppenhäuser, 7 vols in 15 (Frankfurt am Main: Suhrkamp, 1972–1989), 2.1, 152. Henceforth abbreviated as GS, followed by volume number and page reference.

[16] On this level, Benjamin sees an intimate relation between perceiving and naming, '*Anschauung*' and '*Benennung*' as well as a divine objectivity ('von Gott verbürgte Objektivität') (GS, 2.1, 152).

[17] Thus also in the 'language essay' (GS, 2.1, 152). The silent word in the being of things, 'das stumme Wort im Dasein der Dinge', is far below the naming acitivity of humans, 'das benennende Wort in der Erkenntnis des Menschen'. Only in a cognitive language, 'Sprache der Erkenntnis und des Namens', after a process of translating, 'Übersetzung', could the language of things be understood — but then this language would already have to be one of various possible languages, a language that could also function otherwise, and therefore it can no longer contain immanent meaning (ibid.).

[18] See Paul de Man, 'Schlußfolgerungen: Walter Benjamins "Die Aufgabe des Übersetzers"', in Alfred Hirsch (ed.), *Übersetzung und Dekonstruktion* (Frankfurt am Main: Suhrkamp, 1997), pp. 182–230 (see particularly pp. 200–01).

[19] See Sigrid Weigel, *Entstellte Ähnlichkeit* (Frankfurt am Main: Fischer, 1997), pp. 84–85.

[20] This quotation, as well as the 'Translator essay' in general, has been extensively commentated on by Paul de Man (see 'Schlußfolgerungen', pp. 194–95). In this context I should like to stress that the neo-Kantian philosopher Hermann Cohen cannot be regarded as a common background figure for Benjamin and Cassirer. Both Benjamin and Cassirer, independently of each other, did intensively study Cohen's works and even studied with him; but both soon adopted an intellectual position different from Cohen's theory. In the above quoted passage, Benjamin's critical position in relation to Kant as well as in relation to Cohen finds its expression. Benjamin, in letters to Gershom Scholem, even criticized a *Realitätsschwindel*, a fallacy of reality, on the neo-Kantian's part; and this formed one of several reasons for him to separate himself strictly from neo-Kantian epistemology and its deductive method. For further discussion of Benjamin's argument, see Stelio Mazziotti, 'Benjamin und Cohen. Ein Vergleich von Wahlverwandtschaften', in Klaus Garber and Ludger Rehm (eds), *global benjamin*, vol. 2 (Munich: Fink, 1999), 943–48.

[21] See Paul de Man, 'Schlußfolgerungen', pp. 205–07.

[22] The history of the sign and symbol relationship from mediaeval times to the twentieth century is described by Julia Kristeva, 'Der geschlossene Text', in Peter V. Zima (ed.), *Textsemiotik als Ideologiekritik* (Frankfurt am Main: Suhrkamp, 1977), pp. 197–200.

[23] For a more detailed study of the relation between Goethe and Cassirer, see Barbara Naumann, *Philosophie und Poetik des Symbols: Cassirer und Goethe* (Munich: Fink, 1998), especially pp. 175–76.

[24] This is Cassirer's explicit reference to Goethe's concept of the *Urphänomen*, the basis or first phenomenon that Goethe first developed in the context of his botanical studies.

MYTH AND RELIGION IN CASSIRER'S PHILOSOPHY OF SYMBOLIC FORMS

By Louis Dupré

The problem of myth always occupied a central place in Cassirer's thought. The central text of the second volume of the *Philosophy of Symbolic Forms* (1923–1929) had been preceded by 'Language and Myth' (1925) and *Der Begriffsform im mythischen Denken* (Studien der Bibliothek Warburg, 1923). It was followed by the substantial seventh chapter of his *Essay on Man* (1944) and by *The Myth of the State* (1945). In the crucial essay on 'The Problem of the Symbol as the Fundamental Problem of Philosophical Anthropology' (1928), recently published in the posthumous fourth volume of *The Philosophy of Symbolic Forms*, the author once more reviews and extends his earlier views on the subject. The critical response to his work on myth significantly influenced Cassirer's future thought. It was the volume on myth that elicited Heidegger's critique of 1925 in the *Deutsche Literaturzeitung*, a critique repeated at the Davos encounter in 1929.

Heidegger raised the question about the metaphysical foundation of these multiple forms. Where are the roots of Cassirer's alleged *Begründung* of the symbolic forms? The critic praised Cassirer's work for having moved beyond the narrow constrictions of the Marburg neo-Kantians, but he takes its author to task for remaining entirely within the epistemological confinement of Kantian philosophy. Cassirer did not directly respond to Heidegger's challenge, beyond the short replies given in Davos, and some loose notes left in his papers under the title 'Geist und Leben' (published in the fourth volume of *The Philosophy of Symbolic Forms* [*P*, III, §2]), in which he strangely claims to uphold 'the broader, more universal, idealistic meaning of religion', freed from the ontological confinement and dullness of *Dasein*. The essay on 'The Problem of the Symbol as the Fundamental Problem of Philosophical Anthropology' appears to have been part of a projected work, *Zur Metaphysik der symbolischen Formen*, in which he may have intended to provide the metaphysical foundation that Heidegger missed in Cassirer's work. I shall begin my remarks with a discussion of Heidegger's critique. (Did Cassirer ever intend to give an ontological foundation to his theory?) Next, I shall compare Cassirer's main text on myth with his earlier and later discussions of the subject. Finally, I shall deal with the rather ambiguous distinction Cassirer makes between myth and religion.

This much is certain: early and late Cassirer considered his theory of symbolic forms to be grounded in Kant's philosophy. In 'Zur Logik des Symbolbegriffs' (1938), written after his great trilogy, he writes:

> The *Philosophy of Symbolic Forms* attempts to follow the road Kant indicated for critical philosophy. It refuses to start from a general, dogmatic assertion concerning the nature of absolute being, but it poses the question what a statement about being, about an 'object' of knowledge means, in which way and by what means objectivity is attainable and accessible at all. Kant has asserted that the fundamental principles of understanding merely serve to expose appearances; 'the proud name of ontology [. . .] is to yield to the more modest one of a mere analytic of pure understanding.'[1]

But did Cassirer intend to deepen Kant's critical idealism, or merely to complete Kant's system by adding a critique of cultural phenomena to Kant's critique of the natural sciences? Ernst W. Orth, in a thorough article, has attempted to answer that question. Cassirer obviously extended the theory of 'cognition' beyond the *Critique of Pure Reason* (1781).[2] As Dilthey had shown, the *Geisteswissenschaften* required a different method of understanding than the natural sciences. The understanding of cultural symbols presupposes, beyond the categories of objectivity, a connatural presence of the mind's own production. Knowledge includes, besides scientific or ordinary understanding, 'each spiritual activity through which we build ourselves a world in its characteristic form, in its order, and in its essential features (*So-Sein*)'.[3] Still, that does not remove Cassirer from Kant's epistemology altogether. In fact, he owed this extended notion of knowledge in the first place to Kant's *Critique of Judgment* (1790). There Kant had expanded the few dense paragraphs of the *Critique of Pure Reason* on the schemata of the imagination and on the principles of judgement. In the *First Critique* he had shown that sensuous intuitions, in order to become concepts, had to be synthesized in 'schemata' that, generalized the still empirical representations (A 146–47; B 185–86).

The *Critique of Judgment* showed that this intermediate synthesis could serve as the starting-point of a cognitive process without being developed into objective concepts. This allowed Cassirer to broaden the theory of knowledge while still remaining on Kantian ground, as Goethe and Schiller had shown in their poetry.[4] The schemata of the imagination, as well as the images into which they could be developed, laid the foundation for a theory of symbols: they were concrete, particular, and yet universal in significance. Moreover, in the *Prolegomena to Any Future Metaphysics* (1783) Kant had described symbols as representations capable of referring to ideas, to which no direct sensuous intuition corresponds.

Cassirer applies the term Spirit (*Geist*) to the one source of the various kinds of symbolic representation. Yet he persistently rejects Hegel's idea of Absolute Spirit to which his own theory seemed to drive him.[5] His anti-Romantic, anti-idealist position leaves us with the unanswered question: what, then, constitutes the unity of experience which he, as all Kantians, described as essential in a philosophy of consciousness? It was this very question that had caused Fichte to move from critical philosophy to metaphysics, from a theory of self-consciousness to one of the ultimate principle of being. Cassirer did not intend to follow that path. In 'Zur Logik des Symbolsbegriffs' he writes: 'The philosophy of symbolic forms does not want to be a metaphysics of knowledge, but a phenomenology of knowledge.'[6] But, then, how did he account for the one spiritual source of the multiple symbolic forms? He obviously took the question seriously. In his introductory chapter to volume one of *The Philosophy of Symbolic Forms* he asserts that the need to secure a unifying principle of all experience had, since the beginning of Western thought, been considered the essential task of philosophy: 'Philosophical speculation began with the concept of *being*. In the very moment when this concept appeared, when man's consciousness awakened to the unity of being as opposed to the multiplicity and diversity of existing things, the specific philosophical approach to the world was born.'[7] The Presocratics attempted to solve the problem by deriving all reality from one particular part of it (water, the indefinite, etc). But, for Cassirer, any theory of substance, the later philosophy of being as well as the early, uncritically lumps all appearances together within a single entity and fails to justify how a variety of forms could emerge from this unity: 'Metaphysics, as its history shows, is confronted more and more by a logical dilemma. It must either take seriously the fundamental concept of being, in which case all relations tend to evaporate [...] — or it must, in recognizing these relations, turn them into mere "accidents" of being' (PSF, 1, 97). But we have access only to those 'accidents' while their foundation becomes lost in a void of abstraction.

Instead of following the way of being, then, critical philosophy must seek the rules that govern the various *functions* of cognition and establish the *fundamental form* of the judgement that directs the mind's diverse expressions (PSF, 1, 78). Each field requires a different cognitive function and a different rule. Yet these various functions and rules must be determined by one and the same *Urform* that transforms mere *impressions* of consciousness into active expressions of the human spirit: 'Thus the critique of reason becomes the critique of culture' (PSF, 1, 80). Cassirer still appears reluctant to interpret these expressions as defining the nature of the *real*, as metaphysics does. Viewed from that perspective his work appears no more than an enlarged critical reflection on the transcendental conditions of consciousness. Symbolic forms remain subjective forms.

Yet Cassirer's 'anti-metaphysical' attitude is more complex than what emerges from the introduction to volume one. In a commemorative essay on Paul Natorp,[8] he approvingly presents his former teacher's theory of consciousness, a theory that moves well beyond the restrictions of Kant's critical theory. Cassirer mentions that Natorp as early as 1912 in his *General Psychology* had considered Kant's transcendental unity of apperception inadequate for justifying the fact that the cultural universe, despite its great diversity, appears one. Kant's theory fails to explain the very *appearing* of phenomena to oneself. That, according to Natorp, was the fundamental problem of psychology. In his posthumous *Lectures on Practical Philosophy* (1925) Natorp moved even closer to an idealist position. Each field of investigation requires a different attitude, a different intentionality, he argued, and none can be reduced to any other. Philosophy cannot simply take this variety of viewpoints for granted, as if it were a primitive, not-explainable, fact. To do so would threaten the very idea of philosophy. 'This idea has always asserted and will continue to assert the demand of a unity, specifically a unity that, more than an assemblage of given unities or particularities, includes the precondition and the source of all speculations.'[9]

According to Natorp, this could only be a transcendent principle of unity — one that surpasses the finite mind, but that partly reveals and partly conceals itself in that mind. The very nature of the symbolization process presupposes such a transcendent unity. The symbol always implies a finite, empirical reality that both discloses and obscures an infinite *Logos*. The principal quality of the symbol is not the metaphorical transfer of meaning from one thing to another, but rather the *transferring activity* itself, which manifests a unifying *Logos* that expresses itself in all particular domains of meaning-giving.[10] Cassirer rightly points out that Natorp here appears to rejoin the religious-idealistic tradition that began with Nicolas of Cusa and culminated in Fichte. He displays considerable sympathy for his predecessor's project and regrets that a premature death prevented him from bringing it to conclusion. Yet under the admiration one detects a reluctance to follow Natorp's direction. Indeed, in the unpublished essay on 'The Problem of the Symbol as the Fundamental Problem of Philosophical Anthropology',[11] he appears to move further from any kind of metaphysical commitments.

Another related question concerns the number and nature of basic symbolic forms. The ones Cassirer considers in *The Philosophy of Symbolic Forms*, language, myth, and science, can hardly be the only possible ones. Obviously missing are discussions of art and religion, even though Cassirer repeatedly refers to both as symbolic forms. Orth regards this restriction as merely reflecting the chronology of Cassirer's discovery of the forms. Thus, the discussion of language appears to reflect his original awareness that symbols play an important part in the mathematical formalization of physics. This discovery coincided with Cassirer's interest in the function of language in Goethe and Schiller. His awareness of myth as a symbolic form of thinking resulted from his entrance to the Warburg Library, which contained a unique collection of writings on myth and primitive thought. The symbolic process involved in knowledge in general and of scientific knowledge in particular had been with him all these years; he gave it a definitive expression in the third volume, published in 1929. In the projected fourth volume appears a short but important discussion of history. Even the title of Cassirer's early writing on 'The Concept of Symbolic Form in the Construction of the *Geisteswissenschaften*' suggests a comprehensiveness of symbolic form that surpasses the three subjects of *The Philosophy of Symbolic Forms*.[12] The only time Cassirer deals with the symbols of practical reason is in a long essay, 'Form und Technik', originally published as an introduction to a collective work *Kunst und Technik*, in which he treats technology as yet another symbolic form through which the mind gets purchase on the world.[13]

What distinguishes Cassirer's treatise on myth is the radical way in which he transforms the field of studies. He begins by criticizing some earlier modern theories. For Schelling's *Philosophy of Mythology* (1857), the first truly philosophical study of the subject in modern times, he expresses great respect. Once and for all, the romantic philosopher had disposed of the allegorical interpretation, which since late Antiquity and the Church Fathers had dominated European thought on the subject. According to Schelling, the source of mythology lies not in the nature of reality, but in the mind's own powers. Yet Cassirer objected to Schelling's sweeping idealism that, deducing the categories of mythical thought from a priori principles, neglected a serious empirical study of myth. Rather than undertaking such a purely metaphysical, or the opposite, a purely empirical study of myth, the neo-Kantian Cassirer opted for a critical study of the structural form of myth. He equally objected to Schelling's evolutionary thesis that the myth arose out of a primeval, undifferentiated belief in one God, whereby polytheistic mythology had no other purpose but to discover the various attributes of God. Schelling did not sufficiently recognize the dialectical opposition that separated religion proper from mythology.

Yet Cassirer objected far more strongly to nineteenth-century interpretations of myth as a primitive and flawed attempt at scientific knowledge. To be sure, the mythical view of the cosmos as one organic whole anticipated the unifying tendency of modern science. Certainly, myth does play a role in awakening the mind to scientific reflection, as appears in the Ionian philosophers. Still, those who consider mythology a primitive science overlook the specific structure of mythic thought. The differentiated knowledge of science can hardly be compared to the participative one of myth. The latter lacks any awareness of a distinction between subject and object, between representation and reality.

Nor can the relation between myth and forms of language be understood by simply deducing one form from the other, as if ordinary language were merely 'faded mythology' (as Schelling maintained) or no more than misinterpreted language (as Max Müller argued). In 'Language and Myth', an essay Cassirer published while he was still working on his trilogy, we read: 'It is no longer a matter of simply deriving one of these phenomena from the other, of explaining it in terms of the other — for that would be to *level them both*, to rob them of their characteristic features.'[14] Cassirer does not deny that the beginnings of language and myth coincide. They stem from the drive to fixate strong, arresting impressions in verbal sound. Even after myth and ordinary language have broken 'through their original fetters' they remain intimately linked to one another in a move toward universal meanings. But this drive impels myth toward 'concretely defined, distinctly sundered, and individualized mental constructions', while it moves ordinary language toward coherent, logically determined discourse.[15]

Turning now to Cassirer's own structural analysis of myth, we note a fourfold function of myth. First, myth precedes religion before the dividing line between the sacred and the profane, characteristic of religion, has been drawn. It is neither essentially religious, nor is it altogether excluded from religion. Second, myth has a cognitive function. It builds the various impressions derived from the lifeworld into a coherent cosmos, and defines Man's place in it. This is not a premature form of science, but an alternative mode of understanding the unity of the world. Third, myth justifies the existing social order by establishing its institutions on the foundation of a primeval past. Thus some Vedic myths justify the caste system by the story of the aboriginal division. Claude Lévi-Strauss and most Marxists reduce myth entirely to this social function, while leaving the ritual that often accompanies it out of consideration. Fourth, myth guides men through personal and social crises. Although psychological interpretations of myth (especially those of C. G. Jung) have contributed much to its contemporary understanding, an exclusively psychological reading falls short of accounting for the polymorphic richness of mythical structures. Cassirer paid little attention to psychological theories in this context.

The original quality of his theory consists in his having considered the primary significance of myth to lie not in its content but in its symbolic *function*. Three factors here play an essential role. First, myth is first and foremost a primitive reflection on time. Cassirer discusses this indirectly in his treatment of mythical time. Others, particularly Paul Ricœur, have elaborated this aspect as being the most important. The mythical story narrates the primordial acts and gestures performed in a primordial time that differs from ordinary acts. This distinction between primordial, ontologically pregnant, times and actions on one side, and ordinary ones on the other, eventually results in a separation between the sacred and the profane, which still remains implicit in myth. Second, the primordial time of myth is not subject to the transitoriness of ordinary time. It may be endlessly repeated, thereby giving a permanent significance to all aspects of life. Mircea Eliade's well-known definition elucidates what Cassirer had in mind: 'Myth narrates a sacred history; it relates an event that took place in primordial time, the fabled time of the "beginnings"'.[16] The term 'sacred' in this description ought not to be taken in the full, religious sense, nor do the 'beginnings' refer only to what came chronologically first: it includes the ritual repetitions of those beginnings.

Third, explicitly or implicitly, myth is linked to ritual. From all we know, originally myth may always have been accompanied by ritual. One might even describe it as the interpretation of the rite. Later this interpretation became dominant, as we notice in Christian sacraments where the word is the formal element. Eventually it replaces the ritual. In Greek drama almost nothing remained of the original ritual, except a perfunctory sacrifice at the beginning and the ritual dances during the plays. In modern Judaism the Yom Kippur liturgy preserves only the words of the original sacrifice ritual. Cassirer recognizes the priority of the ritual,[17] as well as its overall significance. 'Through rites the monotonous course of existence, the mere "flow" of time, undergoes a kind of religious division; through them each stage of life acquires a particular religious stamp, which gives it a specific meaning' (PSF, 2, 109).[18]

The link between ritual and myth enables men to relive the primeval, so-called mythical, time. For the ritual abolishes precisely ordinary, irreversible time and enables the myth to move beyond the transiency of the narrated events. By repeating the ancient gestures, ritual conveys a lasting significance to myth. Ritual, then, validates myth. Yet in another sense the myth justifies the beginning as sacred time. For without a story that narrates the becoming of things from an unchanging origin that may always be recuperated, the most essential condition for maintaining a link between the primordial events, expressed in the ritual, and the transient ones (of ordinary experience) would be missing. As Cassirer puts it:

> True myth [...] begins only when a genesis, a becoming, a life in time, is attributed to the images of the universe. [...] The mythical world achieves its true and specific articulation only when its dimension of depth, so to speak, opens up with the form of time. (PSF, 2, 104–05)

Time alone enables us to move back to the foundational beginning, and in that beginning to overcome the very transitoriness in which it holds us captive. It conveys meaning to the present by transposing it into the past: 'The past itself has no "why": *it* is the why of things' (PSF, 2, 106). This may well be the original significance of Plato's equation of truth with *anamnesis* (recollection). The mythical past alone is definitive and holds the secret of eternal truth. Mythical time halts the irretrievable flow from past to present to future, and sets up a parallel time-sequence anchored within a permanent past.

In this division between the transitory, unreal, present and the present grounded in that permanent past, lies also the source of religious symbolization. The transient now becomes a sign of the permanent: 'Every natural phenomenon serves rather as a sign for something else, something more comprehensive, which is revealed in it' (PSF, 2, 112). Myth does not make that distinction. It knows nothing of signs or symbols: in it all is real, yet it suggests that some events are more real than others. Without the accents myth places on some facets of reality, religious symbolism would not be possible. Through its notion of time, mythical consciousness effects a transition from a substantial to a symbolic, significatory, view. The temporal order gradually submits the particular powers of nature to its own universal destiny. Cassirer illustrates this by the case of Babylonian-Assyrian religion which, starting from an animistic view of powers, increasingly came to concentrate on the stars, until their movement and the constellations they formed became more important than the particular bodies themselves. All later astrology is based on this same shift: eternal, ever-recurring time determines our destinies, constituting propitious and impropitious, sacred (*fasti* or *nefasti*) and ordinary, times. Cassirer has not spelled out *all* the consequences this entails.

Restrictions of time do not allow a lengthy discussion of that other coordinate of the mythical consciousness, namely, mythical space. The following brief remarks may suffice in the present context. The contiguity of the points of mythical time applies even more to space. Mythical space affects *all* space, even though the special space of myth is clearly distinct from the homogeneous space of ordinary perception, and even more from the geometric space of science. Mythical thought attaches a special significance to such immediate experiences as what is right or left, above or below, with respect to a person's body. Beyond these universal distinctions, it singles out some particular places. They serve as foundations and ordering points of *all* space. Sanctuaries, pilgrimage places, holy grounds, often pre-exist the particular, historical significance that later ages attach to them. Some mountains, some groves, some lakes were 'holy' before the clear distinction between sacred and profane existed. A particular point around which all other space could be ordered was considered to be the centre of the earth. But this centre was neither static nor unique. It was a movable concept. Whenever a new territory was occupied the world had to be founded again, and the centre became transported to a new sacred place.

We now come to the most complex, and also the most controversial, part of Cassirer's treatment of myth: the break-up of mythical consciousness that results in the clear distinction between myth and religion. Can myth survive the reflection which it initiates? Can the mind remain in the mythical state of consciousness once it knows what a myth is? Since myth itself starts the reflective process, must we not conclude that myth drives itself to extinction? Cassirer has no doubt that a transforming dialectic exists:

> Myth would be no truly spiritual form if its unity signified merely a simplicity without contradictions. [...] The progress of myth does not mean merely that certain basic traits, certain spiritual determinations of earlier stages are developed and completed, but also that they are negated and eradicated. (PSF, 2, 235)

At a certain point in human development myth ceases to be credible. Yet upon the drive to surpass mythical consciousness, stemming from myth's own reflective dynamism, follows an equally strong drive to rebuild the mythical world, even after the internal dialectic has lead to a different kind of reflection: 'The process of destruction [of the myth] proves on closer scrutiny to be a process of self-assertion' (PSF, 2, 237). Not to recognize this persistent presence of myth in post-mythical states of consciousness, Cassirer argues in his posthumous *The Myth of the State*, will drive myth underground where, unchecked by reason, it may create major havoc, even — and particularly — while passing for science.

At a certain point the unified vision of myth breaks up into fragments: the mythical narrative turns into poetry, its cosmic interpretation develops into science, even religion distances itself from the ancient saga in which it first found its voice. Myth united these functions, Paul Tillich wrote:

> In the unbroken myth three elements are linked together: the religious, the scientific, and the truly mythical elements: the religious element as relatedness to the unconditioned transcendent, the scientific as relatedness to objective reality, the truly mythical as an objectification of the transcendent through the medium of intuition and conceptions of reality.[19]

Unfortunately, in this statement the special place granted to 'the mythical' reasserts a division in the mythical mind, which the rest of the statement denies.

Cassirer describes how the break-up of myth begins when religion starts assuming a certain independence with regard to myth. 'In the gradual progress of the mythical view a separation begins,' he writes, 'and it is this separation that constitutes the actual beginning of the specifically religious consciousness' (PSF, 2, 238–39). He specifies as such a moment of separation the emergence of the idea of creation. In Babylonian mythology this occurs when the god Marduk defeats the monster Tiamat, establishing the planets as seats for the young gods, and ordering the cosmic structure (PSF, 2, 113). In Vedic myths Prajapati creates time from which all things issue (even in some versions the creator himself) (PSF, 2, 116). The same ambiguity between time and a supreme god-like character marks the creation story of the Avesta, the ancient Persian religion. The creation becomes possible only after one of the gods has acquired a ruling position over all others:

> The further mythical feeling and thinking progress in this direction, the more distinctly the figure of a supreme *creator god* is singled out from among the mere specialized gods and from the throng of individual polytheistic gods. (PSF, 2, 206)

With the emergence of a creator comes the idea of transcendence. The distinction between the sacred and the profane, which is merely implicit in mythical consciousness, now becomes explicit:

> It is this separation that constitutes the actual beginning of the specifically religious consciousness. The further back we follow it toward its origins, the less the content of religious consciousness can be distinguished from that of mythical consciousness. (PSF, 2, 238–39)

Although myth and religion long continue to share a common content, their intentionalities increasingly grow apart. Once religion begins to emancipate itself from myth, it gradually releases the world of everyday life from the all-encompassing power of the sacred. Ordinary reality now becomes 'profane': distinct from the sacred, though still subordinate to it (contrary to the 'secular' of modern culture). In the first chapter of *Mythical Thought* Cassirer describes this process with admirable clarity. Yet precisely on the relation between myth and religion a strange ambiguity runs through the rest of his treatise. Undoubtedly, the more primitive mythical consciousness contains much that will be incorporated within religion. Such notions as taboo, special places, special times, all become eventually adopted by religious consciousness and given a new meaning. But as Lévi-Strauss, Malinowski, and others, have also shown, many myths have more limited social functions that are not necessarily assumed by mature religious consciousness. The term 'sacred' has a far more precise sense than original mythical consciousness allows: indeed, it refers to the very quality that distinguishes religion from myth.

Yet Cassirer fails to distinguish the all-encompassing *sacred* of mythical consciousness from the more specific category of the *sacred* that rules religion. He rightly stresses that religion and myth remain interwoven. At least primitive religion derives its nomenclature and much of its material from mythical sources. But Cassirer, influenced by Hermann Cohen's *Die Religion der Vernunft aus den Quellen des Judentums* (Leipzig, 1919), describes the prophetic religion of Israel as moving away from mythical time determined by the periodic cycles of nature. The absolute monotheism of Judaism remains hostile to the kind of natural symbolization typical of the myth: 'Nature becomes a matter of indifference for the purely ethical-religious pathos of the Prophets'

(PSF, 2, 119). Nor do the prophets refer to the permanent past of myth, but rather to a history that, via the digressions of the past, moves toward the future. Cassirer quotes his master Cohen: 'Time becomes future and only future. Past and present are submerged in this time of the future' (PSF, 2, 120). Theogony and cosmology are surpassed altogether. Even the primeval idea of creation that gave rise to monotheism recedes in post-exilic prophesy.

Cassirer interprets this as the prophets' struggle against the mythical foundations and beginnings of the Old Testament (PSF, 2, 240). That such a struggle occurred cannot be doubted. But the claim that the prophets of Israel succeeded in exorcizing mythology from Old Testament religion conflicts with the facts. Mythological elements often derived from Egyptian and Mesopotamian sources survive in the Psalms, in Genesis and Exodus, indeed in the prophets themselves. In this respect I detect no absolute difference between the radical monotheism of Israel and that of Islam or Christianity. Even today the radically demythologizing movement that started at the end of the eighteenth century continues in Christianity. In Islam the struggle between religion and myth has barely begun.

To be sure, various religions use their mythical past in different ways. The religion of Israel is a strongly historical one, not because the historical books of the Old Testament are uniformly reliable accounts, but because their authors display a persistent intention to place salvation within a historical context. One may claim that Israel transformed obviously mythical accounts in order to incorporate them into its religious history. The French philosopher Henri Duméry uses the neologism 'mythistory' to refer to the Bible's unique mixture of myth and history. Christianity likewise has incorporated mythical elements derived from other, mostly Hellenistic, sources. In its liturgical cycle it has preserved much of the nature mythology of classical civilization. Here also the historical intentionality that determined the accounts of the gospels, has thoroughly transformed these mythical elements. But any attempt definitively to separate the historical from the mythical has proven to be futile. Nor is such a distinction essential, even to a historical religion. Essential is the demythologizing drive itself, even though that drive will never be satisfied. If it were entirely successful, it would drain the life-blood out of religion:

> Undoubtedly, some facets of the myth cannot survive their recognition by the religious, philosophical, or scientific mind. Thus the concepts of space and time of the archaic myth, as well as its loose notion of causality, are incompatible with the scientific worldview. The religious mind, from its side, finds the myth lacking in the radical negativity that transcendence requires. Nonetheless two qualities make the myth indispensable in the religious symbolization process. One is its capacity to reflect *without objectifying* the reality on which one reflects. Outside the myth such symbols cannot be formed nor even properly understood.[20]

Myth possesses a unique ability to reconcile and to integrate opposing facets of life. The other quality that makes myth indispensable to religion is an awareness of the endurance of religious time. Sacred events may not be historically reversible, yet the religious mind nevertheless endows them with a lasting significance that by means of ritual and mythical re-telling can be forever re-actualized.

The fact that an abundance of recent studies on myth has forced us to correct some of Cassirer's theses by no means diminishes the extraordinary significance of his studies on the subject. Others, beginning with Schelling, had shown *that* myth cannot be reduced to any form of primitive science or philosophy. Cassirer's theory of symbolic forms explain *why* the epistemic multiplicity of the mind's symbolic expressions makes such a reduction not unnecessary but mistaken.

Notes

[1] 'Zur Logik des Symbolbegriffs', in *Wesen und Wirkung des Symbolbegriffs* (Darmstadt: Wissenschaftliche Buchgesellschaft, 1956), pp. 228–29.

[2] Erst Wolfgang Orth, 'Zur Konzeption der symbolischen Formen', in Ernst Cassirer, *Symbol, Technik, Sprache*, ed. by E. W. Orth and John Michael Krois (Hamburg: Felix Meiner Verlag, 1985), pp. 165–201.

[3] 'Zur Logik des Symbolbegriffs', in *Wesen und Wirkung des Symbolbegriffs*, p. 208; cf. Orth, 'Zur Konzeption der symbolischen Formen', pp. 174–75.

[4] Ernst Cassirer, *Kant's Life and Thought* (New Haven: Yale University Press, 1981), pp. 271–87; cf. Orth, 'Zur Konzeption der symbolischen Formen', pp. 177–79.

[5] Various authors have differently assessed both this proximity to, and distance from, Hegel. For a discussion of their positions, see Irene Kajon, *Il concetto dell' unità della cultura e il problema della trascendenza nella filosofia di Ernst Cassirer* (Rome: Bulzoni, 1984).

[6] Cassirer, *Wesen und Wirkung des Symbolbegriffs*, p. 208.

[7] Ernst Cassirer, *Philosophy of Symbolic Forms*, vol. 1, *Language*, trans. Ralph Manheim (New Haven and London: Yale University Press, 1955), 73. Henceforth referred to in parenthesis as PSF, 1, followed by a page reference.

[8] Ernst Cassirer, 'Paul Natorp', *Kant-Studien*, 30 (1925), 273–98.

[9] Cassirer, 'Paul Natorp', p. 288.

[10] Paul Natorp, *Vorlesungen über praktische Philosophie* (Erlangen: Verlag der Philosophischen Akademie, 1925).

[11] Ernst Cassirer, *The Philosophy of Symbolic Forms*, vol. 4, *The Metaphysics of Symbolic Forms*, ed. by John Michael Krois and Donald Phillip Verene, trans. by John Michael Krois (New Haven and London: Yale University Press, 1996), 3–114 (esp. p. 61).

[12] *Wesen und Wirkung des Symbolbegriffs*, pp. 171–99.

[13] Leo Kestenberg (ed.), *Kunst und Technik* (Berlin: Volksverband der Bücherfreunde; Wegweiser-Verlag, 1930).

[14] Cassirer, *Language and Myth*, trans. by Susanne K. Langer (New York: Harper and Brothers, 1940; republished New York: Dover Books, 1953), p. 9.

[15] Cassirer, *Language and Myth*, p. 41.

[16] Mircea Eliade, *Myth and Reality*, trans. by Willard R. Trask (New York: Harper and Row, 1963), p. 5.

[17] Ernst Cassirer, *The Philosophy of Symbolic Forms*, vol. 2, *Mythical Thought*, trans. by Ralph Manheim (New Haven and London: Yale University Press, 1955), 39. Henceforth referred to in parentheses as PSF, 2, followed by a page reference.

[18] It is not clear whether Cassirer here refers to the religious attitude in the proper sense or to the purely mythical one that, according to him, precedes it. The argument holds in both cases, I believe.
[19] 'The Religious Symbol', in Sidney Hook (ed.), *Religious Experience and Truth* (Edinburgh: Oliver and Boyd, 1962), pp. 311–12.
[20] Louis Dupré, *Symbols of the Sacred* (Grand Rapids: William B. Eerdmans, 2000), p. 117.

ERNST CASSIRER AND OSWALD SPENGLER: TWO PHILOSOPHIES OF CULTURE IN THE LIGHT OF A POLITICAL POLEMIC

By Dina Gusejnova

It is difficult to imagine two more opposing representatives of the intellectual élite of Weimar Germany than Ernst Cassirer (1874–1945) and Oswald Spengler (1880–1936). Not only did they occupy different political wings at the time: one was a keen supporter of the Weimar Republic, the other an active antagonist. They have also received a very different treatment in recent historiography. Cassirer has often been represented as a liberal but somewhat lethargic philosopher of culture: as somebody who is admirable in his political values but who does not inspire a great deal of political debate. Spengler has experienced the contrary: while he is often marked as a proto-fascist thinker with dangerous conceptions of history, the political appeal of his organic world view of the inevitable decline of cultures in time, which had attracted Arnold Toynbee, is still relatively high.[1] Surprisingly, no attempt has been made so far to discuss the two contemporary philosophies of culture synthetically. Such a view offers the prospect of reconsidering, if not correcting, our impressions not only of their intellectual relationship, but also of Cassirer and Spengler as individual thinkers.

Spengler never mentioned Cassirer by name, though it is unlikely that he did not know his work. Cassirer polemicized with Spengler's works, especially *The Decline of the West* and *Man and Technics*, for twenty years, having first mentioned him in 1928. In what follows I would like to show that Cassirer's Spengler-reception was in many ways contradictory, fluctuating between criticism and a degree of sympathy. A juxtaposition of the two theories helps flesh out the political antagonism of the two thinkers particularly clearly, as it is set against a backdrop of common starting-points. Moreover, presenting Cassirer's engagement with Spengler's *Decline of the West* in the context of the book's reception by other contemporaries shows a Cassirer who is not an apolitical philosopher of culture but a thinker who considered himself to be performing a political duty for his contemporaries with this very philosophy.

At first sight it is understandable why scholars have been reluctant to uncover the intellectual debate between Cassirer and Spengler. Indeed, Spengler's influence on the intellectuals of his time — for example, on Carl

Schmitt — has often been neglected. Cassirer was a well-respected academic, while Spengler was, and still is, being located in the margin between academia and popular science. Raised in a provincial German town, never able to secure an academic position and largely ignored by the academic world, Spengler was something of an outcast until the publication of his best-selling *Decline of the West* in 1918 and *Prussianism and Socialism* in 1919. The German writer Kurt Tucholsky scornfully dubbed him 'the Karl May of philosophy', while Walter Benjamin described him as a 'trivial bastard' (*Sauhund*).

By contrast to many of his contemporaries, though, Cassirer took Spengler's writings very seriously.[2] He described Spengler's style, disclosed in vague terms such as *Kulturseele* ('cultural soul') and *Menschentum* ('humankind'), as 'mystical language' that was a conceptual part of Spengler's prophetic apparatus.[3] For Cassirer, Spengler was an irrationalist in thought and in language, and in that quality also a danger. On the one hand, Cassirer was critical of the fatalism in Spengler's view of history. On the other hand, he was also attracted to some aspects of Spengler's work. For Cassirer, Spengler constituted an example of a return to the astrological and mystical thinking that he studied in his works on the philosophy of the Renaissance.

As I want to suggest, however, Spengler's morphology of human history was more than an example for Cassirer. It also was an excellent case-study for Cassirer's view of history as a symbolic form. Spengler presents one of several ways of reading history as a set of symbols. He looks at history as it is revealed to us in the form of buildings, musical compositions, writings, and scientific discoveries. In a way, this is the most consequential of all possible symbolic readings, for it does not merely seek to describe symbols and their connections; it seeks to extract what these symbols mean.

At the same time, the process of uncovering the meaning of symbols also displays the key difference between Cassirer's and Spengler's understanding of history as a symbolic form. For Cassirer, symbols are expressive functions, the meaning of which can be uncovered only in the context of their emergence. In this sense, the notion of a symbolic form is an innate cognitive tool that allows human beings to understand themselves both in their own time, and in retrospect. Cassirer thinks that the people who create certain symbols could know themselves what these symbols mean, and that we, too, can find out what they meant if we approach their states of mind. In the chapter on the 'Dialectic of Mythical Consciousness' Cassirer writes that religion, for example, is capable of interpreting the symbols that were only used, but not understood, in mythical consciousness:

> Religion carries out the step which remains alien to myth as such: by using the sensual images and signs it *understands* them for what they are — means of expression which, once they have revealed a certain meaning, necessarily stay behind it, 'pointing' at this meaning without ever grasping or exploiting it fully.

[Die Religion vollzieht den Schnitt, der dem Mythos als solchem fremd ist: Indem sie sich der sinnlichen Bilder und Zeichen bedient, *weiß* sie sie zugleich als solche — als Ausdrucksmittel, die, wenn sie einen bestimmten Sinn offenbaren, notwendig zugleich hinter ihm zurückbleiben, die auf diesen Sinn 'hinweisen', ohne ihn jemals vollständig zu erfassen und auszuschöpfen].[4]

Spengler's understanding of a symbol is different. Rather than looking for the meaning of symbols in their context, he tries to combine different symbols in order to extract a message that no single symbol or even set of symbols could have given at any one time. Spengler thinks that the societies and, to an even greater extent, the individuals who create symbols, do so unknowingly, that the meaning of the symbols can only arise to a later-born analyst. His idea of a rise and fall of cultures and the prediction of the imminent decline of Faustian culture is what his study of human symbols across the world has taught him.

Cassirer's ultimate goal or discovery in the participation in and interpretation of symbolic forms was anthropology, the discovery of Man, whose identity is the only thing that is certainly recognizable and unchanging in the continuum of time. For his part, Spengler's goal was to foretell the movements and developments of the masses. Culture was not only how human history is expressed, but it was also the material out of which it can be predicted. For Cassirer, culture was the tool that gives man the opportunity to know himself better. Despite their varying goals and political values, however, their methodology had many things in common.

Method

Both Cassirer and Spengler saw Goethe's notion of the symbol as a key source for their theories of culture. Spengler used Goethe's idea of the *Urpflanze* and other *Urphänomene* for his own theory of the organic growth of cultures out of an *Ursymbol*. Thus, for example, the 'naked body', the 'cave', and 'absolute infinite space' constituted the *Ursymbole* of the ancient, the Arabic, and the Faustian cultural souls, respectively. The latter, in Spengler's words, was best epitomized by German works of art, such as Wagner's *Tristan and Isolde*. The nature of an *Ursymbol* was thus left undefined. For Spengler, culture was the outward, or measurable, appearance of the history of mankind (*Menschentum*), grouped into different 'cultural souls', each of which sought to fulfil its own nature. It was out of an *Ursymbol* assigned to each that every particular culture (*Kulturkreis*) evolved, following its own laws of development entailed in its respective *Ursymbol* in accordance with the Aristotelian principle of *entelechy*.[5] Spengler believed that the individual could play no substantial part in the development of culture because the individual was merely part of a pre-established all-encompassing program. Moreover, he argued with reference to Leibniz, that in their monadic existence, cultures could not influence one another.[6]

Cassirer noticed the tension between Spengler's scientific pretensions and his tendency to give examples instead of defining terms such as *Ursymbol*, criticizing Spengler's statement that 'history ought to be treated poetically'.[7] He observed that Goethe's demand to 'let the *Urphänomene* stand untouched in their majestic and ungraspable quality', which Spengler accepted, was of little use to a systematic philosopher.[8] Cassirer's own notion of *Basisphänomene*, or fundamental phenomena, was indebted to Goethe. Yet it went beyond Goethe's own method in its systematic structure. According to Cassirer, human nature ought to be perceived in terms of three groups of phenomena: the phenomenon of man's consciousness of his historical being; the notion of man's consciousness of his own actions; and the self-perception of man through the medium of his work.[9] In his system, Spengler's *Ursymbol* constituted an analysis of the third kind of *Basisphänomen*, a phenomenology of man's history through man's work, such as an ancient statue or a musical composition. For Spengler himself, however, 'cultures are organisms' and *Ursymbols* were thus aspects of a cultural physique, rather than the result of creation by individuals.[10]

Where Spengler looked at culture from without, and from the point of view of humanity as a whole, albeit presenting it as a morphology of culture developing from within out of the *Ursymbol*, Cassirer used Dilthey's notion of understanding (*Verstehen*) as a basis for exploring the circumstances of an historical event or cultural aspect from the point of view of the historical actors involved. Cassirer's method of symbolic form called for an *understanding* by recreating the spiritual form that was applicable to a particular historical past.[11] Cassirer's aim was to use a '"morphology" of the human spirit', or the study of different symbolic forms such as culture or technology, in order to 'arrive at a clearer and more reliable methodological approach to the individual cultural sciences.'[12] His study of culture would always remain mediated by the analysis of individual perceptions, since beyond analyzing patterns of thought themselves, Man 'can never lay bare the actual and ultimate roots of being'.[13]

The differences between Spengler's and Cassirer's historical approach, so to speak from 'without' and from 'within' the historical actors of the time, are thrown into relief by their respective studies of the Renaissance.[14] Cassirer argued that by studying the 'individual biographies' of artists, thinkers, intellectuals and statesmen of the Renaissance, he came to understand the period better as an epoch characterized by its transitory nature between mythical and scientific, religious and secular thought.[15] Cassirer also argued that 'the world of Renaissance ideas did not have such a direct and permanent effect in Germany as it had in Italy, France and England', for even the most famous

German Renaissance scholar, Nicholas of Cusa, had found a wider reception in Italy than in Germany.[16] By contrast, in Spengler's interpretation of the Renaissance as a phenomenon that began around the year 1000, it was the time of birth of the 'Faustian' cultural soul. He classified it by reference to the cultural products of this period, such as the great Germanic sagas, most of which were the work of an anonymous representative of the people (*Volk*).[17]

Cassirer wrote that while he was 'engrossed in studies of the philosophy of the Italian Renaissance' he recognized in 'some astrological treatises that [he] had quite recently read' a 'close analogy' with Spengler's own semi-mythical, semi-scientific pattern of thought.[18] The analogy informed Cassirer's early observation that mythical thinking confused historical '"time" and "destiny"'.[19] This is certainly applicable to Spengler's conception of history.[20] After all, his law of destiny derived from an interpretation of the chronological sequence of past events, such as the decline of the Roman Empire. Cassirer thus considered Spengler's work to be 'an astrology of history — the work of a diviner'.[21] For Cassirer, Man was the only goal of a morphological approach to history: just as the 'divine creatures of myth mean nothing else but the successive self-revelations of mythical consciousness', so the 'microcosm' of individual persons and societies is reflected in the world or 'macrocosm' that surrounds them.[22] Goethe's notions of microcosm and macrocosm are developed and woven into not only Spengler's mystical language, but also into Cassirer's own philosophy of symbolic forms.

Values

As will become clear, the shared attraction for Goethe's notion of *Urphänomen* and his concepts of microcosm and macrocosm bring about a stronger approximation in method between Cassirer and Spengler than one might have previously assumed. At the same time, just as Cassirer's and Spengler's symbolic readings of human culture lead them to very different forms of analysis, their opposing political value systems permeated even their conceptual thought, as a closer look at their philosophy of culture also reveals.

With regard to culture and history, Cassirer was interested in studying man as a median but single unity, rather than society as such. Accordingly, in his political ideal the highest priority was also given to the individual. Conversely, Spengler's disregard for the role of individuals in the creation of culture also revealed itself — but more strikingly — in his political beliefs. Spengler argued: 'We do not experience the decline of individual or several people, but only the *extinction of an organization*, the "us", as destructive.'[23] For Cassirer, on the other hand, the state could only be the 'final goal of history', as Hegel puts it, 'provided that it recognizes its highest task in the progressive realization of freedom'.[24] By freedom he meant individual, not collective, freedom; that is, he meant, freedom in Humboldt's sense.

In their interpretation and reaction to the two main events of the 1910s, the War and the foundation of the Weimar Republic, Cassirer and Spengler clearly occupied places that were diametrically opposed to each other. The experience of war itself was disturbing for Cassirer.[25] His main occupation was in the sphere of 'ideological' warfare, reading French anti-German propaganda.[26] In Germany, the opposition of German *Kultur*, derived from the spirit of the *Volk*, to French *civilization*, based on the notion of a rationalist state, found resurging popularity.[27] Against this backdrop, Cassirer wrote a history of German idealism, in which individual positive freedom as self-realization and the form of the legitimate state were mutually reinforcing.[28] Presenting Fichte as an idealist and liberal, Cassirer claimed him for his cause, juxtaposing him with the 'chauvinist' Fichte, whom Houston Stewart Chamberlain and Siegfried Wagner involved as a founding father of their 'Fichte Society of 1914'.[29] In the preface to *Freedom and Form*, a work published during the First World War, Cassirer wrote a passage that deserves to be cited at some length:

> The truly creative figures of German intellectual history have always, during the heaviest battles they led for the preservation of the independence of their culture, remained free from the conceit [*Dünkel*] of complete self-complacency with this culture. [...] This is not only true of Lessing, of Herder and Goethe; it is also true for a thinker like Fichte, who in setting up his ideal of the state and the nation always emphasized that this ideal ought not to 'bring forth some kind of special trait of the people' [*Volkstümlichkeit*], but that it ought to 'realize the free citizen'. Likewise, in these days the educated Germans [*deutsche Bildung*] will not allow the misjudgement and scorn brought forward by their enemies, nor a limited small-spirited chauvinism, to move them away from this original path.[30]

For Spengler, war was 'the continuation of Being in a higher form, and states exist for the sake of war; they are an expression of the being ready for war'. It is worth pointing out that Spengler's Heraclitian understanding of war was an important source of influence for Carl Schmitt's friend/foe definition of the political, and one that has been so far ignored.[31] Spengler's political goal was 'an education for the German state and not for a humanism that is removed from the world' ['zur Erziehung *für diesen Staat* [...] und nicht für einen weltfremden Humanismus'].[32] Endorsing the laws of 'life' over mere intellectualism, Spengler insisted that in the face of inevitable cultural decline, technology was a fate that we should embrace as a 'tactics of life'.[33] More precisely, 'using the means of Faustian technology', it was possible 'to melt mankind into a whole' ['durch die Mittel faustischer Technik und Erfindung das Gewimmel der Menschheit zu einem Ganzen zu schweißen'] so as to fulfill the law of destiny at its best.[34] In Geoffrey Herf's words, it was a 'paradox of cultural pessimism' that, unlike Max Weber, Georg Lukács, and Georg

Simmel, who regarded modern technology as disenchanted, for Spengler, technology has become 'ascetic, mystical, esoteric [...] even more spiritual'.[35] For Spengler, the endorsement of technological progress was thus a curious aspect of man's positive liberty, allowing occidental man to fulfil the essence of his Faustian soul. Consequently, the fact that man's use of technology implied domination over nature and other men was a positive notion for him. It was this interpretation of technology as domination that Adorno and Horkheimer criticized in their account of the Odysseus saga.[36]

In Cassirer's terms, by contrast, technology was initially not more than an extension of man's intellectual powers.[37] However, he also recognized that technology could imply domination if consciously employed in this way, for example, by directing other people's thought by means of mass media and other forms of psychological manipulation.[38] Thus modern technology had the potential of creating a 'kind of society according to destiny' in which 'not the individual but the group is the real "moral subject"'.[39] Cassirer's ideal society was composed of responsible individuals, threatened by precisely the form of technology with which Spengler sought to transform this liberal concoction into a unified whole.[40] He wanted to understand technology as the 'means by which man gives the outside world its determinate form' both physically and intellectually, and formed the starting-point for a variety of other 'spiritual functions', including science and religion.[41] Cassirer's words about the cognitive function of technology explain his entire understanding of the history of human culture as a symbolic form: 'If the philosophy of technics has to do with the immediate and mediated sensual and bodily organs with which man gives his surroundings their shape and form, the Philosophy of Symbolic Forms turns its attention to the spiritual expressive functions in their entirety.'[42]

THE AIMS OF A PHILOSOPHY OF CULTURE

It would oversimplify the relationship between Cassirer and Spengler to argue that their differing political values were the only reason for their diverging appropriation of Goethe's terms. Another reason for this circumstance was the actual motivation of their occupation with the history of human culture. Although Spengler's work is so much more aggressive and assertive than Cassirer's balanced style would have ever permitted him to be, Spengler is more of a commentator and creative interpreter of events, while Cassirer has stronger pedagogical motivations. Their respective 'footnotes' on another of Goethe's terms, *Weltenwende*, illustrates in what way the intentions between the two symbolic readings of history differed.

One of Cassirer's central concepts, which was inspired by Goethe, was the notion of 'ethical pregnancy' (*prägnant-ethische Bedeutung*), a term with which Goethe described his sense of intuition for events which had universal political and ethical significance, rather than being part of a linear chain of destiny.[43] Such an event of 'ethical pregnancy' was the experience of the cannonade of Valmy 1792, which Goethe saw as a turning point in world history (*Weltenwende*).[44] Although both Cassirer and Spengler admired Goethe's ability to read and experience history symbolically, they wanted to learn very different lessons from it. Not only did they differ in the values which underlie most of the works; they also differed altogether in their goals when looking at human history. It becomes clear that, for Cassirer, the goal of philosophy was not to find some hidden law underlying human history. On the contrary, we ought to 'resist the temptation to see the totality of forms that surround us here as a final *metaphysical* unity' by explaining it with the 'simplicity of a simple cause of the world (*Weltgrund*)'.[45] Philosophy needed to preserve 'the totality of aspects resulting for different observers.' For 'in precisely this totality the particularity of the viewpoint is not extinguished but preserved and transcended.'[46]

However, Cassirer pushed the goals of his philosophical enquiry even further than merely allowing for infinite self-cognition. For, as he made clear, his view of history as a symbolic form was also motivated by a search for events of — universal — ethical significance, which would constitute a point of orientation for the construction of a present and future cultural and political life. In articles on Jacob Burckhardt and Albert Schweitzer, Cassirer is attracted to the role of not just a close observer of mankind, but of a 'pathologist' of civilization, based on the recognition that knowledge of human culture may lead to a reformation of man himself.[47] Cassirer emphasized the importance of findings in clinical pathology in his *Philosophy of Symbolic Forms*, but also in an independent publication in the French *Journal de Psychologie Normale et Pathologique* from 1929, entitled 'Étude sur la pathologie de la conscience symbolique'. Having addressed specifically studies in clinical pathology relating to distortions of sensation, Cassirer emphasized in this article that distortions in individual areas of sensation were related to a wider problem of the capacity for objectification, affecting the symbolic eye, that would characterize the normal patient. As in the third volume of the *Philosophy of Symbolic Forms*, Cassirer referred his reader to his notion of a *prégnance symbolique* or *symbolische Prägnanz*.[48] Symbolic forms constituted an 'autonomous and independent' space beyond the dichotomy of subject and object. Cassirer's admiration for Goethe's ability to perceive the world symbolically was thus not just based on his admiration for a singular man of genius. It was also an exemplification of an ideal human being endowed with a full sensual capacity, considered in the context of pathological cases that were lacking this range of sense.

It escaped Cassirer's eye that Spengler also picked up on Goethe's term of *Weltenwende*, coining his own term of *Zeitwende* as 'the type of a historical turning-point'. For Spengler, this moment signified the fulfilment of a collective destiny, rendering the witness utterly unimportant and irrelevant.[49] The individual, regardless of whether he is an agent or merely passive commentator of events, is only part of a historical organism to which he belongs by destiny. As became clear in the last section, Spengler thought that war was thus not just the highest form of being, but also a better educator than a philosopher. The symbolic understanding of some human beings, such as Goethe, cannot rank as highly in Spengler's philosophy of culture as it does in Cassirer's because, in Spengler's perception, intellectual qualities cannot change the course of destiny. The ideas of artists and thinkers did not 'make world history'; this, in Spengler's words, was 'just interested chatter of the literati'. Rather, it was important who realized them, 'the statesman and soldier', for ideas 'are only made conscious through blood, like drives, not by abstract deliberation'.[50] Spengler's intentions behind laying out his conception of history were thus very different from Cassirer's, who considered the philosopher to be an educator and trusted the powers of 'abstract deliberation' far more than those of a soldier.

When Cassirer argued in retrospect that Spengler's mythical thinking exerted 'a great political influence' by having 'declared that the modern man cannot avert his fate; he has to accept it', his critique formed something of a summary of the political consequences of Spengler's thought from the early 1920s onwards.[51] In doing so, Cassirer placed his argumentation against Spengler's fatalism within a larger critique of concepts of historical determinism in European thought, such as the notion of 'modifiable fate' epitomized by Hippolyte Taine, who subjected 'the individual Being and Doing' to a 'relentless necessity'.[52] He also argued that Hegel's philosophy of the state, which claimed to be an account of self-realizing freedom, turned 'the individual' into 'a mere marionette in relation to the all-powerful proceedings of the Idea'.[53] Towards the 1930s, Cassirer saw Spengler's contribution complemented by Heidegger's notion of *Geworfenheit*, or the 'being-thrownness', of man, both of which, in Cassirer's interpretation, had turned philosophy into a 'pliable instrument in the hands of the political leaders'.[54]

Cassirer's continued engagement with Spengler's 'sombre predictions of the decline and the inevitable destruction of our civilization' in the late 1930s and 40s was due to his conviction that after this renewed collapse of cultural life, it will be the task of philosophy again to recover for the individual the possibility of an 'active share in the construction and re-construction of man's cultural life'.[55] Ironically, Spengler died in 1936, too early to witness what many called the fulfilment of his prophecies of the 'decline of Western civilization', while Cassirer's death just a month before the end of the Second

World War did not allow him to conceptualize the renewed attempt to rescue civilization from its enemies.

Cassirer and Spengler: A Change of Perspective

In projecting two antagonistic trajectories of liberal and antiliberal thinkers — roughly represented by Goethe and Hegel — Cassirer was not entirely open about his own position. It cannot be denied that he had important agreements with Spengler, Burckhardt and Nietzsche in terms of presenting the line of cultural development between the eighteenth and the twentieth centuries as a declining one. Moreover, Cassirer did not engage adequately with the problem that Spengler rooted his antiliberal philosophy in Goethe rather than in Hegel. The image of Cassirer the 'Olympian' needs to be corrected. His very approach as a 'pathologist' of civilization brings him closer to the thinkers he criticized.

The analysis of the (albeit asymmetrical) polemic between Cassirer and Spengler equally suggests that we look at Spengler's work from a new angle. The immediate tendency to dismiss concepts such as *archsymbol* and *cultural soul* as useless fantasies, as a modern reader might want to do, accusing them of being inconsistent with empirical evidence, is based on a potentially false understanding of the intentions behind the *Decline*. The book is neither one of many 'universal histories', nor, as in Samuel Huntington's 'realist' reading, an *explanation* of cause and effect in world history.[56] There is even less reason to think that it should be valued more because some of its prophetic judgments may 'come true', as a recent republication of the *Decline* in Russian implies.[57]

Spengler's works address one of the key themes of early twentieth-century German thought: the question of the connections between a people, a culture, and the degree of their autochthonic development. Among other things, he thereby presents an elaborate historico-philosophical argument for the autonomy of Faustian culture. Cassirer's understanding of Spengler provides a crucial corrective for our understanding of Spengler's work. It positions it precisely not in the chronology of historical writing, but rather as an element in the development of mystical and astrological thought, as well as a political argument. With Cassirer in mind, Spengler's *Decline of the West* now emerges as a work of historical fiction, a poetically phrased political polemic. Cassirer understood Spengler far better than many other interpreters, because of the degree of conceptual affinity that they shared. Perhaps it could be said that the affinity of Spengler's and Cassirer's 'symbolic' glasses was greater than previously thought, despite the fact that they undoubtedly had opposing political frames and wore them with different intentions.[58]

Notes

[1] See, for example, Jacinta O'Hagan, *Conceptualizing the West in International Relations: From Spengler to Said* (Basingstoke: Palgrave, 2002).

[2] Thomas Mann also devoted much more attention to Spengler than the majority of German intellectuals. By contrast to Cassirer, however, the basis for Mann's interest was an initial sympathy for Spengler's political views. For Mann's most detailed comments about Spengler, see his essay 'Über die Lehre Spenglers' (1924), in Thomas Mann, *Schriften und Reden zur Literatur, Kunst und Philosophie*, vol. 1 (Frankfurt am Main: S. Fischer, 1968), pp. 223–29.

[3] 'I make no attempt to translate this mystical language of Spengler into commonplace idiomatic English; such an attempt would take away its special flavour and spoil the whole effect' (Ernst Cassirer, 'The Technique of our Modern Political Myths' (1945), in Donald P. Verene (ed.), *Symbol, Myth and Culture: Essays and Lectures of Ernst Cassirer, 1933–45* (New Haven: Yale University Press, 1979), pp. 242–72 [p. 261]).

[4] Ernst Cassirer, *Philosophie der symbolischen Formen*, vol. 2, *Das mythische Denken* [1925] (Hamburg: Felix Meiner, 2002) 280. Henceforth referred to as PSF, 2.

[5] For Spengler's views on entelechy, see Oswald Spengler, *Der Untergang des Abendlandes: Umrisse einer Morphologie der Weltgeschichte* [1918], 2 vols, 3rd edn (Munich: Beck, 1923), p. 20. Henceforth referred to as DW (for *Decline of the West*) with a volume and page reference.

[6] For Spengler on Leibniz's reception of entelechy in comparison with Goethe's notion of form, see DW, 2, 36. On the influence of Leibniz on Spengler, see Frits Boterman, *Oswald Spengler und sein 'Untergang des Abendlandes'* [1992], trans. by Christoph Strupp (Cologne: SH-Verlag, 2000), p. 127.

[7] DW, 1, 139. Compare with Cassirer, 'The Technique of Our Modern Political Myths' (1945), in *Essays and Lectures*, pp. 242–72 (p. 260). Spengler's thesis contained a reference to Dilthey's famous dictum 'we explain nature, we understand psychical life' (*Die Natur erklären wir, das Seelenleben verstehen wir*) (Wilhelm Dilthey, *Ideen über eine beschreibende und zergliedernde Psychologie* [Gesammelte Schriften, vol. 5], 8th edn (Göttingen: Vandenhoeck & Ruprecht, 1990), p. 144).

[8] Ernst Cassirer, *Zur Metaphysik der symbolischen Formen* [Nachlass, vol. 1], ed. by John Michael Krois (Hamburg: Meiner, 1995), 131. On Cassirer's Goethe reception, see Johan Michael Krois, 'Urworte: Cassirer als Goethe-Interpret', in Enno Rudolph and Bernd-Olaf Küppers (eds), *Kulturkritik nach Ernst Cassirer* (Hamburg: Felix Meiner, 1995), pp. 297–325.

[9] Cassirer, 'Über Basisphänomene', in *Zur Metaphysik der symbolischen Formen*, pp. 134–36.

[10] DW. 1, 141.

[11] Cassirer, *Zur Metaphysik der symbolischen Formen*, p. 62.

[12] Ernst Cassirer, *Philosophy of Symbolic Forms*, vol. 1, *Language*, trans. by Ralph Manheim (New Haven and London: Yale University Press, 1955), p. 69.

[13] Ernst Cassirer, *Philosophy of Symbolic Forms*, vol. 3, *The Phenomenology of Knowledge*, trans. by Ralph Manheim (New Haven and London: Yale University Press, 1957), p. 35. Cassirer also insisted that 'any attempt simply to transcend the field of form is doomed to failure' (p. 40).

[14] Cassirer's most important works on the Renaissance are *Das Erkenntnisproblem in der Philosophie und Wissenschaft der neueren Zeit*, vol. 1 (Berlin: Bruno Cassirer, 1906), *Individuum und Kosmos in der Philosophie der Renaissance* (Leipzig and Berlin: Teubner, 1927), *Die Platonische Renaissance in England und die Schule von Cambridge* (Leipzig and Berlin: Teubner, 1932), and, with Paul Oskar Kristeller as co-editor, *The Renaissance Philosophy of Man* (Chicago: University of Chicago Press, 1948).

[15] Cassirer, *Das Erkenntnisproblem in der Philosophie und Wissenschaft der neueren Zeit*, vol. 1; see Peter Gay, 'The Social History of Ideas. Ernst Cassirer and After', in Kurt H. Wolff and Barrington Moore Jr. (eds), *The Critical Spirit: Essays in Honour of Herbert Marcuse* (Boston: Beacon Press, 1967), pp. 106–21; and Oskar Schwemmer, 'Cassirers Bild der Renaissance' in Rudolph and Küppers (eds), *Kulturkritik nach Ernst Cassirer*, pp. 255–91 (p. 260).

[16] Ernst Cassirer, 'Deutschland und Westeuropa im Spiegel der Geistesgeschichte', *Inter-Nationes, Zeitschrift für die kulturellen Beziehungen Deutschlands zum Ausland* (Issue 1, v. 4, October 1931), 83–85 (p. 84).

[17] Spengler argued that there was something 'profoundly Gothic in this anti-Gothic movement' (DW, 2, 347).

[18] Cassirer, *The Myth of the State* (New Haven and London: Yale University Press, 1946), p. 291.

[19] In 1922, Cassirer wrote to the Warburg Institute, suggesting he give a talk with the title 'Zeit und Schicksal im mythischen Denken' ('Time and Destiny in Mythical Thought'), Warburg Institute Archive, III, General Correspondence, Cassirer to Gertrud Bing, 29 August 1922. Cassirer also wrote on mythical understanding of time at length in 1925 (see *Philosophy of Symbolic Forms*, vol. 2, *Mythical Thought*, trans. by Ralph Manhein (New Haven and London: Yale University Press, 1955), 117). Enno Rudolph claims that Cassirer's criticism of present political debates failed due to the fact that it remained unconnected to his theory of myth ('Politische Mythen als Kulturphänomene nach Ernst Cassirer', in Rudolph and Küppers (eds), *Kulturkritik nach Ernst Cassirer*, pp. 143–59 [p. 157]). As will become apparent, however, Cassirer's critique of Spengler is deeply connected with his theory of symbolic forms and with myth.

[20] Spengler argued that the understanding of time in physics 'obviously does not relate to the area of life, of destiny, of animated *historical* time', a 'representative phantom' for destiny (DW, 1, 163–64). Like Cassirer, Aby Warburg also read Spengler's works in the context of astrology and mythical thinking. Cassirer thanked Warburg for having opened his eyes for 'the general problem of the intellectual structure of astrology' (letter from Cassirer to Warburg of 26 June 1921; WIA, III). For Warburg's interest in Spengler, see his list of books requested from his library in Hamburg to be sent to Baden-Baden, where he was working whilst taking the waters, including the remark: 'Unfortunately, I also need to have Oswald Spengler's *Decline of the West*' (WIA, III, GC, Warburg to the *Kulturwissenschaftliche Bibliothek*, 19 May 1925).

[21] Cassirer, *Myth of the State*, p. 291.

[22] 'Hier gilt nicht sowohl, daß das Ich sich in den Dingen, daß der Mikrokosmos sich im Makrokosmos spiegelt, sondern hier schafft das Ich sich in seinen eigenen Produkten eine Art von "Gegenüber", das ihm als durchaus objektiv, als rein gegenständlich erscheint. Nur in dieser Art von "Projektion" vermag es sich selbst anzuschauen. In diesem Sinne bedeuten auch die Göttergestalten des Mythos nichts anderes als die sukzessiven Selbstoffenbarungen des mythischen Bewußtseins' (*Philosophie der symbolischen Formen* [1925], vol. 2, *Das mythische Denken*, ed. by Birgit Recki (Hamburg: Felix Meiner, 2002), 255).

[23] 'Als Vernichtung empfindet man nicht den Untergang einzelner oder vieler, sondern das Erlöschen der Organization, des "Wir"' (Oswald Spengler, *Der Mensch und die Technik* (München: Beck, 1931), p. 55).

[24] Ernst Cassirer, *Freiheit und Form* [1916], 4th edn (Hamburg: Felix Meiner, 2001), p. 343.

[25] See Toni Cassirer, *Mein Leben mit Ernst Cassirer*, 2nd edn (Hildesheim: Gerstenberg, 1981). As Barbara Besslich shows, Max Weber similarly criticized the ideological warfare or 'cultural war', in Barbara Besslich, *Wege in den "Kulturkrieg": Zivilisationskritik in Deutschland, 1890–1914* (Darmstadt: Wissenschaftliche Buchgesellschaft, 2000), p. 338.

[26] As Gawronsky remarks: 'He was drafted for [the] Civil Service, and his work consisted of the reading of foreign newspapers' (Dimitry Gawronsky, 'Ernst Cassirer: His Life and Work', in Paul Arthur Schilpp (ed.), *The Philosophy of Ernst Cassirer* [The Library of Living Philosophers] (La Salle, Illinois: Open Court, 1949), pp. 3–37 [p. 23]).

[27] See Raymond Geuss, 'Kultur, Bildung, Geist', *History and Theory*, vol. 35, no. 2 (May 1996), 151–64.

[28] Cassirer, *Freiheit und Form* (1916).

[29] On the Fichte Society, see Besslich, *Wege in den 'Kulturkrieg'*, p. 8, n. 22.

[30] Cassirer, *Freiheit und Form*, p. 393. Interestingly, Aby Warburg expressed a similar thought when he wrote in 1915 that after the war he hoped 'from our Germany a reinvigoration of the

categorical imperative, away from Langbehn and Chamberlain towards Kant and Fichte' (WIA, III, GC, Aby Warburg to Werner Weisbach, 3 April 1915).

[31] 'Krieg ist die ewige Form höhern menschlichen Daseins, und Staaten sind um des Krieges willen da; sie sind Ausdruck der Bereitschaft zum Kriege' (DW, 2, 55). See also Spengler's dictum on how to save Germany, 'in Bereitschaft sein ist alles', in 'Neue Formen der Weltpolitik' (lecture 1924) (in Oswald Spengler, *Politische Schriften*, 3rd edn (Munich: C. H. Beck, 1934), pp. 157–85 [p. 183]). McCormick's work on Schmitt only contains two references to Spengler, and both emphasize Schmitt's opposition to Spengler's pessimism. McCormick voices criticism of Herf for putting Spengler and Schmitt together in a group 'in a reductionist manner' (John P. McCormick, *Carl Schmitt's Critique of Liberalism: Against Politics as Technology* (Cambridge and New York: Cambridge University Press, 1997), pp. 98 and 45, n. 41).

[32] Spengler, *Politische Schriften*, p. xi.

[33] '*Technics is the tactics of life as a whole*' (Spengler, *Der Mensch und die Technik*, p. 7).

[34] DW, 2, 24. For a conceptual history of the term 'Faustian', see Hans Schwerte, *Faust und das Faustische: Ein Kapitel deutscher Ideologie* (Stuttgart: Klett, 1962).

[35] Jeffrey Herf, 'Paradoxes of Cultural Pessimism: Spengler as a Reactionary Modernist', in Alexander Demandt and John Farrenkopf (eds), *Der Fall Spengler: Eine kritische Bilanz* (Köln: Böhlau Verlag, 1994), pp. 97–115 (p. 106).

[36] Theodor W. Adorno and Max Horkheimer, *Dialektik der Aufklärung* (Amsterdam: Querido, 1947), p. 71. Moreover, as Martin Jay observed, Horkheimer's *Habilitationsschrift*, 'The Origins of the Bourgeois Philosophy of History' (1930), 'directly related the Renaissance view of science and technology to political domination' (*The Dialectical Imagination: A History of the Frankfurt School and the Institute of Social Research 1923–1950* (Boston and Toronto: Little, Brown, 1973), p. 257).

[37] Hence the title of Cassirer's work, *Freedom and Form*.

[38] Cassirer's distinction between the different uses to which technology can be put is thus dialectical, similar to the one drawn by the early Marcuse between politicized 'technology' and neutral 'technics' (see Herbert Marcuse, 'Some Social Implications of Modern Technology' [1941], in *Technology, War, and Fascism*, ed. by Douglas Kellner [*Collected Papers of Herbert Marcuse*, vol. 1] (London and New York: Routledge, 1998), 39–67.

[39] John Michael Krois cites here from 'Form und Technik' (1930), 'Der Begriff des Mythos bei Ernst Cassirer', in Hans Poser (ed.), *Philosophie und Mythos: Ein Kolloquium* (Berlin and New York: Walter de Gruyter, 1979), here cited from www.uni-essen.de/sesam/natur/aufsatze/krois.html; accessed 4 May 2005.

[40] See Cassirer's history of the idea of individual rights, in 'Die Idee der Republikanischen Verfassung', his speech on the occasion of the celebration of the Weimar constitution on 11 August 1928, delivered at the Senate of Hamburg, printed manuscript copy with corrections (London, Archive of the Warburg Institute, WIA, III, 29.2.9.1 [*Republican Constitution*], pp. 1–14). The notion of the importance of the individual is traceable throughout Cassirer's philosophical writings; see *Leibniz' System in seinen wissenschaftlichen Grundlagen* (Marburg: Elwert, 1902), and *Individuum und Kosmos in der Philosophie der Renaissance* (Leipzig and Berlin: Teubner, 1927).

[41] Cassirer, *Philosophy of Symbolic Forms*, vol. 2, *Mythical Thought*, pp. 216–17. Here Cassirer is drawing on Ernst Kapp's *Grundlinien einer Philosophie der Technik* (Braunschweig, 1877), which was influential in describing the use of the hand in combination with upright movement as the first technological advancement of Man.

[42] 'Wenn die Philosophie der Technik es mit den unmittelbaren und mittelbaren sinnlich-leiblichen Organen zu tun hat, kraft deren der Mensch der Außenwelt ihre bestimmte Gestalt und Prägung gibt, so wendet die Philosophie der symbolischen Formen ihre Frage auf die Gesamtheit der geistigen Ausdrucksfunktionen' (*Philosophie der symbolischen Formen*, vol. 2, *Das mythische Denken*, 255).

⁴³ Cassirer, *Philosophy of Symbolic Forms*, vol. 3, *The Phenomenology of Knowledge*, 134.
⁴⁴ Cassirer, *Republican Constitution*, p. 18. It was on the same day that the National Convent abolished French monarchy and established a republic in France, and subsequently, in occupied territories. Aby Warburg had used a similar term, that of 'symbolic pregnance'.
⁴⁵ Ernst Cassirer, *Zur Einsteinschen Relativitätstheorie: Erkenntnistheoretische Betrachtungen* (Berlin: Bruno Cassirer, 1921; Hamburg: Felix Meiner, 2001), p. 113.
⁴⁶ Cassirer, *Philosophy of Symbolic Forms*, vol. 3, *The Phenomenology of Knowledge*, 479.
⁴⁷ See Ernst Cassirer, 'Force and Freedom: Remarks on the English Edition of Jacob Burckhardt's "Reflections on History"', *The American Scholar*, vol. 13, no. 4 (Autumn 1944), and Ernst Cassirer, 'Albert Schweitzer as Critic of Nineteenth-Century Ethics', in A. A. Roback (ed.), *The Albert Schweitzer Jubilee Book* (Cambridge Mass.: Harvard University Press, 1946). Accessed as draft, holograph, corrected, in Beinecke Cassirer Papers, GEN MSS 98, II, 50 995 (Envelope #36) (date n.d.).
⁴⁸ 'Désignons le rapport en vertu duquel du sensible se trouve posséder un *sens*, et le représente à la conscience d'une manière immediate, comme celui de "prégnance symbolique" (*symbolische Prägnanz*). Il nous faudra dire alors que le fait de cette "prégnance" ne se laisse ramener ni à des processus purement reproductifs, ni à des processus intellectuals discursifs: il faut l'admettre comme une détermination autonome et indépendente, sans laquelle il ne pourrait y avoir pour nous ni "objet" ni "sujet", et ne purraient exister ni l'unité de l'object, ni celle de "moi"' (Ernst Cassirer, 'Étude sur la pathologie de la conscience symbolique', *Journal de Psychologie Normale et Pathologique*, vol. 26, nos 5–6 (15 May–15 June 1929), 289–337 [p. 328]). See also the *Philosophy of Symbolic Forms*, vol. 3, chapters 2–5, for a discussion of mental illness in the context of an imbalance of symbolic forms.
⁴⁹ 'Ich sah die Gegenwart — den sich nahenden Weltkrieg — in einem ganz andern Licht [...] das war der *Typus einer historischen Zeitwende*, die innerhalb eines großen historischen Organismus von genau abgrenzbarem Umfange einen biographisch *seit Jahrhunderten vorbestimmten Platz* hatte' (DW, 1, 65).
⁵⁰ Oswald Spengler, *Preußentum und Sozialismus* (Munich: Beck, 1919), cited from *Politische Schriften*, p. 86.
⁵¹ Cassirer, 'The Technique of Our Modern Political Myths', in *Essays and Lectures*, p. 262.
⁵² *Essays and Lectures*, pp. 243–44.
⁵³ *Essays and Lectures*, p. 244.
⁵⁴ Cassirer, *Myth of the State*, p. 293.
⁵⁵ See Ernst Cassirer, 'The Concept of Philosophy as a Philosophical Problem' (1935), in *Essays and Lectures*, pp. 49–64 (p. 59).
⁵⁶ Samuel Huntington, *The Clash of Civilizations and the Remaking of World Order* (New York: Simon and Schuster, 1996).
⁵⁷ 'Introduction', in Oswald Spengler, *Zakat Evropy*, ed. by Igor Makhankov, 2 vols (Moscow: Iris Press, 2003), vol. 1, 11–12.
⁵⁸ I would like to thank Martin Ruehl for numerous valuable comments on this paper, and Paul Bishop for further helpful suggestions for improvement.

CASSIRER, WARBURG, AND THE IRRATIONAL

By Edward Skidelsky

Ernst Cassirer has often been viewed as a man out of time, his thought a strange idyll of harmony in the midst of a tragic century. Isaiah Berlin describes it as 'lucid, civilized, [...] and serenely innocent'.[1] This assessment is at best a half-truth. Cassirer was certainly imbued with the spirit of Apollo, but he was by no means unreceptive to that of Dionysos. Much of his work from the mid-1920s onwards is devoted to questions of myth and the irrational. His interest in these subjects is inseparable from his relationship with the great art-historian Aby Warburg, and his famous library. The following essay explores this relationship further, suggesting ways in which it might have influenced Cassirer's mature thought.

Cassirer made the acquaintance of the *Kulturwissenschaftliche Bibliothek Warburg* in 1920, not long after taking up a professorship at the new University of Hamburg. Warburg himself had suffered a mental breakdown in 1918, and was now confined to a sanatorium in Kreuzlingen. It was therefore his assistant, Fritz Saxl, who first showed Cassirer around the library. He later recounted the extraordinary impression it made on the philosopher. 'This library is dangerous,' Cassirer told Saxl, 'I shall either have to avoid it altogether or imprison myself here for years. The philosophical problems involved are close to my own, but the concrete historical material which Warburg has collected is overwhelming.'[2] Cassirer soon became one of the Warburg Library's most treasured users and patrons. With Saxl acting as intermediary, he managed to forge a close intellectual bond with the slowly recovering Warburg. 'When [Warburg] returned cured to Hamburg in 1925,' writes Toni Cassirer in her memoirs, 'countless threads had already been tied between his and Ernst's work.'[3]

It is hard to find words to describe the strange flash of recognition that passed between Cassirer and Warburg. Cassirer himself talked of a 'pre-established harmony' between their viewpoints.[4] And Warburg thanked Cassirer for having made 'the tapping of the rescue party on the other side of the tunnel so perceptible that I once again seized my discarded hammer and tried to find courage to smash through the old rubble'.[5] The metaphor is exact. The two men reached their common destination separately, from different directions, yet each derived enormous strength from the agreement of the other. Warburg in particular drew encouragement from the support of a mind more lucid and systematic than his own. Cassirer became the 'house philosopher' of the Warburg Library, providing its less theoretical members with a usable conceptual framework. But Cassirer also benefited from the relationship. Not only did the Warburg Library place a huge collection of books and a receptive audience at his disposal; it also provided him with *intellectual* corroboration. He immediately recognized it as the objective correlative of his own, germinal theory of symbolic forms; it gave him courage, as he later admitted, to bring that theory to fruition.[6]

What exactly was it that so impressed Cassirer on first entering the Warburg Library? The answer lies to hand. The library embodied a conception of culture very similar to the one taking shape in his own mind. The idea of culture as a system of 'symbolic forms' apparently first came to Cassirer in 1917, as he was entering a street car.[7] The Warburg Library must have struck him as the very incarnation of this thought. It conceived its subject, the classical heritage of Europe, not as a set of texts and monuments but as a system of verbal and pictorial symbols. Its aim was to provide a kind of atlas of European civilization, a panoptic view of its formations and transformations. Iconography replaced authorship or chronology as the basic principle of organization. Cassirer immediately grasped the significance of this novel arrangement. 'From the row of books,' he wrote, recalling his first visit to the library, 'emerged more and more clearly a series of images, of distinct spiritual ur-motifs and ur-forms.'[8]

Cassirer shared with Warburg, moreover, a view of symbolism as *divided* into distinct subspecies. His idea of a plurality of symbolic forms makes its first public appearance in his 1921 essay, *Goethe und die mathematische Physik*.[9] Here Cassirer attempts to adjudicate the famous quarrel between Goethe's intuitive theory of nature and that of modern physics by divesting them both of their ontological status, transforming them into equally valid though incommensurable forms of symbolism. Not only science, but language, art, myth and religion become for us 'different symbolic forms, as it were, in which we accomplish the decisive synthesis of spirit and world'.[10] The conflict between Goethe and Newton now appears in a more tractable light. We can now accept that 'a manifold of nature-concepts is possible, without the objectivity of one absolutely abolishing and destroying that of the others'.[11]

Warburg had already derived a similarly variegated conception of symbolism from the Hegelian philosopher Friedrich Theodor Vischer. In a now forgotten essay of 1887, *Das Symbol*, Vischer locates all symbols on a spectrum between two poles. On the one extreme lies the magical or religious symbol, in which image and meaning are indissolubly fused. In certain primitive mythologies, the bull not only stands for virility, it contains virility, indeed, it can be eaten for its virility. At the other extreme stands the purely arbitrary, conventional symbolism of exact science and allegory, in which image and meaning are recognized as possessing no intrinsic connection. But between these two poles lies the type of symbolism described by Vischer as 'connection with reservation'. Here image and meaning are experienced as related, yet none the less known to be distinct. This is the sphere of poetry proper. The poet *feels* the sunset as 'ominous', even though he *knows* it is no such thing. He sojourns in the realm of myth, but remains a citizen of the realm of science. Art thus mediates between the two poles. It is the crucial first stage in the overcoming of myth, retaining something of its emotional aura while discarding its cognitive claims. In the tranquillity of aesthetic contemplation, the 'dark' force of myth is both neutralized and preserved.[12]

Warburg seized upon Vischer's theory of symbolism as offering an insight into the concrete historical phenomenon of the Renaissance. What the artists of the *Quattrocento* discovered in antiquity, claimed Warburg, was the revitalizing force of pagan myth:

> The unleashing of uninhibited expressive movements which occurred in particular in Asia Minor among the followers of Bacchic cults embraces the whole gamut of kinetic utterance of human nature. [...] Wherever these are represented in works of art they convey the echoes of such surrender to the depths. The marks of the thiasotic mint are indeed an essential and uncanny characteristic of these expressive coinages which spoke, for instance, from ancient sarcophagi to the sensibility of Renaissance artists.[13]

But even as they exploited these ancient images, the artists of the Renaissance were continually on guard against succumbing to their demonic power. They accordingly devised ways of reproducing them in a suitably distanced, metaphoric form: 'The style of simulated classical sculpture (*grisaille* in an engraving or drawing) confines the coinages of the *revenants* in the distant shadowy realm of the explicit metaphor.'[14] In terms of Vischer's theory, techniques such as *grisaille* helped lift the symbol out of the sphere of mythic immediacy into that of aesthetic distance. By means of such devices, the passions of the ancient world were rendered safe for Christian Europe.

Warburg's view of symbolism as divided into mythic, artistic and scientific varieties bears an obvious affinity to Cassirer's nascent philosophy of symbolic forms. But there are also important differences. Cassirer's philosophy of symbolic forms first emerges as an attempt to *mediate* the tension between Goethe's theory of colour and modern mathematical physics. Conciliation is its keynote; it tries to settle disagreement between the branches of culture by taking them symbolically. Warburg, by contrast, portrays culture as inescapably and gloriously conflictual. Renaissance art is torn between the rival forces of *mythos* and *logos*. Dependent upon myth, it at the same time struggles to preserve a reflective distance from it. Its celebrated harmony is not a gift of grace, but a precarious achievement. 'Athens' — in Warburg's famous dictum — 'must always be conquered afresh from Alexandria.'[15]

The contrast between Cassirer and Warburg was as much temperamental as intellectual. Cassirer, the Olympian, 'kindly-indifferent' as Edgar Wind describes him, met his antipole in Warburg, the self-styled *revenant*, passionate and tormented.[16] Style, as usual, is an index of personality. The former's is smooth, elegant and somewhat stereotyped; the latter's tangled, private but occasionally brilliant. Warburg's writings bear the mark of bitter personal experience. He knew at first hand the power of the irrational, and was correspondingly appreciative of the value — and fragility — of reason. Yet even after his return from Kreuzlingen, the demons were never far from the surface. 'An almost awe-inspiring power emanated from him,' wrote Fritz Saxl about the cured Warburg, 'and he lived and worked convinced that the scholar does not choose his vocation but that in all he does he is obeying a higher command. None of those who lived and worked with him in those years could resist this spell.'[17] Max Weber springs to mind. Of all Warburg's contemporaries, he shared most closely his paradoxical combination of demonic charisma and scholarly self-abnegation.

But in spite of — or perhaps precisely because of — their considerable intellectual and personal differences, Cassirer loved and revered Warburg. His funeral oration speaks of his 'might' and his 'tragic grandeur'. It pictures him as a hero of the intellect, dying with his sword unbroken in his hand.[18] The force of Warburg's thought and personality left a decisive mark on Cassirer. It encouraged him to qualify somewhat the cheerful, 'ironic' attitude to cultural plurality he had inherited from Goethe; it persuaded him to view the various symbolic forms as in certain respects *discordant*. But Warburg's influence did not operate in a vacuum. It was reinforced by the breakdown of political order in Germany, and the attendant rise of philosophical and ideological irrationalism. Warburg's emphasis on the tension between *mythos* and *logos* provided Cassirer with the tools he needed to get a handle on these menacing new trends. In his writings on technology and fascism, it is Warburg's tragic perspective, not Goethe's irenic perspective, that ultimately prevails. Warburg, one might say, provided Cassirer with a stepladder down to contemporary social reality. It is thanks to him that the philosophy of symbolic forms is something more than a piece of elegant escapism.

Cassirer and Warburg both identify the unruly element in the system of culture as *myth*. Myth, for both thinkers, is much more than an anthropological category; it is an expression of the primal energy of the human mind. The other cultural forms all bear the stamp of this mythic *arche*. Art, as we have seen, must endlessly distance itself from its own mythical origins; religion continually spiritualizes mythical stories; even science is forever struggling against a 'mythical' interpretation of notions such cause and substance. Myth is both a source of creativity and a threat. It invigorates, but it can also overwhelm. Philosophy's proper task is not to eliminate but to *understand* myth, to accord it its rightful place in the system of culture:

> For knowledge does not master myth by banishing it from its confines. Rather, knowledge can truly conquer only what it has understood in its own specific

meaning and essence. Until this task has been completed, the battle which theoretical knowledge thinks it has won for good will keep breaking out afresh. The foe which knowledge has seemingly defeated forever crops up again in its own midst.[19]

In our therapeutic age, this passage irresistibly suggests the 'return of the repressed'. But Cassirer was thinking not about the psyche but about the contemporary ideological scene. Further down the page we read: 'That no sharp boundary has been drawn between myth and logos is best shown by the recent reappearance of myth in the realm of pure methodology. Today it is openly asserted that no clear logical division can be made between myth and history and that all historical understanding is and must be permeated by mythical elements.' Contemporary readers would have recognized this as a reference to Oswald Spengler's recently published and massively influential *The Decline of the West*. This was only one of a growing number of works which intertwined — with varying degrees of methodological self-awareness — myth and history. Such works were usually inflammatory, often nationalist or racist. When Cassirer and Warburg spoke of the threat posed by myth, they had this kind of literature very much in mind. For them — as indeed for Freud — mythological analysis was a tool for the understanding and exorcism of political irrationalism. All three men were engaged in a rear-guard defence of reason and *Bildung* against the encroachment of mass fanaticism.[20]

This political agenda remains on the whole hidden, and for good reason; the neutrality of research was, after all, part of what Warburg and Cassirer were trying to defend. But it is none the less visible under the scholarly surface. Warburg wrote an essay in 1927 comparing contemporary British and Italian stamps. He shows that while both draw on classical symbols of power, the British stamp employs the familiar *grisaille* to keep them at a metaphoric distance, whereas the Fascist stamp depicts real *fasces* and a real axe.[21] Cassirer gestured to politics in a similarly indirect manner, developing his theory of myth with reference to contemporary right-wing thinkers such as Spengler, Klages, and Heidegger. It is only in his last work, *The Myth of the State*, that he finally makes explicit the political dimension of his thought. Here fascism is interpreted as a technologically orchestrated recrudescence of myth. It signals the final breakdown of distance, the collapse of the *grisaille*. 'In all critical moments of man's social life, the rational forces that resist the rise of the old mythical conceptions are no longer sure of themselves. In these moments the time for myth has come again. For myth has not been really vanquished and subjugated. It is always there, lurking in the dark and waiting for its hour and opportunity.'[22]

Such passages present Cassirer in the familiar guise of the chastened enlightener, realizing only too late the fragility of civilization. But there is more to his thought than this. Neither he nor Warburg regarded the new barbarism as a straightforward *revival* of old mythical habits of thought; both discerned in it the culmination of something distinctively modern. This is the most interesting and original aspect of their social thought, anticipating in many ways Adorno and Horkheimer's more famous *Dialectic of Enlightenment*.

The self-destruction of modernity is a central theme of Warburg's remarkable and bizarre lecture on the serpent ritual.[23] In 1923, still incarcerated in Kreuzlingen, Warburg suggested to his doctors that he might prove his mental fitness by writing and delivering a lecture. They agreed. Warburg took as his theme this famous Indian ritual, which he himself had travelled to New Mexico some thirty years earlier to observe. He had missed the ritual, but managed to collect *en route* many photographs and anthropological observations. Warburg never intended his lecture for publication. In his notes he dismisses it as a product of madness. But he none the less sent a copy to Saxl, accompanied by instructions not to make it public. 'This gruesome spasm of a decapitated frog may be shown only to my dear wife, with the permission of Dr. Embden, and to my brother Max and Professor Cassirer.'[24] Cassirer, who was at that moment working on the second volume of *The Philosophy of Symbolic Forms*, read Warburg's lecture with avid interest.[25] Many of its ideas — and they are profound ideas — work their way into his own writings on myth.

The basic theme of Warburg's lecture is already familiar to us from Vischer. For the Pueblo Indians, the snake symbolizes lightening, the longed-for harbinger of rain. But the connection between the two is not merely conventional. In accordance with the basic law of primitive symbolism, it is perceived as a real identity of essence. The snake in some sense *is* the lightening, and through its magical mediation lightening itself can be summoned. However, Warburg's main interest is not Pueblo mythology as such, but the *tenacity* of that mythology in the face of change. Pueblo culture is not pristine; it has, as Warburg puts it, been 'layered over' twice, first by Spanish Catholicism and secondly by American secular civilization. Yet the native pagan mythology has proved remarkably stubborn. Its symbols are visible on the walls of the local Catholic churches, painted by native artists. And when Warburg asked a class of state-educated Pueblo children to depict a thunderstorm, he was delighted to find that two of them drew the lightening not realistically but in the traditional form of the serpent.[26] Warburg seized upon these pagan residues as proof of the tenacity of the primitive. His lecture is, as he confessed in his notes, a 'search for the eternally unchanging Red Indian in the helpless human soul'.[27]

Given his preference for Athens over Alexandria, one might suppose Warburg to have supported the American authorities in their attempt to eliminate these 'barbarous' residues. But his attitude was more complex. American technocratic civilization was not, in his view, a force for enlightenment; indeed, it was in some respects allied to the very barbarism it opposed. This is the import of his conclusion, a passage of typical metaphorical density and brilliance:

> I was able to capture with my camera in the streets of San Francisco the conqueror of the serpent cult and of the fear of lightening, the heir to the aboriginal inhabitants, the gold-seeking intruder into the land of the Indians. It is Uncle Sam with the top hat proudly striding along the road in front of an imitation classical rotunda. High above his top hat there stretches the electric wire. By means of Edison's copper serpent he has wrested the thunderbolt from nature.
>
> The modern American has no fear of the rattlesnake. He kills and exterminates it but certainly does not worship it. [...] Lightening imprisoned in the wire, captive electricity, has created a civilization that does away with paganism. What does it put in its stead? The forces of nature are no longer conceived as anthropomorphic or biomorphic shapes but rather as infinite waves obeying the pressure of the human hand. By this means, the civilization of the machine age destroys what science, emerging from myth, had painfully conquered, the zone of contemplation [*Andachtsraum*] that became the zone of reason [*Denkraum*].
>
> The modern Prometheus and the modern Icarus, Franklin and the Wright brothers who invented the dirigible airplane, are the fateful destroyers of that sense of distance who threaten to lead the globe back into chaos. Telegram and telephone destroy the cosmos. Mythopoetic and symbolic thought, in their struggle to spiritualize man's relation with his environment, have created space as a zone of contemplation or of reasoning — that space which the instantaneous connection of electricity destroys, unless a disciplined humanity restores the inhibitions of conscience.[28]

One central idea emerges from this complex tangle of images: modern America is permeated by the same mythical forces it arrogantly boasts of having overcome. Its electric cables are serpents, its inventors ancient heroes; the very nation appears in quasi-mythical guise as 'Uncle Sam'. Modern civilization threatens to dissolve into a kind of technological bacchanalia. Yet responsibility for this impending chaos lies with modernity itself. The telegram, the telephone and the airplane have destroyed that *Ferngefühl* on which all civilization rests. Even science, the immediate source of these inventions, is threatened with destruction, for it too, no less than the arts, depends upon the cultivation of symbolic distance. Enlightenment will be consumed by its own children.

To what extent Cassirer was directly influenced by this cryptic piece of prose is impossible to say. What is certain is that similar thoughts punctuate his later writings. Opposition to the positivist instrumentalization of science was central to Marburg neo-Kantianism and to Cassirer's early epistemological writings. But it was only later that Cassirer began to attack positivism and instrumentalism not simply as theories in the philosophy of science but as cultural and political phenomena. Like Warburg, he viewed them as expressions of the hubris of a civilization that has forgotten or 'suppressed' its mythic origins, thus bringing about its own self-destruction. Cassirer cites as an example the degeneration of Comtean positivism into a pseudo-religion, complete with priests and temples of science.[29] And in *The Myth of the State* he shows how the instrumentalization of political reason, initially undertaken in a spirit of enlightenment, eventually gives rise to the myths of modern totalitarianism. Cassirer explicitly conceived his own philosophy as an antidote to the 'forgetfulness' of positivism. Like the Warburg Library, it is an attempt on the part of reason at *mnemosyne* or recollection.[30] It is based on the conviction that reason can understand and feel 'at home' with itself only when it has succeeded in reconstructing its own ascent from the sphere of myth. This grand attempt at reclaiming reason was to be brought to fruition in *The Philosophy of Symbolic Forms*.[31]

Notes

[1] Isaiah Berlin, '[Review of] Ernst Cassirer, *The Philosophy of the Enlightenment*', *English Historical Review*, 68 (1953), 617–19 (p. 619).

[2] Fritz Saxl, 'Ernst Cassirer, in *The Philosophy of Ernst Cassirer*, ed. by Paul Arthur Schlipp (La Salle, Illinois: Open Court, 1949), pp. 47–51 (p. 48).

[3] Toni Cassirer, *Mein Leben mit Ernst Cassirer* (Hildesheim: Gerstenberg Verlag, 1981), p. 126. She has got the date wrong; Warburg returned to Hamburg in the summer of 1924.

[4] Warburg Institute Archive, General Collection, letter from Ernst Cassirer to Fritz Saxl, 24 March 1923.

[5] Warburg Institute Archive, General Collection, letter from Aby Warburg to Ernst Cassirer, 27 March 1923.

[6] See Ernst Cassirer, 'Critical Idealism as a Philosophy of Culture: Lecture to the Warburg Institute, 26 May, 1936', in *Symbol, Myth and Culture: Essays and Lectures of Ernst Cassirer, 1935–1945*, ed. by Donald Verene (New Haven: Yale University Press, 1979), pp. 64–91: 'I was strongly impressed by this first inspection [of the Warburg Library]; and it was by this impression that I was encouraged to pursue a study that I had been planning for many years — to give a systematic analysis of the problem I have attempted to treat in this lecture' (p. 91).

[7] Dimitry Gawronsky, 'Ernst Cassirer: His Life and Work', in *The Philosophy of Ernst Cassirer*, pp. 3–37 (p. 25).

[8] Ernst Cassirer, 'Worte zur Beisetzung von Professor Dr. Aby M. Warburg', in Stephan Füssel (ed.), *Mnemosyne: Beiträge zum 50 Todestag von Aby M. Warburg* (Göttingen: Gratia-Verlag, 1979), pp. 15–22 (p. 17).

[9] Ernst Cassirer, 'Goethe und die mathematische Physik', in *Idee und Gestalt* (Darmstadt: Wissenschaftliche Buchgesellschaft, 1971), pp. 33–80.

[10] Cassirer, *Idee und Gestalt*, p. 69. This, incidentally, is the first use of the term 'symbolic form' in Cassirer's published works.

[11] Cassirer, *Idee und Gestalt*, p. 73.

[12] For more on Vischer and his influence on Warburg, cf. E. H. Gombrich, *Aby Warburg: An Intellectual Autobiography* (Oxford: Phaidon, 1986), pp. 72–75, and Edgar Wind, 'Warburg's Concept of *Kulturwissenschaft* and its Meaning for Aesthetics', in Edgar Wind, *The Eloquence of Symbols: Studies in Humanist Art* (Oxford: Clarendon Press, 1993), pp. 21–35.

[13] Aby Warburg, Introduction to *Mnemosyne*, quoted in Gombrich, *Aby Warburg*, p. 246.

[14] Warburg, *Notebook*, quoted in Gombrich, *Aby Warburg*, p. 247.

[15] Warburg, *Gesammelte Schriften*, quoted in Gombrich, *Aby Warburg*, p. 214.

[16] Warburg Institute Archive, General Collection, letter from Edgar Wind to A. Warburg, 3 September 1928.

[17] See Fritz Saxl, 'The History of the Warburg Library, 1886–1844', in Gombrich, *Aby Warburg*, pp. 325–38 (p. 335).

[18] See Cassirer in Füssel (ed.), *Mnemosyne*, pp. 17 and 22. This tragic and martial language is, incidentally, untypical of Cassirer, and reveals the strong impression made on him by Warburg's otherwise alien personality.

[19] Ernst Cassirer, *The Philosophy of Symbolic Forms*, vol. 2, *Mythical Thought* (New Haven: Yale University Press, 1955), p. xvii.

[20] For further discussion in this connection, see George Mosse, *German Jews beyond Judaism* (Bloomington: Indiana University Press, 1985), pp. 48–54.

[21] Gombrich, *Aby Warburg*, pp. 264–65.

[22] Ernst Cassirer, *The Myth of the State* (New Haven: Yale University Press, 1946), p. 280.

[23] Aby M. Warburg, *Images from the Region of the Pueblo Indians of North America*, trans. by Michael P. Steinberg (Ithica: Cornell University Press, 1995).

[24] Warburg Institute Archive, General Collection, letter from Aby Warburg to Fritz Saxl, 26 March 1923.

[25] Warburg Institute Archive, General Collection, letter from Fritz Saxl to Aby Warburg, 7 May 1923.

[26] Compare with Warburg, *Images from the Region of the Pueblo Indians of North America*, pp. 50–51.

[27] Cited in Gombrich, *Aby Warburg*, p. 226.

[28] I have followed Gombrich's translation here, because it is better and includes slightly more than Steinberg's. I have adjusted only the punctuation in a few place (see Gombrich, *Aby Warburg*, pp. 225–26).

[29] See Cassirer, *The Philosophy of Symbolic Forms*, vol. 2, *Mythical Thought*, p. xvii.

[30] *Mnemosyne* was the Platonic legend selected by Warburg to hang over the entry of his library. But as Cassirer points out, it was intended not so much in Plato's sense as in the sense of Hegel's *Erinnerung*. Cassirer compares and contrasts his own philosophical enterprise with Hegel's (see Ernst Cassirer, 'Critical Idealism as a Philosophy of Culture: Lecture to the Warburg Institute, 26 May, 1936', *Symbol, Myth and Culture*, pp. 77–81).

[31] I would like to express my gratitude to Paul Bishop, Dina Gusejnova, Geoffrey Shullenberger, and Joshua Cherniss, all of whom commented on earlier versions of this paper. Above all, I would like to the thank the Archive of the Warburg Institute for giving me permission to quote from the superbly catalogued correspondence of Aby Warburg.

'EINE GEISTIGE URFORM DER GESCHICHTLICHEN ERKENNTNIS'? CASSIRER AND BACHOFEN ON THE SYMBOL

By Paul Bishop

One of the chief characteristics of philosophical thought in the twentieth century is its concern with the problem of myth, reflected in an astonishing multiplicity of approaches.[1] It is possible to discern a distinct number of schools or approaches to the problem of myth.[2] First, there is the anthropological school, exemplified by the English anthropologist, Sir Edward Tylor (1832–1917), and by the Scottish anthropologist (born in Glasgow), Sir James Frazer (1854–1941), for whom myth constitutes a 'primitive' equivalent to science.[3] Second, there is the position, taken by the Polish-born ethnologist Bronislaw Malinowski (1884–1942) and the Rumanian-born mythologist and philosopher Mircea Eliade (1907–1986), for whom myth is far from being a scientific interpretation of the world, but offers, rather, an existential or religious one.[4] Third, there are the theologians, such as Rudolf Bultmann (1884–1976) or Hans Jonas (1903–1993), who concerned themselves with the biblical New Testament and the ancient writings of the Gnostics respectively, and who saw myth in hermeneutic, and in this sense 'symbolic', terms.[5] Finally, there is the psychoanalytic approach, if it is possible to give a name to what is, in effect, a whole subset of distinct approaches, including those taken by the Vienna-based analysts Sigmund Freud (1856–1939) and Otto Rank (1884–1939), the Zurich-based analyst Carl Gustav Jung (1875–1961), and the Berlin-based analyst Karl Abraham (1877–1925); there was, as is well-known, much discussion and controversy between the various psychoanalytic circles. The major works here include Freud's *Totem and Taboo: Some Points of Agreement between the Menal Lives of Savages and Neurotics* [*Totem und Tabu: Einige Übereinstimmungen im Seelenleben der Wilden und der Neurotiker*] (1913); Rank's *The Myth of the Birth of the Hero: A Psychological Interpretation of Mythology* [*Der Mythus von der Geburt des Helden: Versuch einer psychologischen Mythendeutung*] (1909) and *The Incest Theme in Literature and Legend: Fundamentals of a Psychology of Literary Creation* [*Das Inzest-Motiv in Dichtung und Sage: Grundzüge einer Psychologie des dichterischen Schaffens*] (1912); Jung's ground-breaking work, *Transformations and Symbols of the Libido: Contributions to the Developmental History of Thought* [*Wandlungen und Symbole der Libido: Beiträge zur Entwicklungsgeschichte des Denkens*, translated as *Psychology of the Unconscious*]

(1911–1912), as well as Abraham's *Dreams and Myths: A Study in Race Psychology* [*Traum und Mythus: Eine Studie zur Völkerpsychologie*] (1909), not to mention *Myth and Guilt: The Crime and Punishment of Mankind* (1958) by Theodor Reik (1888–1969), and the Jungian-inspired derivatives of James Hillman, the creator of psychological polytheism,[6] and Joseph Campbell (b. 1904), the author of *The Hero of a Thousand Faces* (1949) and the four-volume study of world mythologies, *The Masks of God* (1960–1968). But how are these various schools of research into myth to be related to the philosophy of Ernst Cassirer? Indeed, can they be related at all? Yet with these thinkers there begins the path from anthropology to politics, on which we encounter Cassirer as a significant path-marker, perhaps even as an important sign-post for a better understanding of the relation to politics of myth.[7]

To begin with, we must remember that, if Cassirer had little to say about these various approaches and distanced himself from them, so they in turn virtually ignored Cassirer, although they recognized his importance.[8] Of Gershom Scholem (1897–1982), Mircea Eliade, and Henry Corbin (1907–1978), whom he collectively dubs the 'historians of religion', Steven M. Wasserstrom has pointed out that 'all three knew the work of Ernst Cassirer on symbolism [...] and acknowledged its importance — even as they distanced themselves from it'. And Cassirer's discussion of psychoanalysis is notably sparse,[9] just as the psychoanalytic tradition seems to have remained, and to remain, largely ignorant of Cassirer.[10]

One of the first studies of myth undertaken by Cassirer was his essay, published as number six in the series, edited by Fritz Saxl, of the *Studien der Bibliothek Warburg*, entitled 'Language and Myth: A Contribution to the Problem of the Divine Names' ['Sprache und Mythos: Ein Beitrag zum Problem der Götternamen'] (1925).[11] This study took as its starting-point the theses of the German philologist Hermann Usener (1834–1905), according to whom etymology can be equated with mythology, inasmuch as the fundamental structures of religion emerge from an analysis of the names of the gods and the heroes.[12] On the first page of this essay Cassirer evokes, in a beautiful passage, the mythical world of antiquity, as reflected in the opening to Plato's dialogue, *Phaedrus*:

> The opening passage of the Platonic dialogue *Phaedrus* describes how Socrates lets Phaedrus, whom he encounters, lure him beyond the gates of the city to the banks of Ilissus. Plato has pictured the setting of this scene in nicest detail, and there lies over it a glamour and fragrance well-nigh unequalled in classical descriptions of nature. In the shade of a tall plane tree, at the brink of a cool spring, Socrates and Phaedrus lie down; the summer breeze is mild and sweet and full of the cicada's song.
>
> [Zu Beginn des Platonischen Phaidros wird geschildert, wie Sokrates durch Phaidros, dem er begegnet, vor die Tore der Stadt an das Ufer des Ilissos gelockt wird. Die Landschaft, in die Platon diese Szene versetzt, hat er bis in

die feinsten Züge ausgemalt — und es liegt über dieser Darstellung ein Glanz und ein Duft, wie wir ihn sonst in antiken Naturschilderungen kaum kennen. Im Schatten einer hohen Platane, am Rande einer kühlen Quelle lassen Sokrates und Phaidros sich nieder, die sommerliche Luft weht milde und süß und ist erfüllt vom Zirpen der Zikaden.][13]

Nevertheless, it would be wrong if we allowed this aestheticized conjuring of myth to lead us to believe that Cassirer had no sense of the dark side of myth. Quite the contrary.

In the same year, 1925, there appeared the second volume of *The Philosophy of Symbolic Forms* [*Philosophie der symbolischen Formen*] (1923–1929), in which Cassirer presented 'mythical thought' precisely as one of the 'symbolic forms', as he had already done with language (volume 1) and as he would do later with science (volume 3), history, and art (see *An Essay on Man* [1944], chapters 10 and 9).[14] We should note here that Cassirer, in his analysis of myth, not only goes back to the thinking of the pre-Socratics (Parmenides, Empedocles, Democritus, Heraclitus), where the question of the significance of myth was posed for the first time, and to the tradition of Platonic philosophy, where the question of myth was discussed at length, but he also turns, and significantly so, to the philosophy of the nineteenth century, to the philosophy of German Idealism, and in particular to the philosophy of Friedrich Wilhelm Joseph Schelling (1775–1854), with whose philosophy of mythology he deals in the introduction to *Mythical Thought*.[15]

According to Cassirer, in his philosophy of mythology Schelling, like Johann Gottfried Herder (1744–1803) in his philosophy of language, *überwindet* ('overcomes') 'the principle of allegory' ['das Prinzip der Allegorie'], and turns to 'the fundamental problem of symbolic expression' ['das Grundproblem des symbolischen Ausdrucks']. Instead of an 'allegorical' interpretation of the world of myth, Schelling offers as a 'tautegorical' ['tautegorische'] one: that is, Schelling looks at 'mythical figures as autonomous configurations of the human spirit' ['die mythischen Gestalten als autonome Gebilde des Geistes'], which 'one must understand from within by knowing the way in which they take on meaning and form' ['aus sich selbst, aus einem spezifischen Prinzip der Sinn- und Gestaltgebung begriffen werden müssen'].[16] For Cassirer, the tautegorical understanding of myth represents a sea-change in the approach to myth, a change he describes as a shift from *analytische Zersetzung* ('analytical disintegration') to *synthetisches Verstehen* ('synthetic understanding'):[17]

> This principle [...] is overlooked both by the euhemeristic interpretation which transforms myth into history and by the physical interpretation which makes it a kind of primitive explanation of nature. [...] True speculation takes an exactly opposite road, aiming not at analytical disintegration but at synthetic understanding, and striving back toward the ultimate positive basis of the spirit and of life itself. And myth must be taken as such a positive basis.

> [An diesem Prinzip geht {...} sowohl die euhemeristische Deutung, die den Mythos in Geschichte verwandelt, wie die physische Auslegung, die ihn zu einer Art primitiver Naturerklärung macht, in gleicher Weise vorbei. {...} Der Weg der wahrhaften Spekulation aber ist der Richtung einer derart auflösenden Betrachtung gerade entgegengesetzt. Sie will nicht analytisch zersetzen, sondern sie will synthetisch verstehen; sie strebt zu dem letzten Positiven des Geistes und des Lebens zurück. Und als ein solches durchaus Positives gilt es auch den Mythos zu betrachten.][18]

As Cassirer is at pains to point out, he is concerned to highlight that Schelling's approach to myth is directed toward understanding myth as, in Cassirer's phrase, 'a positive basis' both for *Geist* — that is to say, it is philosophically sound — and for *Leben*:

> The philosophical understanding of myth begins with the insight that it does not move in a purely invented or made-up world but has its own mode of *necessity* and therefore, in accordance with the idealist concept of the object, its own mode of *reality*. Only where such necessity is demonstrable is reason, and hence philosophy, in place.
>
> [Sein philosophisches Verständnis beginnt mit der Einsicht, daß auch er sich keineswegs in einer rein 'erfundenen' oder 'erdichteten' Welt bewegt, sondern daß ihm eine eigne Weise der *Notwendigkeit* und damit, gemäß dem Gegenstandsbegriff der idealistischen Philosophie, eine eigene Weise der *Realität* zukommt. Nur wo eine solche Notwendigkeit aufweisbar ist, hat die Vernunft, hat somit die Philosophie eine Stätte.][19]

In taking the approach he does, Schelling is not seeking to diminish the religious dimension of myth. Quite the opposite. For, as Schelling asserts in his *Philosophy of Art* [*Philosophie der Kunst*] (1802–1803), the autonomous creations of the spirit, the ideas, are in fact nothing other than the gods themselves:

> These *real*, living, and existing ideas are the gods; general symbolism or the general *representation of the ideas* as real is correspondingly accorded to mythology [...]. Indeed the gods of every mythology are nothing other than the idea of philosophy, only seen as objective or real.
>
> [Diese *realen*, lebendigen und existierenden Ideen sind die Götter; die allgemeine Symbolik oder die allgemeine *Darstellung der Ideen* als realer ist demnach in der Mythologie gegeben {...}. In der Tat sind die Götter jeder Mythologie nichts anderes als die Ideen der Philosophie nur objektiv oder real angeschaut.][20]

Furthermore, according to Schelling, the reality of these gods is proven by their effectiveness, by their activity:

> The gods which followed upon one another really seized successively upon the human consciousness. Mythology as a history of the gods, in other words, real mythology, could only be produced in life; it *had to be experienced* and *lived*.

[Die aufeinander folgenden Götter haben sich des Bewußtseyns wirklich nacheinander bemächtigt. Die Mythologie als Göttergeschichte, also die eigentliche Mythologie, konnte sich nur im Leben selbst erzeugen, sie *mußte* etwas *Erlebtes* und *Erfahrenes* seyn.][21]

In the philosophy of Schelling the process of mythology turns out to be a process of theogony, as Cassirer points out.[22] Yet it remains unclear, particularly in the (even) later works of the increasingly mystical Schelling, whether the gods (or God) are (or is) the expression of human consciousness, or whether human consciousness is testimony to the existence of the gods (or of God).[23]

At the same time, however, as Cassirer was trying to understand myth in terms that were, as he put it, 'phenomenological' and 'immanent',[24] the Romantic interpretation of myth was enjoying something of a renaissance. For myth became the central object and focus-point for research of many academics in Germany, particularly as far as the philologists were concerned. One of them, Walter Burkert (b. 1931), has noted that 'there was a special German path of development in the intellectual history of the first third of the twentieth century' ['Es gibt eine deutsche Sonderentwicklung in der Geistesgeschichte des ersten Drittels des 20. J{ahr}h{underts}']:

> It is marginally touched and influenced by Expressionism, by phenomenology, by the Youth Movement, by the circle around Stefan George; it is far removed from the Christian tradition, opposed to the bourgeois, opposed to reason; it is elitist, latently 'fascistic'. The shock of the First World War was a decisive formative element, but not its sole cause: the rational world of the nineteenth century seemed to have shattered, 'primordial depths' emerged and came to the surface.
>
> [Sie ist in etwa vom Expressionismus, der Phänomenologie, der Jugendbewegung, dem Stefan-George-Kreis tangential berührt und bestimmt; sie ist fern der christlichen Tradition, antibürgerlich, antirational; sie ist elitär, latent 'faschistoid'. Der Schock des Weltkriegs war entscheidend prägendes, nicht aber auslösendes Element: die rationale Welt des 19. J{ahr}h{underts} schien geborsten, 'Urgründe' traten zutage.][25]

In fact, the 1920s and 1930s in Germany were witness to a veritable renaissance, as well as to a discernible radicalization, of the discipline of philology. To this development one might count, among others, Werner Jaeger (1888–1961), Walter F. Otto (1874–1958), Bruno Snell (1896–1986), Ludwig Curtius (1874–1954), Wolfgang Schadewaldt (1900–1974), as well as the academics in the circle around Stefan George (1868–1933).[26] In terms of literature, for many at this time the poet of the moment was, as the extensive secondary literature on him indicates, Friedrich Hölderlin, with his call for a return to ancient Greek ideals that was as impassioned as it was impossible.[27] Like Friedrich Gundolf,[28] Cassirer wrote an essay on Hölderlin,[29] and in the

1940s Heidegger commented in intensive detail in a series of lectures on the work of this very 'mythical', this very 'German', poet.[30] In terms of intellectual history, however, a key thinker for this period turns out to Johann Jakob Bachofen (1815–1887), even if his concept of the symbol was based on that of the earlier, Romantic philologist Friedrich Creuzer (1771–1858).[31] For it was precisely in the early decades of the twentieth century that the reception of the Swiss historian of law and religion was at its most attentive and its most intense. This renaissance of interest in Bachofen was sparked off by a series of editions of his works or selections of his works,[32] as well as by controversy breaking out between two camps of supporters of Bachofen:[33] on the one hand Manfred Schröter (1880–1973), an expert on Schelling, and Alfred Baeumler (1887–1968), an expert on Kant and an editor of Nietzsche's *Nachlass*; and, on the other, Carl Albrecht Bernoulli (1868–1937), a theologian and writer, and Ludwig Klages (1872–1956), the graphologist, characterologist, and 'biocentric' metaphysician.[34]

According to Bachofen, there exists a close — indeed, intimate — relation between the symbol and myth, inasmuch as the latter constitutes an extension, a development, an interpretation of the former:

> Myth is the exegesis of the symbol. It unfolds in a series of outwardly connected actions what the symbol embodies in a unity. It resembles a discursive philosophical treatise in so far as it splits the idea into a number of connected images and then leaves it to the reader to draw the ultimate inference.
>
> [Der Mythus ist die Exegese des Symbols. Er entrollt in einer Reihe äußerlich verbundener Handlungen, was jenes einheitlich in sich trägt. Dem diskursiven philosophischen Vortrage gleicht er insofern er, wie dieser, den Gedanken in einer Reihe zusammenhängender Bilder zerlegt, und dann dem Beschauer überläßt, aus ihrer Verbindung den letzten Schluß zu ziehen.][35]

But what, then, is a symbol? For Bachofen, this can never be stated explicitly, never intellectually articulated — we can only intuit its significance and outline its function:

> The symbol awakens intimations; speech can only explain. The symbol plucks all the strings of the human spirit at once; speech is compelled to take up a single thought at a time. The symbol strikes its roots in the most secret depths of the soul; language skims over the surface of the understanding like a soft breeze. The symbol aims inward; language outward. Only the symbol can combine the most disparate elements into a unitary impression. [...] Words make the infinite finite, symbols carry the spirit beyond the finite world of becoming into the realm of infinite being.
>
> [Das Symbol erweckt Ahnung, die Sprache kann nur erklären. Das Symbol schlägt alle Saiten des menschlichen Geistes zugleich an, die Sprache ist genötigt, sich immer nur einem einzigen Gedanken hinzugeben. Bis in die

geheimsten Tiefen der Seele treibt das Symbol seine Wurzel, die Sprache berührt wie ein leiser Windhauch die Oberfläche des Verständnisses. Jenes ist nach innen, diese nach außen gerichtet. Nur dem Symbole gelingt es, das Verschiedenste zu einem einheitlichen Gesamteindruck zu verbinden. {...} Worte machen das Unendliche endlich, Symbole entführen den Geist über die Grenzen der endlichen, werdenden in das Reich der unendlichen, seienden Welt.][36]

For Bachofen, as for Cassirer, historical progress is a developmental process of *Vergeistigung*, of spiritualization:

> The history of words always begins with the sensuous, natural signification, and only in the course of development arrives at abstract, figurative meanings; and in religion, in the development of the human individual and of humankind, the same progress from the material to the psychic and spiritual can be noted. Likewise the symbols in which the earliest humankind set forth its intuitions of nature and the environing world began with purely physical and material meanings.
>
> [Wie die Geschichte der einzelnen Wörter stets mit der sinnlich-natürlichen Bedeutung eröffnet, und erst im weiteren Fortgang der Entwicklung zu abgezogenen, figürlichen Anwendungen fortschreitet, wie in der Religion, in der Entwicklung des einzelnen Individuums und der Menschheit überhaupt derselbe Fortschritt von dem Stoff und der Materie zu Seelischem und Geistigem zu bemerken ist: also haben auch die Symbole, in welchen die früheste Menschheit ihre Anschauungen von der Natur der sie umgebenden Welt niederzulegen gewohnt war, eine rein physisch-materielle Grundbedeutung.][37]

Indeed, Bachofen divides the early history of humankind into three stages: first, the 'tellurian', the gynocratic or matriarchal, stage, in which Woman, the Earth, and the Primal Mother are venerated; second, as an intermediate stage, the hermaphroditic or androgynous stage of Luna, the Moon; third, the stage of solar development — masculine, *phallisch-zeugend* ('phallic and fecundatory'), patriarchal.[38] In short, it is a journey from the (female) swamp to the (male) city.[39] What constitutes, for Bachofen, 'the sublime dignity and richness of the symbol' ['die hohe Würde und ahnungsreiche Fülle des Symbols'] is the fact 'that it not only allows of but even encourages different levels of interpretation, and leads us from the truths of physical life to those of a higher spiritual order' ['daß es verschiedene Stufen der Auffassung zuläßt und selbst anregt, und von den Wahrheiten des physischen Lebens zu denen einer höhern geistigen Ordnung weiterführt'].[40]

According to Alfred Baeumler, one of the major commentators on (and one of the main champions of) Bachofen in the twentieth century, Bachofen's achievement lay in his appreciation and demonstration of the 'chthonic' nature of antiquity, *das Chthonische*.[41] For Bachofen, Baeumler maintained, the concept of history is based on the concept of myth, such that 'universal history' ['die Universalgeschichte'] is 'the symbolic expression of humankind' ['der symbolische Ausdruck der Menschheit'], and for its part myth is the symbolic expression 'of the development of the essential nature of humankind' ['von der Entwicklung des menschlichen Wesens'].[42] But it is only through an exegesis of the symbol that we accede to the living sense of myth: 'By means of immovable primary symbols, not by means of changeable myths, do the old religions become accessible' ['Aus unbeweglichen primären Symbolen, nicht aus wechselnden Mythen heraus werden die alten Religionen zugänglich']. From these reflections Baeumler draws the following conclusion: 'The era of myth is illuminated for us only in its symbols' ['Das mythische Weltalter leuchtet nur in seinen Symbolen vor uns auf'].[43] On the basis of his reading of Bachofen, Baeumler reads history — to be precise, the First World War — in terms of the mythical aspects of the ritual invocation of the dead and the cult sacrifice in memory of the dead (activities from which, according to Baeumler, Greek tragedy first arose).[44] As it happens, Cassirer devoted an entire chapter of *Mythical Thought* to the topics of cult and sacrifice.[45] And it is also interesting to note that Baeumler's study of intellectual history in Germany in general and of Hegel, Kierkegaard, Winckelmann, Bachofen, and Nietzsche in particular is entitled *Studien zur deutschen Geistesgeschichte* (1937)[46] — a reprise of the subtitle of Cassirer's earlier study of German philosophy, politics, and aesthetic, *Freiheit und Form* (1922)?[47]

What was the intellectual relationship between Cassirer and Bachofen? Was Bachofen the subject of an enthusiastic reception from apparently everyone in the 1920s and 1930s, but not from Cassirer? Bachofen's name is noticeable by its absence in *Mythical Thought*, and in other texts by Cassirer. Yet part of the Cassirer *Nachlaß* shows that Cassirer was by no means ignorant of Bachofen, and that he was as fascinated by him as much as anyone else was. In the planned fourth volume of *The Philosophy of Symbolic Forms* Cassirer refers to several passages from *Der Mythus von Orient und Occident*, a collection of texts by Bachofen selected by the Schelling expert, Manfred Schröter (1880–1973), to which Alfred Baeumler furnished an introduction, and which became the main vehicle by which Bachofen became known to the German-speaking intellectual audience.[48] Cassirer refers to Bachofen at particular length in the section of his *The Metaphysics of Symbolic Forms* [*Zur Metaphysik der symbolischen Formen*] entitled 'The Problem of the Symbol as the Fundamental Problem of Philosophical Anthropology' ['Das Symbolproblem als Grundproblem der philosophischen Anthropologie'].[49] Here he tells us:

> The center of Bachofen's comprehensive view consists of his interpretation of myth as an original intellectual form of historical knowledge. In it we must see the principle of knowledge which animates and guides all his particular investigations. [...] Here we find an *objectivity* in myth which, correctly understood

and made use of, is not only not inferior to mere historical *facticity*, but in a certain regard is far superior to it. [...] Bachofen could develop this interpretation because from the outset he was pursuing a 'tautegorical' understanding of myth, in Schelling's sense, instead of a merely 'allegorical' interpretation.

[Die Auffassung des Mythos als einer geistigen Urform der geschichtlichen Erkenntnis bildet das eigentliche Zentrum von Bachofens Gesamtanschauung. In ihr müssen wir das Erkenntnisprinzip sehen, von dem all seine Einzelforschungen beseelt und gelenkt sind. {...} Hier liegt eine *Objektivität* des Mythischen, die, recht verstanden und gebraucht, der blossen historischen *Faktizität* nicht nur nichts nachgibt, sondern ihr in einer bestimmten Hinsicht weit überlegen ist. {...} Diese Auffassung war Bachofen möglich, weil er von Anfang an, im Sinne Schellings, auf ein 'tautegorisches' Verständnis des Mythos, statt auf eine bloss 'allegorische' Deutung desselben, gedrungen hatte — {...}.][50]

Bachofen, then, constitutes a link back to the philosophical approach to mythology developed by Schelling. But we must be careful to differentiate. It is true that Cassirer, like Bachofen, speaks in terms of a process of *Vergeistigung*: 'The process of spiritualization, the process of the world's "symbolization", discloses its value and meaning where it no longer operates free and unhindered, but must struggle and make its way against obstacles' ['Der Prozeß der Vergeistigung, der Prozeß der "Symbolisierung" der Welt wird seinem Wert und seiner Bedeutung nach gerade dort für uns faßbar, wo er nicht mehr frei und ungehindert sich vollzieht, sondern wo er gegen Hemmungen anzukämpfen und gegen diese sich durchzusetzen hat'].[51] Yet Cassirer's concept of the symbol is, in the end, very different from the Schellingian, or Bachofenian, model; it is far more Goethean, as the following passage shows from volume 2 of *The Philosophy of Symbolic Forms* shows:

> A glance at the development of the various symbolic forms shows us that their essential achievement is not that they copy the outward world in the inward world or that they simply project a finished inner world outward, but rather that the two factors of 'inside' and 'outside', of 'I' and 'reality' are *determined* and delimited from one another only in these symbolic forms and through their mediation.
>
> [Ein Blick auf die Entwicklung der einzelnen symbolischen Formen zeigt uns überall, daß ihre wesentliche Leistung nicht darin besteht, die Welt des Äußeren in der des Inneren abzubilden oder eine fertige innere Welt einfach nach außen zu projizieren, sondern daß in ihnen und durch ihre Vermittlung die beiden Momente des 'Innen' und 'Außen', des 'Ich' und der 'Wirklichkeit' erst ihre *Bestimmung* und ihre gegenseitige Abgrenzung erhalten.][52]

The consequence of this position is that to understand the symbolic forms means to understand how they redefine the limits, and hence the relationship, of Self and World:

If each of these forms embraces a spiritual coming-to-grips of the I with reality, it does not imply that the two, the I and reality, are to be taken as given quantities, as finished, self-enclosed halves of being, which are only subsequently composed into a whole. On the contrary, the crucial achievement of every symbolic form lies precisely in the fact that it does not *have* the limit between I and reality as pre-existent and established for all time but must itself create this limit — and that each fundamental form creates it *in a different way*.

[Wenn jede dieser Formen ihre geistige 'Auseinandersetzung' des Ich mit der Wirklichkeit in sich schließt, so ist dies doch keineswegs in dem Sinne zu verstehen, daß beide, Ich und Wirklichkeit, hierbei schon als gegebene Größen anzusehen sind — als fertige, für sich bestehende 'Hälften' des Seins, die nur nachträglich zu einem Ganzen zusammengenommen würden. Vielmehr liegt die entscheidende Leistung jeder symbolischen Form eben darin, daß sie die Grenze zwischen Ich und Wirklichkeit nicht als ein für allemal feststehende im voraus *hat*, sondern daß sie diese Grenze selbst erst *setzt* — und daß jede Grundform sie *verschieden* setzt.][53]

In these sentences we can hear, as so often in Cassirer, an unmistakable echo of Goethe, here of a late poem, 'Epirrhema':

> *Müsset im Naturbetrachten*
> *Immer eins wie alles achten:*
> *Nichts ist drinnen, nichts ist draußen;*
> *Denn was innen, das ist außen.*
> *So ergreifet ohne Säumnis*
> *Heilig öffentlich Geheimnis.*
>
> You must, when contemplating nature,
> Attend to this, in each and every feature:
> There's nought outside and nought within,
> For she is inside out and outside in.
> Thus will you grasp, with no delay,
> The holy secret, clear as day.[54]

Cassirer's concept of the symbol builds, of course, on that of Goethe who, in one of his maxims, defined the symbol as follows: 'This is true symbolism, where the particular represents the general, not as dream and shadow, but as the living, momentary revelation of what cannot be known' ['Das ist die wahre Symbolik, wo das Besondere das Allgemeinere repräsentiert, nicht als Traum und Schatten, sondern als lebendig-augenblickliche Offenbarung des Unerforschlichen'].[55] Indeed, there is a correspondence between Goethe's notion of the symbolic and his concept of style, from the early essay 'Einfache Nachahmung der Natur, Manier, Stil' ['Simple Imitation of Nature, Manner, Style'] (1789), where he had written that style 'rests on the most fundamental principle of cognition, on the essence of things — to the extent that it is granted us to perceive this essence in visible and tangible form' ['ruht auf den tiefsten Grundfesten der Erkenntnis, auf dem Wesen der Dinge, insofern uns erlaubt ist, es in sichtbaren und greiflichen Gestalten zu erkennen'],[56] through to his later *On the Theory of Colours* [*Zur Farbenlehre*], where he wrote that the symbolic use of colour was one which 'would coincide fully with nature' ['mit der Natur völlig übereinträfe'].[57]

There is another fundamental difference between Bachofen and Cassirer in terms of their concept of the symbol. In the context of his discussion of a tomb painting from a columbarium in the Villa Pamphili in Rome, which shows a group of five young men in deep conversation about the three mystery eggs on the small table around which they are sitting,[58] Bachofen writes:

> Its meaning is not open to doubt. The alternation of light and dark colour expresses the continuous passage from darkness to light, from death to life. It shows us tellurian creation as the result of eternal becoming and eternal passing away, as a never-ending movement between two opposite poles. This idea deserves our fullest attention because of its inner truth, but we must also admire the simple expression of the symbol.
>
> [Ihr Sinn kann keinem Zweifel unterliegen. Der Wechsel der hellen und der dunkeln Farbe drückt den steten Übergang von Finsternis zum Licht, vom Tod zum Leben aus. Er zeigt uns die tellurische Schöpfung als das Resultat ewigen Werdens und ewigen Vergehens, als eine nie endende Bewegung zwischen zwei entgegengesetzten Polen. Verdient diese Idee um ihrer innern Wahrheit willen unsere höchste Aufmerksamkeit, so muß man zugleich den einfachen Ausdruck des Symbols bewundern.][59]

By contrast, Cassirer argues in connection with the mythical image of life after death:

> As in the development of all 'symbolic forms', light and shadow go together. The light manifests itself only in the shadow it casts: the purely 'intelligible' has the sensuous as its antithesis, but this antithesis is at the same time its necessary correlate.
>
> [Wie in der Entwicklung aller 'symbolischen Formen' {gehören} Licht und Schatten zusammen. Das Licht bekundet und erweist sich erst in dem Schatten, den es wirft: Das rein 'Intelligible' hat das Sinnliche zu seinem Gegensatz, aber dieser Gegensatz bildet zugleich sein notwendiges Korrelat.][60]

In the case of Cassirer, we are dealing with not just a symbol, but a *symbolic form*; unlike Bachofen, Cassirer does not play off reason against sensuousness, but rather he tries to show how 'in science and language, in art and myth' ['in der Wissenschaft und in der Sprache, in der Kunst und im Mythos'] there is *Wandlung zur Gestalt*, a transformation into form (and away from chaos):

> Thus in every sphere, it is through the freedom of spiritual action that the chaos of sensory impressions begins to clear and take on fixed form for us. The

fluid impression assumes form and duration for us only when we *mould* it by symbolic action in one direction or another. In science and language, in art and myth, this formative process proceeds in different ways and according to different principles [...].

[Und so ist es überall die Freiheit des geistigen Tuns, durch die sich das Chaos der sinnlichen Eindrücke erst lichtet und durch die es für uns erst feste Gestalt anzunehmen beginnt. Nur indem wir dem fließenden Eindruck, in irgendeiner Richtung der Zeichengebung, *bildend* gegenübertreten, gewinnt er für uns Form und Dauer. Diese Wandlung zur Gestalt vollzieht sich in der Wissenschaft und in der Sprache, in der Kunst und im Mythos in verschiedener Weise und nach verschiedenen Bildungsprinzipien {...}.][61]

As Cassirer emphasizes, this *Wandlung zur Gestalt* is also a *Prägung zum Sein*, a formation into being:

Myth and art, language and science, are in this sense configurations *towards* being: they are not simple copies of an existing reality but represent the main directions of the spiritual movement, of the ideal process by which reality is constituted for us as one and many — as a diversity of forms which are ultimately held together by a unity of meaning.

[Der Mythos und die Kunst, die Sprache und die Wissenschaft sind in diesem Sinne Prägungen *zum* Sein: Sie sind nicht einfache Abbilder einer vorhandenen Wirklichkeit, sondern sie stellen die großen Richtlinien der geistigen Bewegung, des ideellen Prozesses dar, indem sich für uns das Wirkliche als Eines und Vieles konstituiert — als eine Mannigfaltigkeit von Gestaltungen, die doch zuletzt durch eine Einheit der Bedeutung zusammengehalten werden.][62]

This contrast is due to the difference in temperament and methodology between the two men. In his retrospect on his own life (1854), Bachofen wrote:

There are two roads to knowledge — the longer, slower, more arduous road of rational combination and the shorter path of the imagination, traversed with the force and swiftness of electricity. Aroused by direct contact with the ancient remains, the imagination grasps the truth at one stroke, without intermediary links. The knowledge acquired in this second way is infinitely more living and colourful than the products of the understanding.

[Es gibt zwei Wege zu jeder Erkenntnis, der weitere, langsamere, mühsamere verständiger Kombination, und der kürzere, der mit der Kraft und Schnelligkeit der Elektrizität durchschritten wird, der Weg der Phantasie, welche von dem Anblick und der unmittelbaren Berührung der alten Reste angeregt, ohne Mittelglieder das Wahre wie mit Einem Schlage erfaßt. An Leben und Farbe ist das auf dem zweiten Weg Erworbene den Verstandesprodukten mächtig überlegen.][63]

For his part Cassirer, while attaching importance to the imagination, always thought of it in philosophical terms,[64] and the volumes of *The Philosophy of Symbolic Forms* stand as a testimony to his unflinching commitment to what Hegel called 'the labour of the concept': 'To philosophy, which finds its fulfilment only in the sharpness of the concept and in the clarity of "discursive" thought, the paradise of mysticism, the paradise of pure immediacy, is closed' ['Für {die Philosophie}, die sich erst in der Schärfe des Begriffs und in der Helle und Klarheit des "diskursiven Denkens" vollendet, ist das Paradies der Mystik, das Paradies der reinen Unmittelbarkeit, verschlossen'].[65]

Notes

[1] For an example of how the multiplicity of meanings of the term *Mythos* is often acknowledged, only to remain unengaged, and reduced to the semiological conception of Roland Barthes, see Sarah Colvin, 'Introduction' to papers from the WIGS conference 'Myths and Mythmaking', *German Life and Letters*, vol. 57, no. 1 (January 2004), 1–7.

[2] See Robert A. Segal, 'Jung's Twentieth-Century View of Myth', *Journal of Analytical Psychology*, 48 (2003), 593–617.

[3] See Edward Tylor, *Primitive Culture* (1871); and James Frazer, *The Golden Bough* (1890).

[4] For further discussion of Mircea Eliade, see Steven M. Wasserstrom, *Religion after Religion: Gerschom Scholem, Mircea Eliade, and Henry Corbin at Eranos* (Princeton, NJ: Princeton University Press, 1999).

[5] For further discussion of Hans Jonas, see Franz Josef Wetz, *Hans Jonas zur Einführung* (Hamburg: Junius, 1994).

[6] See James Hillman, 'Psychology: Monotheistic or Polytheistic?', *Spring* (1971), 193–208, 230–32; extracts and further texts in Thomas Moore (ed.), *The Essential James Hillman: A Blue Fire* (London: Routledge, 1990), pp. 36–49.

[7] For further discussion, see Paul Bishop, 'Cassirer, Bachofen und der Mythos: Überlegungen zum Weg von der Anthropologie zur Politik', *Studia Neophilologica*, 77 (2005), 31–40.

[8] Wasserstrom, *Religion after Religion*, p. 91. 'In general, [the historians of religion] seemed to prefer more venerable (and less contemporary) authorities. Current theories of symbolism, of which Cassirer's was the best known, interested them only slightly. [...] Goethe was certainly preferable to more recent authorities on the symbol. Corbin, however, did meet Ernst Cassirer [...] [and] also employed Cassirer's phrase "the philosophy of symbolic forms". Scholem eschewed Cassirer. [...] Eliade seems to have cited Cassirer only once, to exemplify a vague "vogue for symbolism"' (p. 91).

[9] Cassirer briefly discusses Freud's psychoanalytic theory of myth as laid out in *Totem and Taboo* (1913), in *The Myth of the State* [1946] (New Haven and London: Yale University Press, 1974), pp. 28–34. His 1896 paper, 'Psychologie und Philosophie', delivered at the Third International Congress for Psychology, held in Munich on 4–7 August 1896, discusses the psychology of Theodor Lipps (1851–1914) (Ernst Cassirer, 'Psychologie und Philosophie', in *Symbol, Technik, Sprache: Aufsätze aus den Jahren 1927–1933*, ed. by E. W. Orth and J. M. Krois (Hamburg: Felix Meiner Verlag, 1985), pp. 161–64).

[10] The possible existence of areas of affinity between Jung and Cassirer has overlooked by most commentators, with the exception of Joy Schaverien, who draws on Cassirer to support and explain her Jungian-inspired style of artistic therapy. See Joy Schaverien, *The Revealing Image: Analytical Art Psychotherapy in Theory and Practice* (London and New York: Tavistock/Routledge, 1992). For further discussion, see Paul Bishop, 'Speaking of Symbols: Affinities between Cassirer's and Jung's Theories of Language', in Cyrus Hamlin and John Michael

Krois (eds), *Symbolic Forms and Cultural Studies: Ernst Cassirer's Theory of Culture* (New Haven and London: Yale University Press, 2004), pp. 127–56.

[11] Ernst Cassirer, *Language and Myth*, trans. by Susanne K. Langer (New York: Dover Publications, 1953); 'Sprache und Mythos', in *Wesen und Wirkung des Symbolbegriffs* (Darmstadt: Wissenschaftliche Buchgesellschaft, 1956), pp. 71–167.

[12] Hermann Usener, *Götternamen: Versuch einer Lehre von der religiösen Begriffsbildung* (1896); and 'Mythologie', *Archiv für Religionswissenschaft*, 7 (1904), 6–32. For further discussion, see Roland Kany, *Mnemosyne als Programm: Geschichte, Erinnerung und die Andacht zum Unbedeutenden im Werk von Usener, Warburg und Benjamin* (Tübingen: Max Niemeyer Verlag, 1987), p. 13.

[13] Cassirer, *Language and Myth*, p. 1; *Wesen und Wirkung des Symbolbegriffs*, p. 73.

[14] Ernst Cassirer, *The Philosophy of Symbolic Forms*, vol. 2, *Mythical Thought*, trans. by Ralph Manheim (New Haven and London: Yale University Press, 1955); Ernst Cassirer, *Philosophie der symbolischen Formen, Zweiter Teil: Das mythische Denken* [*Gesammelte Werke: Hamburger Ausgabe*, vol. 12] (Hamburg: Felix Meiner, 2002). Henceforth cited as *Mythical Thought* and *Das mythische Denken*.

[15] The use of Schelling represents the point of contact between Cassirer on the one hand and Scholem, Eliade, and Corbin on the other: 'The Historians of Religion followed Cassirer in his appreciation of Schelling's late philosophy, borrowing from him, for example, the concept of *tautegory*. On the other hand, they rejected what they felt were both the "bourgeois" and the neo-Kantian elements of his work' (Wasserstrom, *Religion after Religion*, p. 91).

[16] *Mythical Thought*, p. 4; *Das mythische Denken*, p. 5.

[17] For further discussion, see Paul Bishop, 'Analysis or Synthesis? A Cassirerian Problem in the Work of Freud and Jung', in Paul Bishop and R. H. Stephenson (eds), *Cultural Studies and the Symbolic*, vol. 1 (Leeds: Northern Universities Press, 2003), 42–65.

[18] *Mythical Thought*, p. 4; *Das mythische Denken*, p. 5.

[19] *Mythical Thought*, p. 4; *Das mythische Denken*, p. 5.

[20] Friedrich Wilhelm Joseph Schelling, *Texte zur Philosophie der Kunst*, ed. by Werner Beierwaltes (Stuttgart: Reclam, 1982), pp. 153–54.

[21] Friedrich Wilhelm Joseph Schelling, *Historisch-Kritische Einleitung in die Philosophie der Mythologie* [1842], in *Ausgewählte Schriften*, ed. by Manfred Frank, 6 vols (Frankfurt am Main: Suhrkamp, 1985), vol. 5, p. 135; cited in *Mythical Thought*, p. 6; *Das mythische Denken*, p. 7.

[22] *Mythical Thought*, p. 6; *Das mythische Denken*, p. 8.

[23] For further discussion of the late Schelling, see Edward Allen Beach, *The Potencies of God(s): Schelling's Philosophy of Mythology* (Albany, NY: State University of New York Press, 1994).

[24] '[A] critical phenomenology of the mythical consciousness will start neither from the godhead as an original metaphysical fact nor from humankind as an original empirical fact but will seek to apprehend the subject of the cultural process, the human spirit, solely in its pure actuality and diverse configurations, whose immanent norms it will strive to ascertain' ['[Eine kritische Phänomenologie des mythischen Bewußtseins {wird} weder von der Gottheit als einer metaphysischen noch von der Menschheit als einer empirischen Urtatsache ausgehen können, sondern sie wird das Subjekt des Kulturprozesses, sie wird den "Geist" lediglich in seiner reinen Aktualität, in der Mannigfaltigkeit seiner Gestaltungsweisen zu erfassen und die immanente Norm, der jede von ihnen folgt, zu bestimmen versuchen'] (*Mythical Thought*, p. 13; *Das mythische Denken*, p. 16).

[25] Walter Burkert, 'Griechische Mythologie und die Geistesgeschichte der Moderne', in Willen den Boer (ed.), *Les Études classiques aux XIXe et XXe siècles: Leur place dans l'histoire des idées* [*Entretiens sur l'Antiquité classique*, 26] (Geneva: Fondation Hardt, 1980), pp. 159–99 (p. 187).

[26] For further discussion, see Frank H. W. Edler, 'Alfred Baeumler on Hölderlin and the Greeks: Reflections on the Heidegger-Baeumler Relationship', Parts 1, 2 and 3a, in *Janushead*, online. Available http: <http://www.janushead.org> (accessed 28 May 2003); and Ingo Gildenhard und Martin Ruehl (eds), *Out of Arcadia: Classics and Politics in Germany in the Age*

of Burckhardt, Nietzsche and Wilamowitz [BICS Supplement 79] (London: Institute of Classical Studies, 2003), especially pp. 1–6.

[27] See Joseph Suglia, 'On the Nationalist Reconstruction of Hölderlin in the George-Circle', *German Life and Letters*, 55 (2002), 387–97.

[28] Friedrich Gundolf, *Heinrich von Kleist* (Berlin: Georg Bondi, 1922).

[29] Ernst Cassirer, 'Hölderlin und der deutsche Idealismus', in *Logos*, 7 (1917/1918), 262–82; 8 (1919/1920), 30–49; also published in *Idee und Gestalt* (Berlin: Cassirer, 1921), pp. 109–52.

[30] See the essays in Martin Heidegger, *Erläuterungen zu Hölderlins Dichtung* (Frankfurt am Main: Vittorio Klostermann, 1951); for further discussion, see Rüdiger Safranski, *Ein Meister aus Deutschland: Heidegger und seine Zeit* (Munich and Vienna: Carl Hanser Verlag, 1994), pp. 317–26.

[31] For further discussion, see Lionel Gossman, *Basel in the Age of Burckhardt: A Study in Unseasonable Ideas* (Chicago und London: University of Chicago Press, 2000), p. 161; and Josine H. Blok, 'Quests for a Scientific Mythology: F. Creuzer and K. O. Müller on History and Myth', *History and Theory*, vol. 33, no. 4 (December 1994) [Proof and Persuasion in History], 26–52. On the persisting relevance of Creuzer for modernism, see Leon Surette, *The Birth of Modernism* (Montreal and Buffalo: McGill-Queen's University Press, 1993).

[32] The principal publications to be mentioned in this context include J. J. Bachofen, *Oknos der Seilflechter: Ein Grabbild: Erlösungsgedanken antiker Gräbersymbolik*, ed. and introd. by Manfred Schröter (Munich: C. H. Beck'sche Verlagsbuchhandlung, 1923); J. J. Bachofen, *Das lykische Volk und seine Bedeutung für die Entwicklung des Altertums*, ed. by Manfred Schröter (Leipzig: H. Hässel, 1924); Carl Albrecht Bernoulli, *Johann Jakob Bachofen und das Natursymbol: Ein Würdigungsversuch* (Basel: B. Schwabe, 1924); Carl Albrecht Bernoulli, *Johann Jakob Bachofen als Religionsforscher* (Leipzig: H. Hässel, 1924); J. J. Bachofen, *Versuch über die Gräbersymbolik der Alten*, 2nd edn, with a foreword with Carl Albrecht Bernoulli and an appreciation by Ludwig Klages (Basel: Helbing and Lichtenhahn, 1925); J. J. Bachofen, *Urreligion und antike Symbole: systematisch angeordnete Auswahl aus seinen Werken*, ed. by Carl Albrecht Bernoulli, 3 vols (Leipzig: Philipp Reclam Verlag, 1926); J. J. Bachofen, *Mutterrecht und Urreligion: Eine Auswahl*, ed. by Rudolf Marx (Leipzig: Alfred Kröner Verlag, 1926); J. J. Bachofen, *Der Mythus von Orient und Occident: Eine Metaphysik der alten Welt aus den Werken von J.J. Bachofen*, ed. by Manfred Schröter, introd. by Alfred Baeumler (Munich: C. H. Beck'sche Verlagsbuchhandlung, 1926); and J. J. Bachofen, *Selbstbiographie und Antrittsrede über das Naturrecht*, ed. and introd. by Alfred Baeumler (Halle an der Saale: Max Niemeyer Verlag, 1927).

[33] What Baeumler called 'der Konflikt im Lager der Bachofen-Verehrer' (letter to Manfred Schröter of 21 April 1926) began with Klages's polemic, in Bernoulli's edition of *Versuch über die Gräbersymbolik der Alten*, against the 'adoring worship of exploiters and spongers, who live on the desecration of his legacy' ['Anhimmelungen der Ausbeuter und Schmarotzer, die von der Schändung seines Erbes leben'], an implicit reference to Schröter's edition of the section from the *Gräbersymbolik* entitled 'Oknos der Seilflechter' ('Ocnus the Rope Plaiter') ('Würdigung', p. xiii). In his introduction to *Der Mythus von Orient und Occident* Baeumler, who had promised but never published a more detailed response to this criticism, in turn attacked Klages for his 'stubborn dogmatisation and monopolisation of Bachofen's life's work' ['eigensinnige Dogmatisierung und Monopolisierung des Bachofenschen Lebenswerkes']: 'Bachofen, interpreted from an anti-historical spirit hostile to Christianity is no longer Bachofen [...] This can no longer be considered the preservation of his legacy' ['Bachofen, interpretiert von einem antihistorischen und christentumfeindlichen Geiste, ist nicht mehr Bachofen. {...} Eine Wahrung seines Erbes kann dies nicht wohl heißen'] ('Einleitung', pp. ccvi–ccvii). As Werner Deubel, admittedly writing from a position within the Klages circle, if such a thing exists (see Ulrich Hintze, 'Um Werner Deubel: Anmerkungen zur deutschen Geistesgeschichte nach 1914', in Werner Deubel, *Im Kampf um die Seele: Essays und Aufsätze, Aphorismen und Gedichte*, ed. by Felicitas Deubel (Bonn: Bouvier Verlag, 1997),

pp. 9–44 [pp. 15–17]), hints, the difference between the two camps centred on their understanding of Nietzsche ('Der Kampf um Johann Jakob Bachofen' [1927], reprinted in Hans-Jürgen Heinrichs, *Das Mutterrecht von Johann Jakob Bachofen in der Diskussion* (Frankfurt am Main: Campus Verlag, 1987), pp. 161–71). In his letter to Bernoulli of 8 May 1926, Baeumler appealed for unity between the two camps, and in his letter to Schröter of the same day, Baeumler expressed the difference in interpretation in terms of their own predominantly Christian-inspired, as opposed to Klages's predominantly anti-Christian and pagan, interpretation of Bachofen (see Alfred Baeumler's letters to Manfred Schröter from 16 December 1924 to 13 June 1926, in Marianne Baeumler, Hubert Brunträger, and Hermann Kurzke (eds), *Thomas Mann und Alfred Baeumler: Eine Dokumentation* (Würzburg: Königshausen & Neumann, 1989), pp. 111–38 [pp. 134, 135–36]).

[34] Klages, with whom Cassirer also engaged in the fourth planned volume on the metaphysics of symbolic forms, was one of the most excited readers of Bachofen. His enthusiasm for the pre-historic world of Minoan Crete, Mycenean Greece, and the matriarchal culture of ancient Aegean, owed much to Bachofen's notion of *Gynaikokratie* (see *Der Geist als Widersacher der Seele* [1929–1932], 6th edn (Bonn: Bouvier Verlag Herbert Grundmann, 1981), p. 488, note 38, and p. 1252; *Vom kosmogonischen Eros*, 2nd edn (Jena: Eugen Diederichs, 1926), pp. 240–42; *Rhythmen und Runen: Nachlaß herausgegeben von ihm selbst* (Leipzig: J. A. Barth, 1944), p. 17; as well as his 'Appreciation' ['Würdigung'] in Bernoulli's edition of Bachofen's *Versuch über die Gräbersymbolik der Alten*, pp. x–xi). His major philosophical work, *Der Geist als Widersacher der Seele* (1929–1932), culminates in a chapter entitled 'Die Magna Mater (Randbemerkungen zu den Entdeckungen Bachofens)' (pp. 1330–1400). Klages once described Bachofen's *Gräbersymbolik* (1859) as 'one of the greatest intellectual achievements in the history of humankind' and added that he had found in Bachofen 'one of the guides of my life' ['Ich rechne es unter die größten Geisteswerke der Menschheit und habe vor 25 Jahren in Bachofen einen der Führer meines Lebens gefunden'] (cited in Hans Eggert Schröder, *Ludwig Klages: Die Geschichte seines Lebens*, vol. 1, *Die Jugend*, 2nd edn (Bonn: Bouvier, 1996), 225).

[35] *An Essay on Ancient Mortuary Symbolism*, 'Symbol and Myth', in J. J. Bachofen, *Myth, Religion, and Mother Right: Selected Writings*, trans. by Ralph Manheim (Princeton, NJ: Princeton University Press, 1973), pp. 48–50 (p. 48); *Versuch über die Gräbersymbolik der Alten*, 'Symbol und Mythus', in J. J. Bachofen, *Mutterrecht und Urreligion*, ed. by Hans G. Kippenberg (Stuttgart: Alfred Kröner Verlag, 1984), pp. 50–53 (p. 50).

[36] Bachofen, *Myth, Religion, and Mother Right*, p. 50; *Mutterrecht und Urreligion*, p. 52.

[37] Bachofen, 'Ocnus the Rope Plaiter', *Myth, Religion, and Mother Right*, pp. 51–65 (pp. 54–55); 'Der Seilflechter als Symbol (Oknos)', *Mutterrecht und Urreligion*, pp. 53–74 (pp. 59–60).

[38] See Bachofen, 'Introduction' to *Mother Right*, in *Myth, Religion, and Mother Right*, pp. 113–15; 'Vorrede und Einleitung zum *Mutterrecht*', in *Mutterrecht und Urreligion*, S. 134–37.

[39] Gossman, *Basel in the Age of Burckhardt*, pp. 173–74.

[40] Bachofen, 'The Three Mystery Eggs', *Myth, Religion, and Mother Right*, pp. 24–30 (p. 25); 'Das Ei als Symbol', *Mutterrecht und Urreligion*, pp. 21–42 (p. 25). Compare with C. G. Jung's view of the transformative power of the symbol in *Symbols and Transformations of the Libido*: 'The religious myth meets us here as one of the greatest and most significant human institutions which, despite misleading symbols, nevertheless gives man assurance and strength, so that he may not be overwhelmed by the monsters of the universe. The symbol, considered from the standpoint of actual truth, is misleading, indeed, but it is *psychologically true*, because it was and is the bridge to all the greatest achievements of humanity' ['Der religiöse Mythus tritt uns aber hier als eine der größten und bedeutsamsten menschlichen Institutionen entgegen, welche mit täuschenden Symbolen dem Menschen doch die Sicherheit und Kraft geben, vom Ungeheuern des Weltganzen nicht erdrückt zu werden. Das Symbol, vom Standpunkt des real Wahren aus betrachtet, ist zwar täuschend, aber es ist *psychologisch* wahr, denn es war und ist die Brücke zu allen größten Errungenschaften der Menschheit'] (C. G. Jung, *Psychology of the Unconscious: A Study of the Transformations and Symbolisms of the Libido: A Contribution to the*

History of the Evolution of Thought, trans. by Beatrice M. Hinkle (London: Routledge, 1991), §353; *Wandlungen und Symbole der Libido: Beiträge zur Entwicklungsgeschichte des Lebens* (Munich: Deutscher Taschenbuch Verlag, 1991), pp. 230–31).

[41] Alfred Baeumler, 'Nachwort: Bachofen und die Religionsgeschichte', in *Das mythische Weltalter: Bachofens romantische Deutung des Altertums* (München: Verlag C. H. Beck, 1965), p. 316. For further discussion, see Edler, 'Alfred Baeumler on Hölderlin and the Greeks', Part 1; and David Pan, 'Revising the Dialectic of Enlightenment: Alfred Baeumler and the Nazi Appropriation of Myth', *New German Critique*, 84 (Fall, 2001), 37–52.

[42] Baeumler, 'Nachwort', p. 297.

[43] Baeumler, 'Nachwort', pp. 316–17.

[44] *Das mythische Weltalter*, pp. 70 and 74; cf. Alfred Baeumler, 'Der Sinn des Großen Krieges', part 1 (1929), in *Männerbund und Wissenschaft* (Berlin: Junker und Dünnhaupt, 1934), pp. 1–17 (pp. 2–5). For further discussion, see Edler, 'Alfred Baeumler on Hölderlin and the Greeks', part 1.

[45] Part III, chapter 3 (*Mythical Thought*, pp. 219–31; *Das mythische Denken*, pp. 258–73). The topic attracted the interest of Klages, too, who followed the culmination of *Der Geist als Widersacher der Seele* on the *magna mater* with a final chapter entitled 'Nachtrag über den Ursinn des Opfers' (pp. 1401–15).

[46] Alfred Baeumler, *Studien zur deutschen Geistesgeschichte* (Berlin: Junker und Dünnhaupt, 1937).

[47] Ernst Cassirer, *Freiheit und Form: Studien zur deutschen Geistesgeschichte* (Berlin: B. Cassirer, 1922).

[48] *Der Mythus von Orient und Occident: Eine Metaphysik der alten Welt aus den Werken von J.J. Bachofen*, ed. by Schröter (see note 32). Baeumler's preface to this selection was later published separately as *Das mythische Weltalter* (see note 41).

[49] See also Ernst Cassirer, *The Philosophy of Symbolic Forms*, vol. 4, *The Metaphysics of Symbolic Forms*, ed. by John Michael Krois and Donald Phillip Verene, trans. by John Michael Krois (New Haven and London: Yale University Press, 1996), pp. 88–90; see also '"Geist" and "Life"', pp. 3–33 (p. 25); Cassirer, *Zur Metaphysik der symbolischen Formen*, hrsg. John Michael Krois (Hamburg: Felix Meiner Verlag, 1995), pp. 86–87.

[50] Cassirer, *The Metaphysics of Symbolic Forms*, pp. 88–89; *Zur Metaphysik der symbolischen Formen*, pp. 86–87. In this context, Cassirer refers to Bachofen's discussion of the saga of Tanaquil in *Der Mythus von Orient und Okzident* in a section entitled 'Italien und der Okzident' and originally published as *Die Sage von Tanaquil: Eine Untersuchung über den Orientalismus in Rom und Italien* (1870). See *Der Mythus von Orient und Okzident*, pp. 540–41; *Myth, Religion, and Mother Right*, pp. 212–13.

[51] Ernst Cassirer, *The Philosophy of Symbolic Forms*, vol. 3, *The Phenomenology of Knowledge*, trans. by Ralph Manheim (New Haven and London: Yale University Press, 1957), 277; Ernst Cassirer, *Philosophie der symbolischen Formen, Dritter Teil: Phänomenologie der Erkenntnis* [*Gesammelte Werke: Hamburger Ausgabe*, vol. 13] (Hamburg: Felix Meiner Verlag, 2002), 322.

[52] *Mythical Thought*, pp. 155–56; *Das mythische Denken*, pp. 181–82.

[53] *Mythical Thought*, p. 156; *Das mythische Denken*, p. 182.

[54] Goethe, *Werke* [Hamburger Ausgabe], ed. by Erich Trunz, 14 vols (Hamburg: Christian Wegner Verlag, 1948–1960), vol. 1, p. 358; translated by Christopher Middleton in Johann Wolfgang von Goethe, *Selected Poems*, ed. by Christopher Middleton [Goethe Edition, vol. 1] (Boston: Suhrkamp/Insel Publishers, 1983), 159. See also Ernst Cassirer, *Goethe-Vorlesungen: Der junge Goethe — Göteborg 1940–1941, Goethes geistige Leistung — Lund 1941*, ed. by John Michael Krois [*Nachgelassene Manuskripte und Texte*, vol. 11] (Hamburg: Felix Meiner Verlag, 2003).

[55] *Maximen und Reflexionen*, 314, in Goethe, *Werke*, vol. 12, 471. For further discussion, see R. H. Stephenson, *Goethe's Conception of Knowledge and Science* (Edinburgh: Edinburgh

University Press, 1995), pp. 70–71; Barbara Naumann and Birgit Recki (eds), *Cassirer und Goethe: Neue Aspekte einer philosophisch-literarischen Wahlverwandtschaft* (Berlin: Akadamie Verlag, 2002); and R. H. Stephenson, '"Eine zarte Differenz": Cassirer on Goethe on the Symbol', in Hamlin and Krois (eds), *Symbolic Forms and Cultural Studies*, pp. 157–84 (esp. pp. 165–66).

[56] 'Simple Imitation, Manner, Style', in Johann Wolfgang Goethe, *Essays on Art and Literature*, ed. by John Gearey, trans. by Ellen von Vardroff and Ernest H. von Nardroff [Goethe's Collected Works, vol. 3] (New York: Suhrkamp Publishers, 1986), 71–74 (p. 72); 'Einfache Nachahmung der Natur, Manier, Stil', in *Werke*, vol. 12, 30–34 (p. 32).

[57] 'Allegorischer, symbolischer, mystischer Gebrauch der Farbe', in *Zur Farbenlehre* (*Werke*, vol. 13, 520).

[58] A columbarium is a tomb with niches designed to hold urns containing ash; the Villa Doria-Pamphili is situated on the ancient Via Aurelia in Rome, and today contains a museum.

[59] Bachofen, 'The Three Mystery Eggs', in *Myth, Religion, and Mother Right*, pp. 24–30 (p. 25); 'Das Ei als Symbol', in *Mutterrecht und Urreligion*, pp. 21–42 (p. 25).

[60] *Mythical Thought*, p. 245; *Das mythische Denken*, p. 286.

[61] Ernst Cassirer, *Philosophy of Symbolic Forms*, vol. 1, *Language*, trans. by Ralph Manheim (New Haven and London: Yale University Press, 1955), 107; *Philosophie der symbolischen Formen*, vol. 1, *Die Sprache* [*Gesammelte Werke: Hamburger Ausgabe*, vol. 11] (Hamburg: Felix Meiner Verlag, 2001), 41. Cassirer had used the phrase *das Chaos der unmittelbaren Eindrücke* earlier with specific reference to language: 'The process of language formation shows for example how the chaos of immediate impressions takes on order and clarity for us only when we "name" it and so permeate it with the function of linguistic thought and expression' ['So zeigt etwa der Prozeß der Sprachbildung, wie das Chaos der unmittelbaren Eindrücke sich für uns erst dadurch lichtet und gliedert, daß wir es "benennen" und es dadurch mit der Funktion des sprachlichen Denkens und des sprachlichen Ausdrucks durchdringen'] (p. 87; p. 18).

[62] Cassirer had also made reference to the ancient philosophical topos of the One and the Many — used by Leibniz in his definition of consciousness as 'an expression of the many in the one' ['der "Ausdruck des Vielen im Einen", die multorum in uno expressio'] or *expressio multorum in uno* (*Language*, p. 100; *Die Sprache*, p. 32) to explain how the philosophy of symbolic forms offered a solution to a problem posed by Kant: '*Kant* — in his treatise on negative quantities — once formulated the problem of causality as the endeavour to understand why because *something* is, *something else*, of a totally different nature, ought to be and is. [. . .] Here, in the most general terms, lies the critical solution of Kant's question as to how it is thinkable that because "something" is, something "other", totally different from it, must also be. The relation, which inevitably seemed more and more paradoxical the more sharply it was examined and analyzed from the standpoint of absolute being, becomes necessary and immediately intelligible when it is considered from the standpoint of consciousness. For here there is not from the very start an abstract "one", confronted by an equally abstract and detached "other"; here the one is "in" the many and the many is "in" the one: in the sense that each determines and represents the other' ['*Kant* hat einmal — in seiner Schrift über die negativen Größen — das Problem der Kausalität dahin formuliert, wie es zu verstehen sei, daß, weil *etwas* ist, darum zugleich *etwas anderes*, von ihm völlig Verschiedenes sein solle und sein müsse. {. . .} Damit erst ist die allgemeinste kritische Lösung für jene Frage Kants erreicht, wie es zu denken sei, daß, weil "etwas" ist, dadurch zugleich ein "Anderes", von ihm völlig Verschiedenes sein müsse. Das Verhältnis, das, vom Standpunkt des absoluten Seins betrachtet, um so paradoxer erscheinen mußte, je schärfer es betrachtet und analysiert wurde, ist das notwendige, das aus sich unmittelbar verständliche, wenn es vom Standpunkt des Bewußtseins gesehen wird. Denn hier gibt es von Anfang an kein abstraktes "Eines", dem in gleich abstrakter Sonderung und Loslösung ein "Anderes" gegenübersteht, sonder das Eine ist hier "im" Vielen, wie das Viele "im" Einen ist: in dem Sinne, daß beide sich wechselseitig bedingen und sich wechselseitig repräsentieren'] (*Language*, pp. 97 and 105; *Die Sprache*, pp. 29 and 39).

[63] Bachofen, 'My Life in Retrospect', *Myth, Religion, and Mother Right*, pp. 3–17 (p. 11); 'Lebens-Rückschau', *Mutterrecht und Urreligion*, pp. 1–18 (p. 11).

[64] And specifically, in terms derived from Goethe — 'as Goethe said' ['um den *Goetheschen* Ausdruck zu gebrauchen'] — of 'an "exact sensory imagination"' ['eine "exacte sinnliche Phantasie"'] (*Language*, p. 87; *Die Sprache*, p. 17). See Goethe's review, 'Ernst Stiedenroth, *A Psychology in Clarification of Phenomena of the Soul* (Part One, Berlin: 1824)' ['Ernst Stiedenroth, Psychologie zur Erklärung der Seelenerscheinungen. Erster Teil. Berlin 1824'] (*Werke* [Hamburger Ausgabe], vol. 13, 42).

[65] *Language*, p. 113; *Die Sprache*, p. 49.

THE SYMBOLIZATION OF CULTURE: NIETZSCHE IN THE FOOTSTEPS OF GOETHE, SCHILLER, SCHOPENHAUER, AND WAGNER

By Martine Prange

Aged only twenty-five, as professor of classical philology and languages at the University of Basle, Friedrich Nietzsche (1844–1900) instantly rose to fame with the publishing of his début book entitled *The Birth of Tragedy* [*Die Geburt der Tragödie*]. In this still-controversial study of ancient Greek art and contemporary German culture, Nietzsche states that the ideal set by Weimar Classicism to reproduce Greek tragedy can only be fulfilled by the 'music-dramas' of his friend Richard Wagner (1813–1883). Widening the scope to contemporary culture, and opening fire on scholarship without the slightest qualm while advocating a more artistic culture, the professor exceeded the academic rules so violently, that his colleague Usener declared Nietzsche 'scientifically dead' ['wissenschaftlich tot'].[1] I am not in a position to judge the philological quality of the book, but the aesthetics expounded remains today very challenging, and very influential on twentieth-century art: the sum of artists who have found strong inspiration in the book — the painters like Giorgio de Chirico (1888–1978),[2] Wassily Kandinsky (1866–1944),[3] the 'action-painter' Jackson Pollock (1912–1956), as well as his opponent Marc Rothko (1903–1975) — is testimony to its quality and living relevance.

Nietzsche's idea that art can actually raise culture is my central topic in this essay. Central to this view is the argument that art must be *symbolic* in order to raise culture. In brief, without reaching for the level of the symbolic, an artist will never surpass the subjective, sentimental age he lives in and grasp the metaphysical truth of life. In attaching so much importance to the symbolic power of art, Nietzsche is following in the footsteps of Goethe, Schiller, and Schopenhauer. An artist must strive for the objective in things, as Goethe indicated to Eckermann. He must bring out the general in the particular, the symbolic in daily live, in order to express the true world (which is discursively inexpressible),[4] and to position himself as someone who strives for cultural progress.[5] This ambition is obligatory, according to Goethe, so as not to fall back into subjectivity and artificiality, which are signs of weakness and decadence. Progress, on the other hand, hints at energy and a strong will.[6] Hence Goethe and Schiller, and Nietzsche after them, aim to gain a purchase on life by means of aesthetic appearance.[7] At the very least, they appreciate aesthetic appearance rather than 'conceptual art' and 'discursive thinking' as the proper gateway towards reality, and, accordingly, as the appropriate instrument to raise cultural powers.

Commentators on Nietzsche's aesthetics have often underlined his interest in *myth*, and this might be the reason that they have neglected his positive reception of the symbol.[8] But it is not only art that Nietzsche sets against science, and not just mythical art he contrasts with discursive thinking; it is art's *symbolic* powers that represent the truth of life and conquer movements hostile to it. Not only does Nietzsche write that 'without myth [...] every culture loses its healthy, creative, natural power' ['ohne Mythus ... geht jede Cultur ihrer gesunden schöpferischen Naturkraft verlustig'] (GT, §9; KSA, 1, 145), but he also claims that 'understanding the world in "symbols" is the precondition of a great art' ['Verständniß der Welt in "Symbolen" ist die Voraussetzung einer großen Kunst'], adding that the modern world lacks symbols (KSA, 7, 9[92], 308). Without symbolic powers, art neglects life as much as discursive thinking; without symbolic powers, art is as conceptual as science is. Hence, in the context of revivals of interest in Cassirer's and Warburg's theories of symbolization, it is appropriate to discuss the symbol in Nietzsche's (early) aesthetics systematically, and to recognize its significance in Nietzsche's philosophy of art and culture.

With this aim in mind, I shall first discuss Wagner's centenary essay *Beethoven*, which influenced Nietzsche's view of music as a symbolic form of art substantially. Second, I shall deduce Nietzsche's musical aesthetics and related cultural ideal from notes belonging to his literary remains of 1870–1871.[9] These notes were made while Nietzsche was working on *Die Geburt der Tragödie*. I have chosen to concentrate on those instead of the book itself, because they show in greater detail than the published text the deeply penetrating influence exercised by Friedrich Schiller, Arthur Schopenhauer, and Richard Wagner on Nietzsche's early aesthetics. As I hope to demonstrate, Nietzsche tried to bring together Schillerian views, Schopenhauer's metaphysics, Wagner's music-drama, and his own concept of the tragic Dionysian in one unifying philosophy of art, in which the symbol plays a central role.

WAGNER'S BEETHOVEN-ESSAY OF 1870
WAGNER AND SCHOPENHAUER'S METAPHYSICS OF MUSIC

In *Die Geburt der Tragödie* Nietzsche maintains that Wagner's music will resolve the artistic crisis in which Europe finds itself due to Italian opera and French Naturalism. In his centenary essay on Ludwig van Beethoven (1770–1827) of 1870, Wagner displays a similar confidence in Beethoven's music as the rescuer of European culture. He proclaims that Beethoven's *Ninth*

Symphony contains a typically German depth, which not only elevates German culture, but should enrich other European countries, like France and Italy, so as to save them from their decadence. This decadence is caused by a tendency to superficiality, characteristic (according to Wagner) of Catholic nations. With Luther and Beethoven as examples, Wagner advocates an artistic reformation of Europe. Without ever mentioning the general idea that Beethoven was, in terms of music, nothing less than a revolutionary, in this essay Wagner attempts to demonstrate instead that Beethoven was to music what Martin Luther previously had been to religion — a reformer. But the essay not only commemorates Beethoven's hundredth birthday, it also contains an exposé of Wagner's own ideas on music's importance to culture. (In fact, according to Nietzsche, Wagner not only advances his own philosophy of music, but *the* philosophy of music.)[10]

Wagner proffers his essay with the question about the nature of Beethoven's relationship to his native country, Germany. Music, it is widely supposed, speaks an 'absolute' language, because it enters the hearts of people directly, irrespective of nationality. Nevertheless, Wagner advocates the idea that musicians, like painters and poets, do express a national identity. On the other hand, he sticks to the idea that music is a 'universal' form of art. Moreover, the union of universality and national identity characterizes *true* music. So Beethoven, according to Wagner, is the only musician who actually succeeded in making true music. But what exactly *is* true music?

To support his exposition, Wagner calls to his aid Schopenhauer's metaphysics of music, as articulated in *The World as Will and Representation* [*Die Welt als Wille und Vorstellung*] (1819). Here Schopenhauer argues, in line with Kant, that the world in which we live is a world of *phenomena*, behind which a world of *noumena* is obscured. Because this world of *noumena* is unknown, Kant called it 'the thing-in-itself' (*Ding an sich*). In Schopenhauer's philosophy, however, the noumenal world is conceived as one, omnipresent 'Will' (*Wille*), that is, a blind, unstoppable force and the motor of life; and a glimpse of the true nature of the world can be caught in 'ideal' knowledge. Ideal knowledge, Schopenhauer further argues, is only passed on by music, not by other forms of art, nor by science, because they all limit themselves to the world of phenomena. An 'idea' (*Idee*) in the Schopenhauerian sense is a *symbol* (*Abbild*) of the Will or, as he says, 'the immediate and adequate objectivity of the thing-in-itself, of the will' ['die unmittelbare und adäquate Objektität des Dinges an sich, des Willens'].[11] As music issues forth from the Will directly, music *symbolizes* the essence of life. Schopenhauer even concludes that 'we could just as well call the world embodied music as embodied will' ['man könnte demnach die Welt ebensowohl verkörperte Musik als verkörperten Willen nennen'].[12] Speaking the language of the Ideas, the unique quality of music lies in its universality. This universal, 'metaphysical' power, which forms music's *status aparte* among the arts, has nothing to do with German superiority whatsoever for Schopenhauer. Wagner, by contrast, says that this metaphysical strength forms *German* music's uniqueness. How, again, are universality and nationality linked?

For Wagner, music is a source of true knowledge, just as Schopenhauer posited. Music expresses the knowledge that all things in nature, including man, stem from the same source, the Will. Fundamentally, music is a *symbol* of truth. Beethoven, Wagner argues, made symbolic music; that is, he did not just formally *compose* music, but in his music he *revealed* the secret of music (and life) itself, and, in so doing, led his audience towards the experience of the *sublime*. Thus the experience of the sublime is accomplished by insight into the deepest soul of all being, because this insight *fills* us with the experience that, on a deeper level, limiting-categories — as Wagner, in line with Schopenhauer, calls them — such as time and space have no say. There is only the experience of infinity, imparted by the feeling of the sublime. Consequently, Wagner's answer to the Faustian exclamation 'where do I grasp you, infinite nature?' runs: in Beethoven's symbolic and sublime music. The question remains, however: why is this typically German?

Germany as Europe's Saviour

In Wagner's view, art in Europe generally finds itself in a state of decadence. Italian opera, Italian post-Renaissance painting, Jesuit architecture, and French naturalistic theatre are, as he says, 'weakened and sweetened' forms of art. He regards all these forms of art as decadent forms of earlier, strong ones such as Hellenistic architecture, Italian Renaissance painting, Greek tragedy, and Shakespearean poetry. This artistic decadence, Wagner proclaims, is to be ascribed to an increasing 'Roman', or 'Catholic' sway in Europe, which, while figuring out all kinds of new *forms* in art, neglected the metaphysical *spirit*. Fortunately, Germany will help European culture to escape its own dissolution; Wagner asserts:

> We know that it was the '*German spirit*', so much feared and hated 'over the mountains' [i.e., in Italy — MP], which everywhere, also in the field of art, met the artistically conducted decadence of the spirit of European nations, in a redemptive manner.[13]

> [Wir wissen, daß der 'über den Bergen' [in Italien — MP] so sehr gefürchtete und gehaßte 'deutsche Geist' es war, welcher überall, so auch auf dem Gebiete der Kunst, dieser künstlich geleiteten Verderbnis des europäischen Völkergeistes erlösend entgegentrat.]

The Italian and French Counter-Reformation triggered the fall of European art and religion, Wagner claims. However, thanks to such German artists as

Lessing, Goethe, and Schiller, and above all the music of Beethoven (in which the German '*Volksgeist*' was supremely active, according to Wagner), the decadence was interrupted and European culture took a turn for the better. German art in general, he says, and Beethoven's music in particular, showed the way back to the true essence of art, away from mere amusement and superficial beauty to the metaphysical and the sublime. With Beethoven, music returned to its very self, that is, in Wagner's words, to its sublime innocence in style, its philosophical apprehension, and its musical representation of the Will. It is herein, Wagner concludes, that the relationship between the great Beethoven and Germany is established.

BEETHOVEN AS THE MUSICAL COUNTERPART TO MARTIN LUTHER

Wagner has now answered his own chief question: Beethoven is the sublime expression of the national, German spirit. And as an artistic reformer, Wagner adds remarkably, Beethoven is the musical counterpart of Martin Luther, the great German religious reformer. Of course, it is quite odd to put a musician who was raised a Catholic on a par with the father of Protestantism. Wagner, aware of this curiosity, nevertheless starts to bear out that Beethoven, though coming from a Catholic family, had a Protestant (or, in other words, *reforming*) frame of mind. How does Wagner defend this curious assertion? Beethoven's reformatory spirit is emphatically clear in Beethoven's Eighth Symphony, which Wagner describes as a highlight of 'German natural peculiarity' ['die Eigentümlichkeit der deutschen Natur'] —

> which is so innerly, deeply and richly gifted that it knows how to impress its essence on every form, by transforming the form from within, which saves it from the necessity of outer revolution. That is why the German does not have a revolutionary, but a reformatory spirit. (DuS, 9, 64–65)
>
> [welche so innerlich tief und reich begabt ist, daß sie jeder Form ihr Wesen einzuprägen weiß, indem sie diese von innen neu umbildet, und dadurch von der Nötigung zu ihrem äußerlichen Umsturz bewahrt wird. So ist der Deutsche nicht revolutionär, sondern reformatorisch.]

The old revolutionary Wagner, who, in the Forties, was a close friend of the illustrious Russian revolutionist Michael Bakunin, and who was banned from Prussia and in exile in Switzerland as a consequence of his revolutionary activities in the years 1848–1849, here condemns revolution in general. He compares artistic revolution with political revolution, and regards both as the results of the same, revolutionary, spirit. By reasoning so, Wagner also holds the political and social Revolution in France responsible for the French artistic idea that poetical and musical forms should be destroyed so that a new, better form can rise spontaneously from their ruins. Wagner thinks this view to be erroneous. By contrast, he expounds the view that Germans know how to work with different forms, because they do not replace forms with others, but rather seek to enrich them with the deep, German spirit. Artistic Reformation therefore comes down to the 'pervasion of the [Italian — *MP*] musical form with the [German — *MP*] genius of music' ['die Durchdringung der {italienischen — *MP*} musikalischen Form von dem {deutschen — *MP*} Genius der Musik'] (DuS, 9, 65).

What makes the difference is the German spirit, and it is the German spirit to which the decline of spirit and taste in Europe (of which Italian opera, religious Counter-Reformation, and French fashion,[14] in short everything 'Roman', are the clearest symptoms) bowed. Such German artists as Schiller and Goethe, he concludes, already fought the Roman tendency to superficiality, but only recently had Beethoven's music overcome it completely. Beethoven's music, in brief, is a testimony to true 'Germanism' (*Deutschtum*). Beethoven, Wagner writes with great relief, finally freed music from Roman superficiality, whereby he proved its tremendous importance for German culture. Beethoven *deepened* German culture. Now the time has come, Wagner presumes, for music to undertake the task of deepening, hence elevating, culture in decadent European countries like France and Italy too.

Nietzsche's Notes of 1871

Now, having outlined Wagner's objectives (in particular, his main idea concerning the task of German music in relation to European culture), I turn to how Nietzsche approaches the same matter in section 9 of KSA, 7. This section consists of a collection of notes Nietzsche made in 1871, while he was working on the never-finished essay 'Musik und Tragödie', which was later to be, in a rather different form, *The Birth of Tragedy*.[15] Although the form of these notes and Nietzsche's conception of the essay deviate distinctly from the later book, the subject, its purposes, and its method are the same. In these notes, Nietzsche, on the one hand, analyzes Ancient Greece as a Dionysian and tragic culture, and, on the other, spells out what art should be like.

The German Reformation of Italian Opera

Section 9 of KSA, 7, opens with a reflection on Wagner's great enemy, the Italian opera. Although these reflections are clear evidence of Nietzsche's indebtedness to Wagner's *Beethoven*-essay, they also introduce some formulations and ideas we have not encountered there. For example, the metaphysical depth which Wagner regarded as typically German by associating it with a reforming, Lutheran spirit, is called 'Dionysian' by Nietzsche. For that reason this spirit, in place of the 'Protestantism' of Beethoven, is connected to Greek religious art. Nevertheless, Nietzsche pursues Wagner's depth-superficiality opposition, assigning 'superficiality' to Italian opera and regarding German depth as its rescuer. For Nietzsche, this 'depth' means: first, the ability to view Dionysos behind every living thing; and second, that to live out the Dionysian is to exist *zum Tode*, as Heidegger was to express it.

Now, despite the fact that Italian opera intended to make music like the Greeks, it did not succeed, because it always lacked this Dionysian worldview, this metaphysical depth. Instead, it remained 'externalized', focused as it was on phenomena like the performances of the individual singers and the stage-setting. Hence Italian opera expresses the nature of the 'Roman, unartistic man' (KSA, 7, 9[10], 275), that is the individual who lacks depth and has a trivial taste. Wagner, on the other hand, changes opera into the materialization of an artistic (*künstlerisch*) world, Nietzsche continues. His music has succeeded in escaping the non-artistic tendency of Italian opera, of favouring text and other outer aspects over music. His music distinguishes itself through its '*germanische Begabung*' (KSA, 7, 9[10], 275), which is to be understood as a national talent for metaphysical depth and truth. Here Nietzsche uses an important Wagnerian parallel, and Wagner's religious justification, when he writes that Wagner, in so doing, follows in Luther's footsteps: like Luther, he acquaints us with the Dionysian.[16] Thus, the German, Dionysian depth first came to the fore in Luther. This statement is at least equally remarkable as Wagner's defence of Beethoven as a Lutheran. The Dionysian Luther is not regarded as a composer here (which, of course, he was as well), but as a reformer, who battled the Italian, Catholic, frivolous spirit. 'Dionysian', hence, means 'reforming', and Nietzsche explains this as a 'deepening' of the opera, as musical form of the Roman, 'non-artistic' individual with the German gift, and so elevating opera to the level of true art. Next Nietzsche, like Wagner, equates Beethoven's artistic reformation to Luther's reforming spirit, and anchors Beethoven's musical reformation in his transformation of Schiller's poem 'An die Freude'. Through Beethoven's musical arrangement the poem finally became true art, Nietzsche writes in agreement with Wagner:

> We see, how the poet tries to transform his German, deep emotion into images; how he, though, as a modern individual, can do nothing but stumble ineptly. When Beethoven then brings out the actual, Schillerian foundation, we have the infinitely higher perfection. (KSA, 7, 9[10], 275)

> [Wir sehen, wie der Dichter sich seine germanisch tiefe dionysische Regung in Bildern zu deuten versucht: wie er aber, als moderner Mensch, nur schwerfällig zu stammeln weiß. Wenn jetzt Beethoven uns den eigentlich Schillerschen Untergrund darstellt, so haben wir das unendlich-Höhere und Vollkommene.]

What Nietzsche means is that Schiller, by virtue of his (German) nature, possessed a tendency to metaphysical depth that brings humankind into contact with the Dionysian. However, Schiller, as a poet, was 'governed by words' more than by music,[17] and hence failed to provide his Dionysian depth with the right — that is, musical — mode of expression.[18] The depth sought by Nietzsche and Wagner is only apparent in Beethoven's musical transformation of the hymn, because only music can make the metaphysical depth audible and attainable.

Schiller indeed ushered in a Reformation, but never took us to the catacombs of Greek art and culture. That is exactly what Nietzsche, varying Wagner's expression that Beethoven fulfilled the fight Goethe and Schiller fought, writes later on: 'Wagner fulfils what was started by Schiller and Goethe' ['Wagner vollendet, was Schiller und Goethe begonnen haben'] (KSA, 7, 9[23], 280).[19] Nevertheless, Nietzsche was subtle enough to understand Schiller's own hopes of music and opera, and to value and elaborate Schiller's theory of the chorus.[20] In order to define more specifically the changes Nietzsche introduced, and to define more precisely where Nietzsche is thinking in line with Schiller, Schopenhauer, and Wagner, and where he seems to surpass them, I shall outline Schiller's theory of the chorus, as that is set out in his essay 'On the Use of the Chorus in Tragedy' ['Über den Gebrauch des Chors in der Tragödie'] (1803), since this text paves the way for Nietzsche's interpretation of music's central role in Greek tragedy, as well as for his criticism of Wagner.

Schiller's Theory of the Chorus

Long before Wagner and Nietzsche, Schiller claimed that a tragic poem finds its completion in the performance: 'The tragic poem reaches perfection in the theatrical performance alone: the poem gives nothing but words; music and dance must be added to experience them' ['Das tragische Dichtwerk wird erst durch die theatralische Vorstellung zu einem Ganzen: Nur die Worte gibt der Dichter, Musik und Tanz müssen hinzukommen, sie zu beleben'] (NA, 10, 7). Play (*Spiel*) and seriousness (*Ernst*) must coincide, so as to become 'poetic play' (*poetisches Spiel*) and to ennoble (*veredeln*) the joy of the audience: 'All art is dedicated to joy, and there is no higher and no more serious task than making people happy' ['Alle Kunst ist der Freude gewidmet, und es gibt keine höhere und keine ernsthaftere Aufgabe, als die Menschen zu beglücken'] (NA, 10, 8). Against theatre which offers nothing but 'an amusing delusion of the moment' ['ein gefälliger Wahn des Augenblicks'], 'a passing illusion' ['eine vorübergehende Täuschung'], Schiller stresses that 'true art does not aim at a passing play; it is a serious thing to true art, not to place people in a momentary dream of freedom, but indeed and actually to *set* them free' ['die wahre Kunst {...} hat es nicht bloß auf ein vorübergehendes Spiels abgesehen; es ist ihr ernst damit, den Menschen nicht bloß in einen augenblicklichen Traum von Freiheit zu versetzen, sondern ihn wirklich und in der Tat frei zu machen'] (NA, 10, 8). This art tries to appeal to a power in the beholder, by which he is able to recreate the sensual world that he used to regard as 'a blind power' (*eine blinde Macht*) and 'rude material' (*roher Stoff*). Through the play, he experiences that he has the power to change the material world with his (aesthetically modulated) mind. Therefore, Schiller concludes, 'true art founds its ideal building on the truth itself, on the fixed and deep ground of nature' ['auf der Wahrheit selbst, auf dem festen und tiefen Grunde der Natur errichtet sie ihr ideales Gebäude'] (NA, 10, 9).[21] That is why art should be 'completely ideal and yet, in the deepest sense, real' ['ganz ideell und doch im tiefsten Sinne reell']. If art were to base itself on reality alone, then it would show nature as nothing more than *mere* appearance, without capturing the essence of reality (*der Geist der Natur*). Such art would be without joy (*Freud*) and would be serious in the sense of 'not enjoyable' (*unerfreulich*). According to Schiller, such art would be, for example, French naturalism.

On the other hand, art should not be a mere product of someone's fantasy. Such art, Schiller thinks, would not care for any truth at all, and would merely wish to surprise its audience: 'Just to link fantastic forms at random does not mean to go into the ideal, and to represent reality by imitation does not mean to represent nature' ['Phantastische Gebilde willkürlich aneinanderreihen heißt nicht ins Ideale gehen, und das Wirkliche nachahmend wiederbringen heißt nicht die Natur darstellen'] (NA, 10, 9). The aim of art should be 'to build and found something in the heart of the beholder' ['im Gemüt {des Zuschauers — *MP*} {etwas} erbauen und begründen'] (NA, 10, 9). For this, art should unite truth and (aesthetic) illusion. French naturalism has not understood this, and therefore, has not captured the Greek spirit. It has interpreted the demand of unity of place and time purely empirically 'as if there was another place here than the merely ideal space, and another time than the merely continuous series of the action' ['als ob hier ein anderer Ort wäre als der bloß ideale Raum, und eine andere Zeit als bloß die stetige Folge der Handlung'] (NA, 10, 10). Schiller, on the other hand, says that everything outward in the drama should not give the illusion of empirical reality, but it should be a *symbol* of reality, which renders the universal essence of things and men. This symbolic power is made dependent on the *chorus*. The introduction of the chorus into the tragedy, to Schiller, was a decisive step in art: now it was able to unite illusion and truth, to render the truth in an (aesthetically) illusionary, free, poetic play. How does this work? As a 'living wall', the chorus isolates itself from the empirical reality. Hence, it preserves art's 'ideal' fundament — that is, its poetic freedom — and it declares war on naturalism

— that is, the mere imitation of reality. Instead, tragedy becomes a symbolic art-form.

Schiller remarks that Greek tragedy — 'as one knows', he says, suggesting that this was common knowledge — sprang from the chorus, and that the chorus, at that time, was a natural result of the poetic crystallization or formation of life. In modern times, this is no longer a natural result, but an 'artificial organ', which helps to call forth poetry. This has everything to do with the modern aberration of the 'living word': to our times, the *written* word has become more natural. 'The people' used to be a 'living mass', a 'rude mass', but in modern times has formed itself into a 'state', a 'skimmed concept' of the 'original' people. Now, the poet, for Schiller, should bring Man back to his original, prehistoric situation. He should strip Man of everything artificial about him and lead him back to his inner nature by presenting this inner nature to him. At the same time, the poetical power of the whole is enhanced by dance and music, and by isolating reflection from the action. The chorus brings *life* back into *language*, it raises the lyricism of the tragedy, and it forces the poet to *enliven* his material, that is, to give it 'tragic greatness' (*tragische Größe*). On the other hand, the chorus, apart from lyricism, renders to the whole, peace (*Ruhe*), or, as Schiller calls it — 'the beautiful and high peace, in which the character of a noble artwork must consist' ['die schöne und hohe Ruhe, die der Charakter eines edlen Kunstwerkes sein muß'] (NA, 10, 14). This peace sees to it that 'the heart of the beholder [...] [will] retain his freedom, even in the most vehement passion' ['das Gemüt des Zuschauers ... auch in der heftigsten Passion seine Freiheit behalten {kann}'] (NA, 10, 10). This sort of freedom implies that the audience does not fall prey to emotive impression, to the 'violence of affects' (*Gewalt der Affekte*), to 'mere illusion' (*Täuschung*). Instead, this freedom guarantees that the audience remains 'clear and cheerful (*klar und heiter*), able to discriminate between heart (*Gemüth*) — and the emotions it undergoes — and mind. In order to bring this about, the artist must build in the audience a balance between 'passivity' (*Leiden*) and 'activity' (*Aktivität*). He does this through the breaking of the action by the chorus, which relieves the passion with reflection and distance: 'By separating the parts and stepping forward between the passions with its soothening reflection, the chorus gives us back our freedom, which was about to get lost in the storm of affections' ['Dadurch, daß der Chor die Teile auseinanderhält und zwischen die Passionen mit seiner beruhigenden Betrachtung tritt, gibt er uns unsre Freiheit zurück, die im Sturm der Affekte verlorengehen würde'] (NA, 10, 10).

The chorus constrains (*bändigt*) the passion (*Leidenschaft*), which means it 'motivates the contemplation' ['motiviert die Besonnenheit'] (NA, 10, 10). At the same time, everyone, actors and chorus, act on a symbolic level, which means that they are ideal persons, 'representations of their sort, giving voice to the depth of humanity' ['Repräsentanten ihrer Gattung, die das Tiefe der Menschheit aussprechen']. What Schiller precisely means by this 'depth of humanity' is not made clear here. Is it more than that Man's insight is his own natural freedom and his freedom to form his freedom, or is it just, for Schiller, something biological and social, but not metaphysical? Nietzsche and Wagner, under Schopenhauer's influence, understood it metaphysically. And although they agree in great part with Schiller, and — and as he does — demand that art be symbolic, and — as he does — that tragedy be symbolic and musical, for them this level of symbolic depth has everything to do with a metaphysical conception of nature. The main point of difference between Schiller and Nietzsche, then, is their conception of nature and the nature of Man; or, as Nietzsche marks the distinction: Schiller adheres to a 'joyful' (*heiter*) view of nature, while he regards nature as 'tragic' (KSA, 7, 9[142], 327).

The Importance of the Chorus to Nietzsche

In my view, Nietzsche uses, and changes, Schiller's theory of the chorus with three objectives in mind: first, he wants to demonstrate the musical roots of Greek culture; second, he intends to put forward a suggestion about how Wagner could get rid of the dramatic singer by extending the part of the chorus; and third, he wants to show that Wagner, due to his enormous symbolic powers, is a true servant of Dionysos.[22]

The chorus is to Nietzsche the only *communicative* body in drama, meaning that it is the only element in drama that expresses immediately the Will. As the immediate representation of the Will it is, by implication, the solely musical element of the whole drama. Therefore, it is in the chorus that the enrichment of words by music takes place. The musical potency of the chorus is exactly the reason why Schiller had such high hopes for opera, as a form of art that would break with naturalistic theatre. Wagner and Nietzsche adopt Schiller's hope, but adjoin it to a Schoperhauerian, metaphysical, and 'tragic' content. Nietzsche, with Schiller, is advocating the re-institution of the chorus: he protests against the single, dramatic singer, who sings clear words and stories like a rhapsodist or a troubadour. In his view, no instrument other than the tones of the singing chorus and a playing orchestra, supported only by mime,[23] should express the story (KSA, 7, 9[10, 11], 275–77), as was the situation in Greek tragedy. Restoring the chorus might help Wagner solve his difficulty with the dramatic singer, Nietzsche explains, and his *Tristan* was well on the way to fulfilling this idea of Nietzsche — 'the choir that has a vision and describes what it sees in an enthusiast manner! *The Schillerian idea intensified endlessly!*' ['der Chor, der eine Vision hat und begeistert beschreibt was er schaut! *Die Schillerische Vorstellung unendlich vertieft!*'] (KSA, 7, 9[11],

277). Following this path, Wagner would free himself from an important dilemma, and rejuvenate the Greek, musical spirit at one stroke.

Wagner's tragic art, Nietzsche supposes, might be the starting point of a substantial period in which the tragic or Dionysian view of life dominates German culture. For Nietzsche, this would entail the re-establishment of Germany's identity, a 'return of the German spirit to itself' ['Rückkehr des germanischen Geistes zu sich selbst'] (KSA, 7, 9[31], 283). It is the result of the Dionysian spirit seeking revelation, which it finds at last in Wagner's music: 'Effects of Wagner. Birth of tragedy out of music' ['Wirkungen Wagner's. Geburt der Tragödie aus Musik'] (KSA, 7, 9[31], 283). And he adds: 'I recognize the only form of life in the Greek: and regard Wagner as the most sublime step towards its rebirth in the German soul' ['Ich erkenne die einzige Lebensform in der griechischen: und betrachte Wagner als den erhabensten Schritt zu deren Wiedergeburt im deutschen Wesen'] (KSA, 7, 9[34], 284).[24]

MUSIC AND TRAGEDY

Not only does the German spirit return to itself with Wagner, the Greek spirit too is revived in Wagner's music. 'Greek' and 'German' become interchangeable predicates for Nietzsche or, rather, it is his ideal that they will mean the same one day, as a fragment from the literary remains of the year 1871 shows us (KSA, 7, 16[44], 408). According to this note, Nietzsche considered using the title 'The Rebirth of Greece out of the Rejuvenation of the German Spirit' ['Die Wiedergeburt Griechenlands aus der Erneuerung des deutschen Geistes'] for his first book. This title is an indication of how close Nietzsche thought the bond between Greece and Germany was and had to be. The ideal culture would be the one in which 'our music', that is, Wagnerian music, would be generally understood. However, what, to Nietzsche's mind, is the specific merit of Wagner's music? What makes this music so different that present culture would not be able to understand it?

Another fragment from this period, Note 9[36], provides the beginning of an answer to these questions and sheds some light on the question *why* Nietzsche aspired to a new culture. It opens with the remark that modern art lacks 'insight into the primordial phenomena' ['Einblick in die Urphänomene'] (KSA, 7, 9[36], 284). Its subjects, instead, are 'artificially imitated models' ['künstliche nachgemachte Vorbilder']. Modern art offers nothing more than a shallow copy of Greek artworks, whereas it should originate from insight into the primordial. Only Richard Wagner, we read in this note, produces art out of such insight: 'Having seen the phenomenon Wagner live, it has been explained to me, at first in a negative way, that we have not understood the Greek world yet' ['Für mich erläutert das leibhaft geschaute Phänomen Wagner's zuerst negativ, daß wir die griechische Welt bis jetzt nicht verstanden haben'] (KSA, 7, 9[36], 284). In other words, if we want to understand Wagnerian art, we can do so by understanding the Greek world. The same applies the other way round: if we are to grasp Greek culture, we can attain understanding by listening to Wagnerian music. Nietzsche confirms this in several other notes, for example in the following:

> In world history, we have seen this enormous capacity of music reach the *creation of myths* twice: and we are so fortunate to experience this stunning process ourselves right now, in order to clarify analogously with our time the first time as well. (KSA, 7, 14[3], 376)
>
> [Dieses ungeheure Vermögen der Musik sehen wir zweimal bisher in der Weltgeschichte zur Mythenschöpfung kommen: und das eine Mal sind wir beglückt genug, diesen erstaunlichen Prozeß selbst zu erleben, um von hier aus auch jenes erste Mal uns analogisch zu verdeutlichen.]

In his *Nachlass*, Nietzsche perceives the process of modern Western civilization as a 'mighty fight' against 'the spirit of music' (KSA, 7, 9[36], 284). To regain a musical spirit, and hear the truth about life, we have to turn our ears to a civilization whose soul depended on music, ancient Greece. Because Nietzsche considers ancient Greece to be 'the only and deepest possibility for life' ['die einzige und tiefste Lebensmöglichkeit'] (KSA, 7, 9[36], 284) and this world to be fundamentally musical, Wagner — as a composer of tragic music — functions, among others, as a vehicle for Nietzsche, one which promises access to his beloved Greek world. Through Wagner, Nietzsche achieves a better understanding of his beloved Greek culture. What is more: through Wagner modern culture might actually become Greek again, through him 'a German rebirth of the Hellenic world' ['eine deutsche Wiedergeburt der hellenischen Welt'] will take place, Nietzsche predicts in this note, a rebirth, he comments in addition, 'to which we want to devote ourselves' ['der wir uns widmen wollen'] (KSA, 7, 9[36], 284). Wagner has the ambition and the ability to change or, in Nietzsche's words, to *redeem* modern culture with his symbolic, metaphysical music-dramas. Since this change is Nietzsche's main purpose as a philosopher, a lover of art and a lover of humankind, he is prepared to become Wagner's assistant and servant. For the sake of German culture, Nietzsche is even willing to withdraw from university so as to accompany Wagner in his fight against superficiality.[25]

Myth

What should culture look like to match Wagner's music? What spirit must culture turn into in order to understand art's message, to understand the metaphysical truth art reveals? In another note, Nietzsche relates this truth to

Dionysos, and ponders the relationship between music and language, speaking of 'scholarship' (*Wissenschaft*) as the 'murderer' of tragedy. The question with which this note ends — 'under which conditions do we conceive of the rebirth of tragedy?' ['unter welchen Bedingungen denken wir uns die Wiedergeburt der Tragödie?'] — is a kind of Kantian question; namely, under what conditions culture would be able to understand and to perform Wagner's music (KSA, 7, 9[38], 286–87)? Unfortunately, this question is not answered here. However, we already know that it must become deeper and must be opened up to the tragic truth of life, which means that culture must become *mythical*. Contrary to modern opera, Wagner restores the place of myth in musical art and deepens opera with a tragic view of life (KSA, 7, 9[41], 287–88). Against the tendency to abstract and conceptual thought, Nietzsche places myth as an expression of life's essence, its joy and sorrow (KSA, 7, 9[58], 296–97). Abstraction stands in the way of the tragic culture. Myth has to set art free, liberate it from theory and scholarship, and, accordingly, deepen culture with tragic, metaphysical insight. In a further note, Nietzsche writes that music has to lead the image back to myth, away from Socratism, that is. In other words, music replaces the image as concept with the image as imagination (KSA, 7, 9[59], 297).

Myth, we learn in another note, is, for Nietzsche, 'in its totality interpretation of music' ['als Ganzes Interpretation der Musik'] (KSA, 7, 9[125], 320).[26] He regards myth as a literary form, a pre-historical period, and a model for the future. In the pre-historical period, human beings maintained a tragic view of life and were driven by the desire to express this artistically.[27] To Nietzsche, this strong desire is a sign of suffering from an abundance of life as well as of lust for life, or to put it differently, in pre-historical individuals life is present in a very strong, persistent way, so strong that it drives them insane. Hence, it is a constructive and destructive power at the same time. Only with the help of artistic transformation can Man succeed in controlling these enormous powers and finding the balance not to be torn apart and destroyed.[28] Contrary to science, as it is dominated by the desire to control life logically, this process is not hostile to life. Science resists life by trying to grasp its truth in an abstract way, in logical concepts. However, logic lacks the power to justify life. Contrarily, it resists life's metaphysical pain (*Urschmerz*). Myth, on the other hand, exploits the powers of life, its joy and sorrow, in an extraordinary extension of human imagination.

The Idyll

Another note compares the relationship between Italian Renaissance painting and the rediscovery of ancient culture. Elaborating Schiller's notions of the idyllic and the sentimental as expounded in the treatise *On Naïve and*

Sentimental Poetry [*Über naive und sentimentalische Dichtung*], Nietzsche states that the rediscovery of ancient culture and opera are signs of the return of an idyllic tendency, of a sentimental bent (KSA, 7, 9[45], 292).[29] Elsewhere, Nietzsche uses the adjective 'sentimental' to describe contemporary art (KSA, 7, 7[126], 283–84).[30] Modern art, according to this note, is sentimental, because it aims at the creation of the 'idyll'. Here, he opposes sentimental art to 'Dionysian' and 'naïve' art. Hence, the sentimental and the idyll attain a negative meaning. However, in the fragments contained in section 9, the idyllic gains also a positive connotation, especially in combination with the adjective 'tragic' and in combination with Wagner.

In his *Nachlass*, Nietzsche writes that we want from art the 'idyllic-elegaic' (*das Idyllisch-Elegische*), because this gives us joy: as he puts it, 'the cult of nature: *that is our true experience of art*' ('der Kultus der Natur: *das ist unsere wahrhafte Kunstempfinding*') (KSA, 7, 9[85], 305). To this he adds that 'the more powerful and magic nature is being represented, the more we believe in it [...] *art to us means the expulsion of non-nature*, flight from culture and education' ['je mächtiger und zauberischer die Natur dargestellt wird, um so mehr glauben wir an sie ... *Die Kunst* ist für uns *Beseitigung der Unnatur*, Flucht vor der Kultur und Bildung'] (KSA, 7, 9[85], 305).[31] This idea, now, he seeks to unite with Wagner's tragic art, in a sequence of fragments (KSA, 7, 9[136] to 9[151], 324–31). Here Nietzsche tries to define Wagner's art with the help of Schiller's definition of the idyll, as the poetic representation of an innocent and happy humanity.[32] Nietzsche supports Schiller's definition of the idyll as the enjoyable (restored) unity of reality and the ideal of Man living in harmony with himself and nature (KSA, 7, 9[142], 327). He even regards Wagner's compositions *Siegfried* and *Tristan* as idyllic, in which, however, not the Schillerian 'cheerful' (*heiter*) view of nature is active, but Wagner's tragic, Dionysian worldview. In Wagner's and Nietzsche's view, life means, first and foremost, suffering. However, enjoying the unity of reality and the ideal on the symbolic level in tragedy does encompass, at times, joy. For this reason, Nietzsche says, we enjoy Tristan's death, instead of weeping over it, because in his death reality and the ideal have become one and true. What makes Wagner 'idyllic', albeit 'idyllic' with a tragic worldview, is the fact that he exploits the idyllic aspects of opera, like the recitative, verses, and myth, to its limits (KSA, 7, 9[149], 329). His 'total artworks' (*Gesamtkunstwerke*) are the products of an 'undivided Man' (*ungetrennter Mensch*) or 'primordial Man' (*Urmensch*). Wagner possesses a metaphysical insight into Man, into Man as a primordial, natural being.[33] He shows Man what his true nature is, besides being a modern who, according to Schiller's analysis of modernity in his *Letters on the Aesthetic Education of Man* [*Briefe über die aesthetische Erziehung des Menschen*], lives alienated from nature, or who is ripped into pieces by the *principium individuationis* (KSA, 7, 9[149], 331).[34] The idyllic artist Richard

Wagner creates 'primordial music' (*Urmusik*), which comes down to a form of music which is free of any plastic bent. This music brings the message to modern Man that he might find union with nature again, when he succeeds in liberating himself from the Roman tendency, and that his idyllic situation of happiness and innocence might be restored.

THE SYMBOL

Still reflecting on the idyll, Nietzsche shifts his attention to its relation to the symbol (KSA, 7, 9[76], 302). Here Nietzsche, referring to Schiller's idyllic poem 'The Walk' ['Der Spaziergang'], remarks that the essence of modern German poetry is the cult of nature ['der Kultus der Natur'].[35] By nature he means the 'German-comprehended nature', that is, divine nature as opposed to non-divine, empirical nature, which is the object of science. To Schiller's mind, as Nietzsche points out, Shakespeare mastered the art of capturing the 'non-representative' side of nature in symbols, he grasped the spirit of nature ['der Geist der Natur'] by using symbols 'where nature can not be presented' ['wo die Natur nicht kann dargestellt werden'] (KSA, 7, 9[77], 302).

Nietzsche further remarks that, 'in the original period' ['in der ursprünglichen Periode'], the symbol used to be used as the language of 'the general' ['das Allgemeine'], but later became reduced to a mere token of the concept (KSA, 7, 9[88], 305). What Nietzsche means here is that what Shakespeare did, and what reminded Schiller so much of ancient Greek tragedy, was never achieved afterwards by any artist. Only music, Nietzsche contends, may be able to master the original art of symbolising. Obviously, modern opera does not show this, since Nietzsche is convinced that 'in opera music became the symbol of concepts' ['in der Oper wurde {die Musik} zur Symbolik des Begriffes gebraucht'] (KSA, 7, 9[88], 306). In fact, the present world in its totality lacks symbols, that is, a universal level, or insight into its universal essence. Nietzsche holds this shortage of symbols responsible for the contemporary lack of great art: 'Understanding the world in "symbols" is the precondition of a great art' ['Verständnis der Welt in "Symbolen" ist die Voraussetzung einer großen Kunst'] (KSA, 7, 9[92], 308). The only art that provides us with a truly symbolic understanding of the world is music. Other forms of art only force bare abstractions, bloodless ideas, upon us. Wagner's art, however, recalls an 'artistic era' by utilising the original, symbolic character of music. Preserving the symbolic level of the 'universal', Wagner's music bridges different periods in history and different nations. On top of this, it becomes the only redeeming art modern times have at their disposal: '*Music as general-unnational-untimely form of art* is the *only* blossoming *form of art*. It represents for us the *entire* art and the artistic world. Therefore it redeems' ['Die Musik als allgemein-unnational-unzeitliche Kunst ist die einzig blühende. Sie

vertritt für uns die *ganze* Kunst und die künstlerische Welt. Darum erlöst sie']
(KSA, 7, 9[90], 307). *Grasping the world in symbols* becomes Nietzsche's first
demand of art (KSA, 7, 9[92], 308), and it is in *symbolization* that he sees a new
possibility for art. By drawing on the original art of symbolising, music is able
to create an idyll, a 'Schillerian' world in which the reality and the ideal are
united. Wagner's *Siegfried-Idylle*, according to Nietzsche, is such an idyll.[36]
What distinguishes Wagner and, in his footsteps, Nietzsche from Schiller,
however, is their view of reality. While Wagner has a *tragic* view of nature,
Schiller adheres to a view which is 'joyful' (*heiter*).

Conclusion

According to *Über naïve und sentimentalische Dichtung*, the 'idyll' is a poetic
form, next to the 'elegy' and the 'satire'. The idyll portrays humankind in a
state of innocence and happiness ('Die poetische Darstellung unschuldiger
und glücklicher Menschheit ist der allgemeine Begriff {der Idylle}'), that is,
'in a state of harmony and peace with itself ('in einem Zustand der Harmonie
und des Friedens mit sich selbst' (NA, 20, 467). However, the idyll is not only
a poetical form, but also a human condition and a historical period. Innocence (*Unschuld*) and happiness (*Glück*) were the human condition in the
'childish period' in human history, that is, the pre-cultural period (which
Nietzsche, with a more metaphysical term, calls 'primordial'): 'But such a
state does not only occur prior to the beginning of culture, but it is also what
culture aims at as its final purpose' ['Aber ein solcher Zustand findet nicht
bloß vor dem Anfange der Kultur statt, sondern er ist auch, dem die Kultur
[...] als ihr letztes Ziel beabsichtet'] (NA, 20, 467). According to Schiller,
Man should strive to regain this state of innocence and happiness, yet this
does not mean that Man should return to his childhood, but rather should
strive to become *more Man*. Man should aim at a state of 'maturity'
(*Mündigkeit*), freedom of speech and resistance to tyranny (NA, 20, 472).
Here Schiller baptizes this ideal with the utopian term 'Elysium' — the
idyllic poet must not direct us back into 'Arcadia', but lead us to 'Elysium',
where we (the public) will find the 'higher harmony' that is the reward for all
warriors and victors (NA, 20, 467). Consequently, whereas Schiller agrees
with Kant — that Man must leave the state of nature to develop himself — at
the same time he assumes that the idyll could help us to found a cultural state
in which the goods things of our natural state are preserved.

The idyll offers rest and peace, which are far removed from the turbulence,
lassitude, and complexity of modern life. For Schiller, art activates the imagination of the beholder: by projecting an idyllic world, the beholder sees how
his future world could be, and he is prompted to believe in his power to
materialize this idyll. According to Schiller, Man's emancipation, his future

independence, his maturity, and freedom, all begin with his receptive and creative imagination. While Schiller, with the aid of the artistic imagination and the aesthetic appearances (*Schein*), wants to make the public aware of its social circumstances *and* of its ability to change its situation, Nietzsche seeks to make the people aware of its tragic fate and its collective powerlessness regarding that fate. For Schiller, the action must take place, not in the empirical sphere of the real, of 'the common' (*das Gemeine*), but in the symbolical and 'poetical' sphere of the idyll, so as to supply the public with hope and determination to fight for their freedom. In this sphere, the real and the ideal[37] come together in a bond. Nietzsche, holding to the view that Man's experience of freedom is limited to short moments of sublime aesthetic experiences, cannot go along with Schiller's hopes for a future maturity. Genuine humanity to Schiller means (political and social) freedom, but Nietzsche in these notes cannot accept with this *heiter* view of humanity. For him, Man can only experience the aesthetic illusion of freedom, when he, through art, forgets his individuality and his dependence on blind Will. In these fragments notes which precede *Die Geburt der Tragödie*, Wagner, next to Schiller, appears as, on the one hand, a major source of inspiration for Nietzsche's ideas on music and culture, and, on the other, as the successor to Greek, tragic art and culture.[38] Nietzsche draws on Wagner's ideas about the essence of true music and music's central task, as evoked in his *Beethoven*-essay.

Now, which ideas exactly do Wagner and Nietzsche share, and in what respect does Nietzsche deviate from his musical friend? As we saw, for Schopenhauer music held a unique position amongst the arts. Other than poetry and sculpture, true music was a universal, sublime, symbolic, and metaphysical form of art. Schopenhauer warns of the danger for opera of sticking too closely to the words; yet for him the true musician was the Italian Rossini, a composer particularly famous for his operas. Wagner agrees with Schopenhauer's metaphysical aesthetics, but he confines the ability of making true, universal, symbolic, and sublime music to Germans, and above all to Beethoven. For Wagner, the ability for metaphysics is linked to the reformating spirit, a typically German spirit. More than Schopenhauer, Wagner turns his back on opera, because it, instead of aiming at metaphysical knowledge and at representation of that knowledge, has the more limited ambition of merely amusing and impressing the public. To this extent Nietzsche agrees with Wagner, although he considers Wagner, rather than Beethoven, to be the one true musician. Furthermore, he suggests that Wagner would be an even better musician, if he would start making more use of the chorus. But what is most characteristic of Nietzsche is his idea that Wagner is the only true musician, not so much because he is German or creates out of an inner vision of the Will, but because he is Greek, or rather, because he is Dionysian.

Contrary to Schopenhauer, Wagner and Nietzsche set cultural aims for music, and trusted in German superiority in this respect. Jointly they wished to combat the modern bent for theory and discursiveness, as Goethe and Schiller had done before them. For Wagner and Nietzsche, however, it is the art of music that, thanks to its immense symbolic powers, will accomplish the return to Greek theatre and culture. Music, they expect, will redeem the superficiality of present-day, to which amusement is central, by enriching it with metaphysical and symbolic — hence, 'German' — depth. This desire for *symbolization* constitutes Nietzsche's main demand of art and, hence, of culture. This, however, is not only in line with Schopenhauer and Wagner, but also with Goethe and Schiller, who also wanted art to be symbolic, so as to go beyond the mere imitation of French naturalistic theatre and the sentimental poetry created out of subjectivity. Nietzsche agrees with Goethe that a higher symbolic activity saves culture from decadence, from falling back into subjectivity and a naturalism orientated towards the phenomenal world. For Goethe, Schiller, and Nietzsche, the imagination takes us to the heart of life, whether this is 'idyllic' or 'tragic'. But where Goethe and Schiller, according to Nietzsche, lacked music and a tragic worldview, Wagner succeeded in making the desired deeply symbolic, metaphysically objective, form of art. Thanks to his 'understanding of the world in symbols', he accomplished what Goethe and Schiller had set out to achieve — the revitalization and heightening of culture through symbolic art.

Notes

[1] See Nietzsche's letter to Erwin Rohde of 25 October 1872 (Friedrich Nietzsche, *Sämtliche Briefe: Kritische Studienausgabe*, ed. by Giorgio Colli and Mazzino Montinari, 8 vols (Munich; Berlin and New York: Deutscher Taschenbuch Verlag; Walter de Gruyter, 1986), vol. 4, 70–71. Henceforth referred to as KSB, with volume and page reference. Nietzsche's works are cited from Friedrich Nietzsche, *Sämtliche Werke: Kritische Studienausgabe*, ed. by Giorgio Colli and Mazzino Montinari, 15 vols (Munich: Deutscher Taschenbuch Verlag; Berlin/New York: de Gruyter, 1980); henceforth referred to as KSA, with volume number, followed by section and page reference (*Die Geburt der Tragödie* is signified by GT). English quotations are taken from Friedrich Nietzsche, *The Birth of Tragedy*, ed. by Raymond Geuss and Ronald Speirs (Cambridge, New York: Cambridge University Press, 1999).

[2] De Chirico was especially attracted by its metaphysics; see his painting 'Great Metaphysical Still-Life' of 1918.

[3] Kandinsky treated colours and lines as if they were sounds; see, for example, his 'Composition' series.

[4] For further discussion, see R. H. Stephenson, 'The Proper Object of Cultural Study: Ernst Cassirer and the Aesthetic Theory of Weimar Classicism', in Paul Bishop and R. H. Stephenson (eds), *Cultural Studies and the Symbolic* vol. 1, (Leeds: Northern Universities Press, 2003), 82–114 (p. 82).

[5] See Goethe's conversation of 29 January 1826 (Johann Peter Eckermann, *Gespräche mit Goethe in den letzten Jahren seines Lebens* (Munich: Hanser, 1986), pp. 155–56). Compare with Goethe's definition of *Stil* in his essay 'Einfache Nachahmung der Natur, Manier, Stil' (1788).

⁶ Goethe's conversation of 29 January 1826; compare with his conversation of 11 June 1825 (*Gespräche mit Goethe*, p. 144).

⁷ 'Was *ist, ist* schon Symbol, und die Dichtung hat das nur aufzudecken' is how Wolfgang Binder summarizes Goethe's position ('Das "offenbare Geheimnis": Goethes Symbolverständnis', in Gaetano Benedetti and Udo Rauchfleisch (eds), *Welt der Symbole: Interdisziplinäre Aspekte des Symbolverständnisses* (Göttingen: Vandenhoeck & Ruprecht, 1989), pp. 146–63 (p. 160).

⁸ For an exception, see Berhard Lypp, 'Der symbolische Prozess des Tragischen', *Nietzsche-Studien*, 18 (1989), 127–40.

⁹ As collected in KSA, 7, Notebook 9 = U I 4 a (1871), 269–331.

¹⁰ See Nietzsche's letter to Richard Wagner of 10 November 1870 (KSB, 3, 156–57).

¹¹ Arthur Schopenhauer, *Die Welt als Wille und Vorstellung* [*Sämtliche Werke*, vol. 1] (Frankfurt am Main: Suhrkamp Verlag, 1986), §36, p. 265; Arthur Schopenhauer, *The World as Will and Representation*, vol. 1, trans. by E. F. J. Payne (New York: Dover, 1966), 184.

¹² *Die Welt als Wille und Vorstellung*, §52, p.366; *The World as Will and Representation*, pp. 262–63. Note the strong similarity with Goethe's definition of 'Stil' as based on essential knowledge and Goethe's aesthetic appreciation of nature, 'one that cannot be reduced to an empirical object or to an intellectual idea. Nature is rather — and, in this respect, like Art — the embodiment of (symbolic) significance' (Stephenson, 'The Proper Object of Cultural Study', pp. 84–85).

¹³ Richard Wagner, *Dichtungen und Schriften*, ed. by Dieter Borchmeyer, 10 vols (Frankfurt am Main: Insel Verlag, 1983), vol. 9, 38–109 (p. 63). Henceforth cited as DuS, followed by volume number and a page reference. English translations by the author.

¹⁴ Like Schiller, Wagner speaks often of 'French fashion', when he means the latest French fashion in every domain of life, such as daily life, art, and politics. Wagner's criticism of French fashion probably inhibits Wagner from repeating what he had written one year earlier in 'On Conducting' ['Ueber das Dirigiren'], namely, that only in Paris in the year 1839 did he start to understand the secret of a good musical performance, when he attended a performance of Beethoven's *Ninth Symphony* performed by the Parisian conservatory orchestra. Moreover, he remarks that German performances are often so bad, because conductors conceive of music in an abstract manner. Hence, French art may be superficial and German art deep, but in *performing* the French seem to be better (Richard Wagner, *Wagner on Conducting*, trans. by Edward Dannreuther (New York: Dover, 1989), pp. 15–16).

¹⁵ The genesis of *The Birth* is quite complicated, because the notes relevant to this book stretch over fourteen different notebooks. For further discussion, see M. S. Silk and J. P. Stern, *Nietzsche on Tragedy* (Cambridge, London, New York: Cambridge University Press, 1981), pp. 41–52.

¹⁶ According to Nietzsche, 'the German gift', which was 'revealed in Luther for the first time', is the talent for insight into and expression of the Dionysian wisdom. By articulating this in music, Man gets acquainted with *die künstlerische Weltbetrachtung, den Mythus* (KSA, 7, 9[10], 275). With regard to Schiller's *germanische Begabung*, Nietzsche speaks of 'seine [i.e., Schiller's — MP] germanisch tiefe dionysische Regung'.

¹⁷ Despite Nietzsche's awareness of Schiller's musical inspiration; see GT §5 (KSA, 1, 43).

¹⁸ Schiller had already noticed this himself, as a letter of 21 October 1800 to his close friend Körner shows: 'The *Ode to Joy* is, according to my feeling now, truly inaccurate; [. . .] Because it met the inaccurate taste of that time, it has received the honour of becoming a national poem, to a certain extent' ['Die *Freude* ist nach meinem jetzigen Gefühl durchaus fehlerhaft; [. . .] Weil sie aber einem fehlerhaften Geschmack der Zeit entgegen kam, so hat sie die Ehre erhalten, gewißermaaßen ein Volksgedicht zu werden]' — in fact, the poem 'An die Freude' was published for the first time in the *Rheinische Thalia* in 1785 (Friedrich Schiller, *Werke: Nationalausgabe*, ed. by Julius Peterson and Gerhard Fricke, im Auftrag des Goethe- und Schiller-Archivs, des Schiller-Nationalmuseums und der Deutschen Akademie, 43 vols

(Weimar: Hermann Böhlaus Nachfolger, 1943-), vol. 30, 206). Henceforth cited as NA, followed by a volume number and page reference.

[19] Compare with GT §20 (KSA, 1, 131).

[20] In *The Birth of Tragedy*, Nietzsche finds himself forced to admit that Schiller, by his lyrical inspiration and by his 'sentimental bent' indeed showed us the way to Greek culture, but because of a lack in musicality and an 'idyllic tendency', both Goethe and Schiller never showed us the heart of life, nor of Greek art and culture. Nicholas Martin is correct when he remarks that Nietzsche views Schiller as 'an exemplary character whose works, while hinting at the importance of music, fail to fulfil their promise' (Nicholas Martin, *Nietzsche and Schiller: Untimely Aesthetics* (Oxford: Clarendon Press, 1996), p. 22), but he has missed Nietzsche's struggle with 'the idyllic tendency' and their common interest in 'symbolization'. By merely stating that Goethe and Schiller inspired in so far as they reflected on a 'self-sufficient German culture', Martin neglects the fact that Nietzsche at first struggled to combine Goethean, Schillerian, Schopenhauerian, Wagnerian, and his own aesthetic insights, before he, as shown in *The Birth of Tragedy*, decided that Goethe's and Schiller's 'idyllic tendency' could not be united with a tragic, Dionysian view of life.

[21] Schopenhauer offers the same interpretation of the world as a blind power and rude material, but he states that, in the end, the world is this blind power, and Man is not able to change anything in the material world with his ideas. To him there is nothing more than a moment of apparent freedom.

[22] As chapters 2 and 3 of *The Birth of Tragedy* reveal, to Nietzsche 'Greek' means: a high development of symbolic powers. The stronger these powers, the better the artist serves Dionysos (but *why* he should serve Dionysos has not yet been revealed).

[23] Compare with Goethe and Schiller, 'Ueber epische und dramatische Dichtung' (1797), in Johann Wolfgang Goethe, *Werke* [Hamburger Ausgabe], ed. by Erich Trunz (Hamburg: Christian Wegner, 1948–1960), vol. 12, 249–51.

[24] The problem of circular reasoning turns up here: first Nietzsche describes how Wagner could transform himself into a truly tragic man, a real Greek, and then goes on to prove and state that Wagner is the only 'German Greek', by building upon Greek tragedy.

[25] Compare with the preface to *The Birth of Tragedy* (KSA, 1, 24) and Nietzsche's letter to Wagner in a letter of 24 January 1872 (KSB, 3, 276).

[26] From notes 9[125] to 9[149], Nietzsche again reflects openly on Wagner's *Beethoven*-essay, especially with regard to Schopenhauerian metaphysics, Shakespearean poetry, and myth (KSA, 7, 320–31).

[27] Schiller speaks of 'poetry', Nietzsche of 'myth', but both refer to the time of ancient Greek mythology. To Schiller the modern world is 'common' (*gemein*), the ancient or old world 'poetical'.

[28] In section 21 of *The Birth of Tragedy*, this is understood as the Apollonian drama that protects the beholders from the destructive Dionysian effects of music.

[29] Whereas Schiller discriminates between the naïve idyll and the sentimental elegy, Nietzsche considers them together. This move is quite problematic, especially because the idyll is directed towards the future and the elegy to the past: the idyll is ruled by hope, the elegy by melancholy.

[30] The notes recorded as section 7 of this part of the *Nachlass* in KSA, 7, were written during the period from the end of 1870 until April 1871; those recorded in section 9 originate from 1871. Compare with KSA, 7, 8[29], 9[123], 9[126], 9[129], 9[137], 232–33, 287, 321, 322, 325. When Nietzsche writes 'modern', sometimes he uses it with reference to the development of Italian opera from the Renaissance period onwards, sometimes with reference to contemporary, or in an even broader sense of nineteenth-century art. What he means is to be inferred from the context.

[31] Nietzsche also refers to Goethe's 'Introduction to the Propyläen' here, in which Goethe writes that the young man believes he has entered the innermost sanctuary, in nature and art. (As a more mature man, Goethe understands that he still finds himself in the atrium.)

[32] The notion of the 'tragic', which so often is taken as an autonomous and major concept, plays a minor role in this part of the notes; remarkably, it even appears in this set of notes as subordinate to the idea of the idyll.

[33] In section 8 of *The Birth of Tragedy*, Nietzsche asserts that for the Greeks the figure of the satyr represented this *Urmensch*.

[34] Here Nietzsche takes over a Schopenhauerian notion and combines it with the myth of Dionysos Zagreus, who was torn into pieces by the Titans. For Nietzsche, the experience of individuality encompasses grief, because in this experience Man understands that he is not one with nature and his fellow men.

[35] 'Der Spaziergang' was published for the first time in 1795 in *Die Horen*, the journal that Schiller, in cooperation with Goethe, edited between 1795 and 1798. The poem cherishes nature's power to refresh and stimulate Man (*Auch um mich, der, endlich entflohn des Zimmers Gefängniß / Und dem engen Gespräch, freudig sich rettet zu dir*). This is the joyful side of nature. The poem is quite lyrical in its celebration of the natural beauty that surrounds Man, yet it transcends the mere description of nature's beauty. It also points out what beauty means to Man, what powers he finds in beauty, how nature offers balsam to his soul. Schiller would not be Schiller, however, if this beauty was not linked to the moral and educational qualities of nature: nature is also *fromm*, and has a *züchtiges* effect.

[36] Even in *Ecce Homo*, where he verbally attacks the combination 'German' and 'music', he makes an exception for the *Siegfried-Idyll*: 'I shall never tolerate that a German could *know* what music is [...]. I make an exception for Wagner's Siegfried-Idyll, for three reasons' (KSA, 6, 290–91). Unfortunately, Nietzsche did not record the three reasons for this exception.

[37] In 'Zu Gottfried Körners Aufsatz über Charakterdarstellung in der Musik' (1795) Schiller writes: 'To idealize something to me means only, to strip off all its accidents and supply it with the character of inner necessity' ['Etwas idealisieren heißt mir nur, es aller seiner zufälligen Bestimmungen entkleiden und ihm den Charakter innerer Notwendigkeit beilegen'] (NA, 22, 293).

[38] In other words, precisely as Nietzsche describes him later in his 'Preface to Richard Wagner', which precedes *The Birth of Tragedy*.

SCHILLER'S 'CONCRETE' THEORY OF CULTURE: REFLECTIONS ON THE 200TH ANNIVERSARY OF HIS DEATH

By R. H. Stephenson

> 'You cannot think without abstractions; accordingly it is of the utmost importance to be vigilant in critically revising your *modes* of abstraction.'[1]

Under the somewhat vague — and misleading — rubric of 'German Culturism: Hermeneutics and Historicism', Schiller is at least afforded a (rare) mention in a recent book on contemporary cultural theory.[2] Cited — along with Novalis(!) and Goethe — as one of the 'key figures in German Romanticism', the niggardly reference none the less indicates the growing awareness of Schiller's thought amongst today's cultural theorists.[3] In fact, in view of attempts since the 1980s to come to terms with Schiller's cultural theorizing from the perspective of that 'deconstructionist turn' that is said to constitute Postmodernism,[4] it is perhaps disappointing, indeed surprising, that not more notice is taken of Schiller in this context. After all, Schiller's influence has been strong, if often unacknowledged, in the unbroken line of reflection on culture in the last 200 years. It is unnecessary to retell in detail here the transmissions that mark the spread of Schiller's thought in that time.[5] But a selective sampling of some of the representative acceptions of his work helps highlight what is at important issue in today's reception of Schiller.

The mixed reception on publication of Schiller's letters *Briefe über die ästhetische Erziehung des Menschen* (*Letters on the Aesthetic Education of Humankind*; 1795) seems to have owed a good deal to the central role played in his theory by the unsettling idea of 'sincere semblance'.[6] The relative neglect into which the *Aesthetic Letters* fell (pretty well until the early 1920s, when C. G. Jung picked them up again with enthusiasm) may be attributed to the centrality of what appeared to many to be a highly dubious idea. It certainly sat uneasily with the public image foisted on to Schiller of *the* great moral-didactic writer, an image which Nietzsche deftly caricatured as the 'Moral-Trompeter von Säckingen' ('The moral-trumpeter of Säckingen') in his *Götzen-Dämmerung* (*Twilight of the Idols*).[7] Schiller's sophisticated doctrine of the need for an aesthetic *Umweg* of indirection to mediate between moral, intellectual, practical, political, and other realms of life was clearly incompatible with such a simple, straightforward view of the poet's office. None the less, despite — or perhaps, rather, because of — this widespread public repudiation of 'sincere seeming', it exerted a powerful influence over Nietzsche's conception of art in particular and aesthetics in general. But on the few occasions when Schiller's doctrine of illusion was noted, outside academic discussions of aesthetics, by other nineteenth-century German writers it merely served to attract either the support of the extreme political Right (commending such a-political disengagement with reality) or the condemnation of the extreme Left (on the same grounds).

Hegel, like Kant, was enthusiastic about the *Aesthetic Letters* on their appearance; they were, he told Schelling in a letter (16 April 1795) 'ein Meisterstück' ('a masterpiece').[8] And in the very next year, in collaboration with Schelling and Hölderlin, he produced the so-called 'Ältestes Systemprogramm des deutschen Idealismus' ('Oldest Systematic Programme of German Idealism'), setting out the new Romantic attitude to art, science, and philosophy.[9] The influence of Schiller's ideas is obvious; but so, too, is their subordination to the Platonic Idea of beauty as the highest reason.[10] For Hegel, however, any tender regard for the quiddity of form would constitute a betrayal of the onward rush of the Spirit towards the Absolute, would constitute indeed an *illusion* (but with a negative accent); even in the loveliest of paintings 'this element of truth as thus exhibited is manifested only in a sensuous mode, not in its appropriate form' ('dies Wahre [ist], wie es *erscheint*, nur in der Weise eines Sinnlichen, nicht in seiner ihm selbst gemäßen Form').[11] The Spirit cannot tarry in the aesthetic realm, for this is but a step to the next levels, those of Religion and Philosophy. And the orthodox Marxist view of Schiller's attachment to *Schein* as a regrettable, if understandable, escapism in the face of Germany's social and political misery in the late eighteenth and early nineteenth centuries contrasts markedly with Karl Marx's own well-documented admiration for, and indebtedness to, Schiller. In particular, in its crudity it expunges the many tell-tale traces, in formulation as well as in conceptualization, of the powerful hold that Schiller's modes of thought seem to have had over Marx. The remarkable passage, for instance, in the introduction to the *Grundrisse* (1858) where Marx turns not only Hegel, but the philosophical tradition on its head — by the simple expedient of reversing the usual hierarchy of abstraction: high, concretion: low — is a continuation of a tradition in which Schiller participates too.[12] For Marx seems to be juxtaposing there, in terms reminiscent of Schiller's oppositions of 'true (frank, sincere) semblance' and 'false (logical) semblance', a kind of concreteness (Hegelian) that is false with another kind that is true-to-reality (and therefore higher than mere abstraction):

> The concrete is concrete because it is the concentration of many determinations, hence unity of the manifold. It appears in the process of thinking, therefore, as a process of concentration, as a result, not as a point of departure, even though it is the point of departure in reality and hence also the point of departure for observation (*Anschauung*) and representation.

[Das Konkrete ist konkret, weil es die Zusammenfassung vieler Bestimmungen ist, also Einheit des Mannigfaltigen. Im Denken erscheint es daher als Prozeß der Zusammenfassung, als Resultat, nicht als Ausgangspunkt, obgleich es der wirkliche Ausgangspunkt und daher auch der Ausgangspunkt der Anschauung und Vorstellung ist.][13]

Marx, in 'rising from the abstract to the concrete', seems to be working with a sophisticated doubling of his favoured metaphor of the 'veil' of illusion: in the sense of (Hegelian) 'false consciousness' on the one hand and, on the other, in the sense of the true veil of aesthetic consciousness in Schiller's sense. Certainly Marx's insistence on the 'autonomy' of the real individual, existing outside the abstractions of thought, would, like his use of that key-term of Weimar Classicism, *Anschauung*, seem to suggest so.[14] The fact that this reading is also supported by Marx's distinction, developed in the same text, between negative, illusory *Verdinglichung* ('reification') and positive *Vergegenständlichung* ('objectification' in the sense of 'self-realization') is equally suggestive of Schiller's influence.[15]

Understandably, no such intensity was generated outside Germany by Schiller's aesthetic theories. The enthusiastic response of Wilhelm von Humboldt had the ironic effect of reinforcing the tendency of British (and French) colporteurs of contemporary German culture to an undifferentiated conflation of quite disparate positions amongst the German thinkers of the time: Humboldt's views, heavily reliant as they were on Schiller's as well as Goethe's, become in many a mind indistinguishable from theirs. So Schiller, shorn of key-elements of his entire thesis and, in particular, its relation to the political sphere, appeared before the English public as if he were advocating not an aesthetic theory but the kind of substitute religion of individual self-improvement for which Humboldt's position, increasingly identified with Schiller's, was to be impugned.[16] Nevertheless, Schiller's idea of 'freedom-in-appearance' found other channels of transmission to Britain, and to France. Although the question remains open of the exact degree and nature of the assimilation of German thought by Coleridge, which clearly led to a naturalization of German ideas in William Morris, Matthew Arnold, F. R. Leavis, and the New Critics,[17] it is clear that the illusion-component became downgraded in the transmission, to be replaced by pragmatic policy-making and a theory that does not really distinguish the aesthetic from any other modality of imagination.[18] It seems clear that John Stuart Mill's often aggressively anti-Platonic stance against one-sided intellectualism enabled him to discern the far-reaching potential for life of Schiller's conception of aesthetic experience as a special type of illusion. And it was seized upon by Walter Pater and his followers, though they overlooked the fact that, in spite of Schiller's having *distinguished* the aesthetic and moral, his whole concern was not to *separate* them — but rather, precisely by means of judicious use of 'sincere seeming' in flexible articulation with ethics (and intellect, and politics, and so on), to sustain a dynamic interplay. Though Pater's championing of the aesthetic transformation of daily life, like his (and Wilde's) advocacy of art for art's sake, in *The Renaissance* (1893), may sound very like some of Schiller's down-to-earth formulations, as both Pater and Wilde liked to point out, both men's accounts lack what, for Schiller, is a vital condition of successful living. The whole point of aesthetic experience for Schiller is that it is *not* an ultimate, Platonic, end in itself (although it must *seem* so); its justification lies in the fact that aesthetic freedom is the necessary condition of that rebirth of the personality as a whole that energizes us sufficiently to face as best we can the moral, and the many other, challenges of this world. That is why the apparently dubious concept of 'true illusion' is central to Schiller's whole cultural programme: it alone can set us free, to be open to formative, civilizing — indeed, civic — influence.[19]

Given the established channels of transmission between the two countries it is hardly surprising that the English Romantics should have been indebted to Schiller for some of their most 'original' aesthetic doctrines.[20] It is difficult to imagine, for instance, a closer, more precise, evocation of concrete aesthetic perception, as Schiller understood it, than the primordial realism of the *Suspiria de Profundis* (1845) by Thomas De Quincey:

> Far more of our deepest thoughts and feelings pass to us through perplexed combinations of *concrete* objects, pass to us as *involutes* (if I may coin that word) in compound experiences incapable of being disentangled, than ever reach us *directly*, and in their own abstract shapes.[21]

All that is missing here is an explicit statement of what is implied by such 'concrete' perception: since quality inheres in felt contrasts and likenesses between things, any attempt to articulate the qualitative aspect of experience will require a form that is equally dynamic and concrete, or at least *appears* to be so: the frank illusion of living form.

Certainly, in twentieth-century reflection on cultural issues Schiller's influence seems to be equally widespread, if as often unacknowledged. For example, the remark of Alfred North Whitehead, reportedly made in 1939, to the effect that he preferred Schiller's down-to-earth thought to Goethe's more exalted 'Romantic' flights, reminds us that there is much in Whitehead's philosophy that seems identical with Schiller's fundamental tenets:

> Goethe's thinking is too special, and [...] the world would be better off for the sound, sane, sensible, second-rate sentiments of Schiller. They never rise beyond a certain level but they are safe and serviceable.[22]

Since Whitehead held, like Schiller, that 'an actual fact is a fact of aesthetic experience,' and that 'all aesthetic experience is feeling arising out of the realization of contrast under identity,'[23] he may have had no more in mind (if he is being correctly reported) than that, of the two Weimar Classicists — as Schiller himself generously acknowledged — Goethe had the greater scope and, therefore, the greater ('Romantic') tendency to lead too far afield. However that may be, the remark, once set in the context of Whitehead's own philosophy, neatly makes the point that Schiller's aesthetic theorizing is profoundly realistic in firmly setting art, and aesthetic experience in general, in their often subordinate, 'second-rate' place within the broad framework of human needs and aspirations. Like Schiller (and Goethe), Whitehead, too, saw 'the animal body [as] the great central ground underlying all symbolic reference':[24] since every occasion of experience is dipolar, integrating mental experience with physical experience, all experience, at whatever level, is in some sense a physical-mental synthesis, that is, it is aesthetic.[25]

But, in general, the philosophical discourse of the twentieth century, certainly in the case of the major thinkers of the time, has not concerned itself chiefly with aesthetics. Whitehead is a rarity in this respect, as is his pupil Susanne K. Langer, who freely acknowledges her deep indebtedness to Schiller's theorizing.[26] On the whole, twentieth-century philosophy has stood under the sign of what Hegel called, in a famous remark defining the task of the modern novel, the 'prose of circumstance' — in 'the conflict with the poetry of the heart' ('den Konflikt zwischen der Poesie des Herzens und der entgegenstehenden Prosa der Verhältnisse').[27] Indeed that very model of a modern thinker, Max Weber, in his *Zwischenbetrachtung* of 1915, declared unambiguously that, in a world of unceasing rationalization of life, art (and, by implication, aesthetics) is degraded to the ancillary role of providing a pseudo-salvation from the prosaic and soul-destroying constraints of everyday life, and especially from the pressures of theoretical and practical rationalism. Art has, admittedly, a redemptory function; but without the faith that sustained earlier ages. The tendency to Ivory-Tower aestheticism at the turn of the nineteenth to the twentieth century seems, from this perspective, a mere symptom of the shift from the now unsustainable moral to the aesthetic evaluation of conduct, a touching if doomed resistance to the crushing machinery of society. And yet, as a consideration of just two representative thinkers of the era — Adorno and Habermas — indicates, Schiller's doctrine of the 'freedom-in-appearance' of frank illusion is still detectably at work in not unimportant junctures of current thought. In the case of Theodor W. Adorno the links with Schiller, on the surface at least, are striking. If Weber's melancholy analysis of modernity gave rise to the Frankfurt School's critique of instrumental reason (*Zweckrationalität*) and of the 'repressive tolerance' of mass culture, it also stimulated in Adorno a theory of art and aesthetic value that shares Schiller's faith in what Whitehead called 'the efficacy of beauty'.[28] For all his animus against (Platonic) ideals of harmony and plenitude, and for all his (and Horkheimer's) insistence on the need to resist the established status quo,[29] Adorno also expresses what some have seen as an almost 'theological' belief in art's capacity to reveal insight, in an epiphany or *'apparition'*[30] By contrast with the subordination by the mass media of aesthetic effect to mere mythical reification of reality, art — as in Schiller — has an emancipatory function. A work of art is the site of 'promise' (*Versprechen*), of a *sensuous*, child-like, happiness: for art, according to Adorno, transcends, in utopian fashion, the (Weberian) constraints of existence (though such joyful realization is constantly ruptured).[31] And it does so by virtue of its autonomy (as a kind of 'windowless monad'), which is a vital form of resistance to the social system. The 'seriousness of works of art' consists for Adorno precisely in their enigmatic quality of never being fully reducible to interpretation; in the fact that, in terms Schiller employed to make the same point, their 'import' (*Gehalt*) is not reducible to their 'content' (*Inhalt*).[32]

As Jürgen Habermas has pointed out, Adorno's (and Horkheimer's) recourse to the notion of aesthetic 'mimesis' is open to the criticism that it is a regression to an occult property, analogous to 'a piece of unpenetrated nature' ('ein undurchschautes Stück Natur'), an 'organic cuddling-up to the Other' ('organische Anschmiegung ans Andere').[33] But, while the underlying notions of truth and reason in Critical Theory may be, as Martin Jay has suggested, very nebulous,[34] what is important in the present context is that Adorno was concerned to make room in sociological thinking for aesthetic experience, and in terms that are strikingly familiar to readers of Schiller.[35] The shift of focus, away from Marxist class-conflict, to that between humankind and nature,[36] seems very much like a return to Schiller, especially since it is claimed that the proper function of art to 'reconcile' this contradiction and to keep us in remembrance of natural being ('Eingedenken der Natur').[37] The apparently moralistic seriousness of the Frankfurt School's castigation of twentieth-century popular culture has apparently hidden, Critical Theory's reliance on Schiller's (profoundly serious) concept of playful frank illusion. Adorno's rhetorical dependence on the German Classical tradition is incontrovertible: his texts are saturated, for example, in the key-terms of Weimar Classicism. What merits further investigation are the indications of a *conceptual* indebtedness, suggested, for example, in his theory of the moment of 'sublimation' (*Vergeistigung*) in works of art providing epiphany. Is this not Schiller's 'ennoblement' (*Veredelung*)? —[38] and, if so, are there significant differences as well as continuities? For one of the differences between Adorno and Schiller would seem to be that, while for Adorno escape from Weber's famous 'iron cage' ('eisernes Gehäuse') of social repression, is unreliably fleeting and transient, for Schiller the application of 'frank illusion' to social activity ('schöner Umgang') promises sustained personal liberty (*Aesthetic Letters*, XIX, 12).

On this latter point, Habermas is far closer to Schiller than the Frankfurt School (and than he himself seems to recognize). After all, the whole burden of Habermas's concern is the question of how to defend what he calls 'the lifeworld' of intrinsically meaningful forms of life that are endangered in his view by the 'colonializing' encroachments of the purposive rationality of the socio-economic 'system.' Like Habermas, Schiller, too, aims 'to mark out within the positive State an area in which personal and social contact is governed by criteria other than those of law, politics, or the received morality of public opinion'.[39] But for Habermas the 'expressive' function of the aesthetic is no more than a distinctive species of 'communicative action'.[40] This much is clearly revealed in his 1984 essay 'Exkurs zu Schillers Briefen über die ästhetische Erziehung des Menschen' ('Excursus on *Schiller's Letters on the Aesthetic Education of Humankind*'), where Habermas reduces Schiller's concept of art and aesthetics to his own (Hegelian) notions, and, above all, Schiller's complex notion of 'beautiful communication' ('schöne Mitteilung') to his own of communicative action.[41] As Schiller made clear (for example, in his letter to Körner of 10 November 1794), the aesthetic in his view does *not* appeal to universalizing Reason at all, but rather to that 'generalized individuality' ('generalisierte Individualität') of the coordination of sensuous delight and mental apprehension that constitutes aesthetic experience alone can bring forth. Hence what Schiller means by 'thinking presentationally' ('darstellend denken') is far away indeed from the kind of abstract rationalizing Habermas obviously has in mind.[42] Yet, despite Habermas's acceptance of Walter Benjamin's thesis, to the effect that art has in the modern era lost its 'aura' (of aesthetic semblance?) and its 'classical' autonomous status,[43] he still seems attached to certain key-concepts of Schiller's theory (even if he does not always seem alive to their full implications). For example, he sees 'sincerity' (*Wahrhaftigkeit*) as the defining criterion of aesthetic value. Admittedly, he sees such 'authentic expression' as a *reason* to be adduced for the validity of aesthetic judgement, one which can be 'measured' —[44] as opposed to Schiller's insistence that such sincerity could only ever be appreciated in terms of the aesthetic form, the 'schöner Schein', giving it articulation. In the light, however, of Habermas's overriding concern for lifeworld values, for transparent, mutual understanding between individual people in terms of *Verständigungsformen*, and, above all, in view of his concept of 'dramaturgical action' as a form of self-presentation (derived from the mediation of the play-concept via Ernest Goffman and T. R. Sorbin), his distance from Schiller seems much reduced —[45] bringing out anew the serious political and social engagement driving Schiller's commitment to aesthetic play.

But perhaps the most promising context of all in which to seek to establish the ongoing relevance of Schiller's 'sincere semblance' to twentieth- (and twenty-first-)century thought is the work of Ernst Cassirer. Essential elements of Cassirer's thought on art and the aesthetic derive from Schiller's reflections. The striking similarities between Cassirer's and Schiller's thinking seem less remarkable, perhaps, when one recalls what a sensitive, as well as critical, reader of Cassirer was.[46] Perhaps most significantly, Cassirer is rare among commentators of his era in taking Schiller seriously as a philosopher. In tackling the question of how something sensuous becomes a carrier of meaning, Cassirer developed a theory of the 'symbolic pregnance' ('symbolische Prägnanz') of expressive symbolism that is remarkably close, at all major points, to Schiller's conception. For Cassirer, as for Schiller, the body-mind relationship is the prototype of symbolization (letter to Goethe, 24 August 1798): the body, as for Schiller, is the seat of meaning. Taking his cue from Gestalt-psychology, Cassirer attempts to develop a general theory of the image in its most basic sense, the perceptual *Gestalt*, in barely translatable terms that are redolent of Schiller's formulations of the 'living form' of the aesthetic symbol:

> The specific particularization of 'Prägnanz' is what first founds and makes possible the specific differences among 'Gestalten'; all representation is always representation in a specific 'sense'.
>
> [Die spezifische Besonderung der Prägnanz begründet und ermöglicht erst die spezifische Verschiedenheit der 'Gestalten'; alle Vergegenwärtigung ist immer Vergegenwärtigung {literally 'making present'} in einem bestimmten Sinne.][47]

Although closer at times to Kant, for whom symbols are always indirect presentations of the concept, than to Goethe, for whom symbols can have an inherently sensuous meaning, Cassirer is, like Schiller, yet respectful of the boundaries marking poetry off from science. And, again like Schiller, he came to see that Goethe's conception of a 'concrete' symbolism could be conceptually conciliated with the view of the symbol as an abstraction of thought. For out of this subtle tension Cassirer conceives the notion of 'symbolic pregnance', as a complement to his idea of 'symbolic form'. Cassirer's profound insight into the nature and significance of Goethe's doctrine of sincere seeming applies equally to Schiller, and may be summed up in the following remark, taken from his *Freiheit und Form*: '[Schiller] penetrated the play of becoming as "true illusion", as a semblance which does not conceal, but reveals, Being' ('[Schiller] hat das Spiel des Werdens als "wahrer Schein" durchschaut, als einen Schein, der das Wesen nicht verhüllt, sondern offenbart').[48]

This doubling of the meaning of the key-concept, 'semblance' (*Schein* and its synonyms), is but one instance of Schiller's reliance on a mode of argumentation usefully called 'binary synthesis'.[49] The sophistication of this key theoretical tool, so close to current conceptions of Deconstruction, and yet subtly — and decisively — different, may well be one of the main reasons for the comparative neglect of Schiller in the ongoing theoretical ferment of 'postmodernism'. William James offered an illuminating analysis of just this kind of synthesis as a variation of the principle of *coniunctio oppositorum* in a discussion of mystical modes of experience:

> The keynote [...] is invariably a reconciliation. It is as if the opposites of the world [...] were melted into unity. Not only do they, as contrasted species, belong to one and the same genus, but *one of the species, the nobler and better one, is itself the genus and so soaks up and absorbs its opposite into itself.*[50]

In binary synthesis, found throughout Weimar classical aesthetics, the name of one element in a pair of antitheses is also applicable to the synthesis, which thus represents *both* a richer concept, *and* one that tends towards one of the original antitheses in an ascending hierarchy.[51] For instance, the Goethean 'permanence in change' ('Dauer im Wechsel') which experience of the aesthetic illusion vouchsafes, yields both Dionysian import — 'the content in your heart' ('den Gehalt in deinem Busen') — and Apollonian form — 'the form in your mind' ('die Form in deinem Geist') — in the characteristically binary synthesis characteristic of art and beauty (Hamburger Ausgabe 1, 247–48).[52]

It is hardly surprising, given Schiller's indebtedness to the Scottish School of commonsense philosophy, that, in terms that are uncannily reminiscent of Thomas Reid's own, Schiller should have formulated an account of aesthetic experience as a (binary) synthesis of Sense (*Stofftrieb*) and Mind (*Formtrieb*) that constitutes the kernel idea of Weimar Classicism.[53] Aesthetic knowledge of objects arises in a co-ordination of sense and mind, rather than in the initial subordination postulated by Rationalists and Empiricists alike. The epistemological gap of the Cartesian tradition derives for Schiller from the incapacity of discursive reason to connect coherently what the senses, as the organism's media of the mind's interaction with the environment, deliver, from its point of view, as isolated particulars. For Schiller, aesthetic experience is the way in which Idea and Experience converge. In terms very reminiscent of Reid, Schiller insists (in a letter to the Duke of Augustenburg, 21 November, 1793) that in 'presentational thinking' ('darstellend denken', i.e., aesthetic contemplation) there is no question of sense itself being able to think, though intellect is at work in co-ordination with sense. Schiller, who felt that one could learn a good deal about human beings in general but all too little about beauty in particular from Kant's aesthetics (letter to Goethe, 19 February 1795), seems to have accepted Kant as the best-available philosophical account of the cognitive aspects of aesthetic experience, while missing a satisfactory treatment of the sensuousness that, for Schiller, is constituent of the content of true aesthetic perception. Glad as he is to have Kant's philosophical support for the validity of the aesthetic, Schiller is well aware that Reason has the upper hand in Kant's account ('taste is formed for us as a regulative principle by a still higher principle of reason'),[54] and that the co-ordination of Mind and Sense, essential to aesthetic experience, is neglected.

It was Schiller's conviction that objectification of the inner life is the distinctive function of all art and of all aesthetic experience. An object of aesthetic perception articulates *feeling* (in the broad, eighteenth-century sense of the word, i.e. the whole continuum from tactile sensation to thought — thought not yet reduced to the either-or categories of discursive language, and thus highly ambivalent). In this way an analogue of the felt-life within is presented to our contemplation, something that can be achieved only if this analogue — this 'semblance' (*Schein*) — exhibits the same sensuous-abstract quality as the felt-thought it may serve to express. Where this illusion is achieved the direct benefit to our minds is twofold. On the one hand we gain in self-awareness, and self-control. On the other, aesthetic insight is knowledge and, like any other form of freshly acquired knowledge, enables us to conceive the world with a new tool. Commonly shared but dimly apprehended feelings become, through aesthetic experience, no less shared but now articulated 'convictions' or 'attitudes' — *Gesinnungen* — upon which we act and base our reasoning, but to which (for the reason that they are still tethered to sensation) we find it impossible to give adequate intellectual expression. Such sensuous-abstract schemata permit us to 'see into the life of things'. 'Import' (*Gehalt*) is that aspect of our felt life that the aesthetic phenomenon 'contains' for us. Feeling has distinctive patterns; it exhibits a 'morphology':[55] the structure of the inner life is an organic, developmental one in which thinking-feeling-sensation are interfused. Moreover, it is in constant interaction with the external world: we internalize ideas and impressions — what Schiller called 'content' (in the sense of 'material', *Stoff*) — by aligning them with the felt, dynamic, patterns incessantly at work within us. Because of different life-experiences the felt-life of one individual will, to a lesser or greater extent, differ from that of another. But, because we share the same, or at least a similar, natural-cultural-social environment, the overlap will be considerable and therefore significant. The more fundamental and encompassing the felt-thought is that an aesthetic object symbolizes, the more 'universal' its appeal will be, the greater its significance. If what is within is to be projected outwards on to it, the aesthetic phenomenon must exhibit the same organic structure as the morphology of the inner life; it must, as Schiller argued, evince 'manifest freedom' ('Freiheit in der Erscheinung'): it must appear to be both self-regulating and self-regulated. In order to achieve this, peculiarly aesthetic, illusion, the relations discernible in the aesthetic object must inhere in its physical medium, so that its aesthetic order does not appear to be imposed from outside, but *seems* rather to be immanent in the object itself.

One distinct advantage that Schiller's mode of theorizing has over contemporary cultural theory is that, as a hybrid poet-philosopher, he is able to embody his (in theoretical contexts, necessarily) abstract thinking in the concretion of aesthetic discourse — not only in his philosophical treatises, but in the full-blown particularity of his poetic productions. As if in response to Karl Marx's challenge to '*rise* from abstraction to the level of the concrete', much of Schiller's literary works may profitably be read as the vivid crystallization of his ideas.

This is already evident, for example, in his early poem, 'An die Freude'. Schiller's 'Ode to Joy' of 1786 celebrates, as the root of a cultural community, precisely that quality that Hegel, throughout his *Lectures on the Philosophy of History*, had deemed a trivial matter: namely, *happiness*. The German word '*Freude*' is close to the French term *jouissance*, and has earthier connotations than does its English equivalent, 'joy', indicating 'pleasure' and 'delight' as well as 'near-bliss', as is clear in Faust's rejoinder to the Devil's offer of earthly pleasures in Goethe's *Faust*: 'Pleasure doesn't come into it' ('Von Freud' ist nicht die Rede'; l.1765). Contrary to the widely received image of Schiller, there is no discrepancy here between duty and the joy of living; rather, what we have is a return to the Ancient view of a concurrence of the two. Schiller sees joy as embracing the whole of existence; and, like say Alexander Pope, he seeks to give poetic form to this inspiring, because life-enhancing, feeling. Both Hegel's and Faust's rejection of the kind of joyful happiness Schiller eulogizes in this poem is an accurate indication of the low status to which this once-great value had sunk by the end of the eighteenth century. (Indeed, throughout the modern era, as pessimism has grown into the very badge of our modernistic sensibility, the mark of the truly intellectual, alienated, spirit – this downward trajectory has continued almost unabated. It is wholly typical of Schiller's (still radically unfashionable) philosophical poetry to take such material and to revalue it by means of what the rhetoricians call an 'epideictic' presentation, i.e. by a celebration, in the language of public discourse, of shared, communal values which would otherwise go without saying. What Schiller is doing in his 'An die Freude' can be illustrated by recourse to a sardonic observation on the irresistible decline of common cultural property by his contemporary, G. C. Lichtenberg, who offers a summary of a debate stretching back to the impact made by the printing press:

> One thinker gives birth to the idea, the second lifts it out of the font, the third produces children with it, the fourth visits it on its deathbed, and the fifth buries it.
>
> [Einer zeugt den Gedanken, der andere hebt ihn aus der Taufe, der Dritte zeugt Kinder mit ihm, der Vierte besucht ihn am Sterbebette, und der Fünfte begräbt ihn.][56]

The thoughts deployed by Schiller in his philosophical poems are not simply commonplaces but — to borrow Lichtenberg's metaphor — 'on their deathbed'. Schiller shared the deep anxiety of his age about the possibilities of cultural continuity: how was the apparent 'triviality' of such in reality vital truths to be overcome, so that they would once more seem important and significant? Sharing, too, Dr. Johnson's opinion that 'the task of an author is, either to teach what is new, or to recommend known truths',[57] Schiller sets out in 'An die Freude' to recommend what is, to his mind, a disastrously debased value. But, unlike Johnson, Schiller is not content to appeal to the mind alone: if such apparent banalities are to come home to the reader, they must engage feeling; and to do this, they must be made sensuous. For, it is the peculiar office of the poet — as Schiller insists in one of his epigrams, 'To the Poet' ('An den Dichter') to exploit the bodiliness of language, 'as lovers use their physical bodies', to give (aesthetic) expression to what discursive language cannot possibly capture.[58]

Read merely as a discursive statement, 'An die Freude' traces an ever-widening perspective on the cosmic ubiquity of joy. From the apostrophe to its personification as the 'daughter of Elysium' in the first strophe, where its revolutionary potential to transcend the conventional dimensions of society is celebrated; to the second, where the quite ordinary experiences of love and friendship are cited as paradigmatic cases of joy, requiring an *ability* to relate one to another; to the strophe in which the participation of 'all creatures, in a realm beyond good and evil', is evoked:

> All drink joy from Mother Nature,
> All she suckled at her breast,
> Good or evil, every creature,
> Follows where her foot has pressed.
>
> [Freude trinken alle Wesen
> An den Brüsten der Natur,
> Alle Guten, alle Bösen
> Folgen ihrer Rosenspur.]

In the fourth, a definition of joy is offered as the driving-force of life: 'the spring of all contriving, / In eternal Nature's plan'; before, in the fifth strophe, we move back — in a way reminiscent of the baroque hymnal poetry to which Schiller owed so much — from the macrocosm to the microcosm, the joyful human experiences of the pursuit of truth, right conduct, and faith. The Christian morality of the sixth strophe is integrated as an effect of joyful living, while in the seventh we return to the sheer exuberance of 'the joy of sparkling potions / In the goblet's liquid gold' ('Freude sprudelt in Pokalen, / In der Traube goldnem Blut'). The eighth strophe — now the final one, since Schiller deleted the ninth of an earlier version — recapitulates the whole panoramic survey in an appropriately climactic condensation of language. This whole, magnificent edifice is given cohesion and coherence, not by logical links, nor by a self-consistent pattern of imagery; but by a masterly rhetorical structure. The poem can perhaps best be seen as built upon a figure of thought, the technical term for which is *expolitio* (the re-presentation of a central thought by variation of the formulation, especially of subsidiary thoughts). And this sense of development-with-return is underlined by the use of a dramatic chorus added to each strophe, one that is repeated over and over again, with more or less minor variations which yet signal important modulations. Similarly, a well-judged choice of synonyms, antonyms, homonyms and, perhaps most simply effective of all, plain repetitions (sometimes with tiny variations) make for a sense of coherence. The reader — addressed directly by the stirring imperatives and rhetorical questions — is drawn along (and then sent back) — through a network of inter-related figures. For example, in the third strophe, the word '*Küsse*' ('kisses') sends us back to the chorus of the first strophe where the singular '*Kuss*' stands; and the changes rung in the epithets for God — 'a loving father' (strophe 1), 'the Unknown' (strophe 2), 'the Creator' (strophe 3), 'the good spirit' (strophe 7) — provide an object-lesson in the effective use of rhetorical synonymization, here with the purpose of pointing to, and yet avoiding dogmatic limitations of, the mystery of being. With these, and a variety of other techniques, Schiller enacts a semblance in language of that 'holy circle' that the final strophe proclaims as the work of joy. Schiller's talent for the grand manner of high rhetorical style, however, must not blind us to the fact that its function here is to transfigure and (to use a favourite term of his) 'ennoble' (*veredeln*) what is an everyday experience. We are told (in the third strophe), it is true:

> E'en the worm was granted pleasure,
> Angels see the face of God.
>
> [Wollust ward dem Wurm gegeben,
> Und der Cherub steht vor Gott.]

But the clear implication of this is that the human condition lies between these extremes, sharing something of both. For Schiller, 'ennoblement' retains its alchemical meaning of 'enhancement', of raising — without loss — to a higher degree of complexity. The re-iteration in the poem of the motif of wine ('that maketh glad the heart of man', as the Psalmist has it) is enough to indicate that this is no prim exhortation to some 'ideal', other-worldly purity of feeling. Rather, in its revaluation of radiant worldly happiness, it is as radically challenging to many of our modern cultural snobberies as is Nietzsche's summons to 'love the earth'.[59] But the earthiness of the poem is most powerful in the non-discursive, sensuous configurations that Schiller weaves into his rhetorical structures. In strophe seven, for instance, the original German evinces profoundly meaningful patterns that are simply untranslatable:

> *Trinken Sanftmut Kannibalen,*
> *Die Verzweiflung Heldenmut*
>
> (Savages drink gentler notions
> While the meek learn to be bold)

The syntactical ambiguity of the second line here expresses an exquisitely subtle thought (*something* like 'heroism owes as much to despair as despair to heroism'), one amplified by the homeoteleuton play on 'Sanft*mut*' and 'Helden*mut*': both seem, in their poetic concretion, to be species of 'courage' ('*Mut*'), a felt-thought utterly lost on the discursive level of translation. Similarly, the figure (again, syntactical ambiguity — a favourite resource for Schiller) in the opening line of the seventh strophe's chorus: 'Den der Sterne Wirbel loben' ('Him whom the stellar eddies praise') can be taken to mean what the literal translation indicates, *and* 'den' can also be taken as the definite article of (the singular) '*Wirbel*', and '*loben*' as an infinitive-imperative: we then have a linguistically concrete articulation of the pantheistic identification of God-and-Nature. Or consider how, in the penultimate line of this chorus, the simple device of alliteration — again a much-used Schillerian poetic technique — tethers the sublimity of God, or rather the 'good spirit', with the everyday yet powerful symbol of the glass of good cheer: 'Dieses Glas dem guten Geist' ('This glass to the good spirit'). As Frank M. Fowler has rightly insisted, 'it is the emotional value of [...] ideas that is predominant in [Schiller's] poetry'.[60] It is surely this quality, of deeply felt thought, that inspired Beethoven's enthusiastic admiration for the poem (which Schiller himself judged harshly — and quite wrongly! — in later years), using the first three strophes and the first, third, and fourth choruses in his Ninth Symphony. Doubtless, too, Schiller's poetic exploitation of the idiom of public discourse has also contributed to the success of Beethoven's setting as the 'national anthem' of a united Europe.

This tendency of Schiller's to concretize highly abstract thoughts is perhaps most blatant, as successive commentators have demonstrated, in his dramas,[61] eminently so in his treatment of that newly relevant topos, central to so much current cultural theory: the nexus of violence-identity-and-the-aesthetic. Schiller thematizes this violence over and over again, insisting, in a passage that has proved controversial, that the secret of artistic creation resides in the artist's power to make form 'annihilate' (*vertilgen*) content.[62] Indeed, beauty, on Schiller's view, is only possible if the difference between concept and percept, between universal and particular, is destroyed[63] — i.e., if the conceptual basis of rhetorical analysis is 'annulled' (*aufgehoben*): 'destroyed and preserved', in a proto-Hegelian sense.[64] While Kleist in the *Marionettentheater*, as Paul de Man argues, is content to try 'to articulate [. . .] phenomenal particularity' by reference to a formalized abstraction such as a line or curve,[65] Schiller clearly has in mind a much more robust notion of the aesthetic symbol as 'concrete universal', as a phenomenon displacing other phenomena.

Nowhere is Schiller's shrewd insight into the complicity between forceful self-assertion on the one hand and self-presentation on the other clearer than in his dramatic work. In the ungovernable violence of his feelings (grotesquely, almost comically, evident in his smashing of the violin in Act III, scene 4), Ferdinand in *Kabale und Liebe* (1784) in no way distinguishes himself from, say, Karl Moor in *Die Räuber* (1781) or the titular hero of *Die Verschwörung des Fiesko zu Genua* (1783): all are typical eighteenth-century 'Enthusiasts' (*Schwärmer*), in whom head and heart, thinking and feeling, are unrelated, indeed in conflict, and whose behaviour violently oscillates from cool detachment to passionate frenzy. In *Kabale und Liebe* Schiller analyses this psychological pathology by presenting a whole array of slight variations on it. Luise, the apparently sensible lower middle-class heroine, evinces the same lack of integration of body and mind: so shocked is she by the 'wild desires' ('wilde Wünsche') that the aristocratic Ferdinand excites in her that she loses any sense of perspective (III. 4), coming to see her love for him not just as a sacrilege but as threatening the very foundations of society, indeed of cosmic order! Even those apparently so unfeeling, calculating characters, Wurm and the President, reveal this same precarious, insecure, queasy imbalance between head and heart. Their very choice of language, like the rhetorical coarseness of Luise's father in the opening scene, suggests murky sexual emotion lurking just below the surface-polish of court intrigue, ready to break out at any moment in destructive — and sadistic — fury (II. 6). As Luise notes (III. 6), these people understand how to use their political power to torture and torment those (notably, women) unfortunate enough to be subordinate to them – just as her father threatens her mother with physical abuse in order to silence her (I. 2). So when Ferdinand denounces his father at the end of the play (V. 8) with the words, 'Here, barbarian, gorge yourself on the terrible fruit of your mind' ('Hier, Barbar! Weide dich an der entsezlichen Frucht deines Witzes'), the audience/reader is well aware that this 'mind' (*Witz*) is little more than rationalization born of repressed desire. It is thus brought home to us that the corrupt, repressive state pilloried in the play is both cause and effect of a perverted 'thinking' in which concrete feeling and abstract reflection are related by rigid subjugation, punctuated only rarely by a violent overthrow of now the one, now the other, oppression.

The theme of political suppression as a co-implicate of personal, psychological, repression becomes ever more elaborated in Schiller's later work, both theoretical and poetic. It takes, for example, a strikingly violent turn in Schiller's representation of the havoc and chaos of the Thirty Years War in that most brutally realistic practitioner of Might-is-Right ethics, the eponymous central figure of the *Wallenstein* trilogy of 1798, as is clear from the following statement expressing his *Weltanschauung*:

> If you don't want to be displaced, you must displace others; struggle rules supreme, and only the strong are victorious.
>
> [Wer nicht vertrieben sein will, muss vertreiben; Da herrscht der Streit, und nur die Stärke siegt.] (*Tod*, II. 12. 791–92)

There is no doubt that Wallenstein is a man of (annihilating) power; a good deal of the first part of the trilogy, *Wallensteins Lager*, is devoted to reinforcing this image (ll. 332–24) of 'absolute Gewalt' (l. 848) — 'absolute power' certainly, but in German (by virtue of the word *Gewalt*) it smacks, too, of actual (physical) violence. In fact we learn in the second part of the trilogy, *Die Piccolomini* (II. 3. 722), that, also in the private sphere, Wallenstein subjugates those around him (his wife and daughter, notably) as surely as in the public arena he 'enslaves' his followers (II. 3. 786). Moreover, he *loves* his power: 'It gives me pleasure to exercise my power' ('Es macht mir Freude, meine Macht zu üben'; II. 5. 868), he confesses in a poetically charged formulation that defies adequate translation. The remarkable thing about this play — and it will be a feature, too, of all Schiller's dramas after *Wallenstein* — is that the central character is shown to *change* radically. When he appears in Act V, scene 1 of the third part of the trilogy, *Wallenstein's Tod*, we are told, reliably (ll. 3214ff.), that the people of Eger were moved by his entrance to their town, and saw in him a 'prince of peace' (*Friedensfürst*). Wallenstein is said (IV. 2. 2460–63) to have achieved that synthesis of right action and fair seeming for which Schiller, in his theoretical writings, reserved the (quite ordinary eighteenth-century German) term, 'schöner Umgang' ('handsome behaviour'; see *Tod*, IV. 2. 2508–09). The psychological acumen with which Schiller motivates this change, like the linguistic virtuosity with which he embodies this metamorphosis in the very body of his poetry, are topics for a separate study. The important point in the present context is to register that Schiller envisages an overcoming of the propensity to violent will-to-power by cultural self-definition in aesthetic terms.

It is helpful when reading Schiller to bear in mind, not so much his technical theoretical terms (which has led to oversimplified schematizations of his thought, poetry, and dramas), but rather what he *meant* by them, in particular by the term, 'aesthetic', as in the title of one of the most influential works of modern times, his *Aesthetic Letters*. He certainly does not mean 'art for art's sake', or anything of that anaemic kind. What he has in mind is the reality of the concrete, sensuous-mental complex that constitutes human experience.[66] As a medical practitioner he knew a good deal more about the body than many a philosopher, and his whole outlook turns on the proper co-ordination of the physical medium with mental function, whether in language or in artful self-presentation. The connection that Schiller discerned between the psychological and sociological 'given' of (physically based) violence and its (necessary) overcoming in aesthetic activity is, perhaps, at its clearest in two plays he wrote about powerful women, *Maria Stuart* (1800) and *Die Jungfrau von Orleans* (1801).

In choosing Mary Stuart as material for his play Schiller has once again chosen one of those charismatic but highly problematic characters that so fascinated his generation: the 'genius'/'super[wo]man' (*der Kraftmensch*). But, unlike some of his contemporaries, Schiller's aim is not glorification, but rather the presentation, against the realistic, socio-political background of a seething chaos of egoistic ambition in both the Scottish and English camps, of what he, like the humanistic tradition he consciously renewed, considered to be the whole point of being human: the development from socio-cultural repression to personal autonomy, with minimum loss of vitality and effectiveness. As in *Kabale und Liebe*, characters who on the surface seem so different turn out to share a fundamental psychological identity. Elisabeth, apparently closed to emotion and motivated only by rational calculation, and Maria, led by passion, are in fact (as is clear from their encounter in Act III, scene 4) very alike. Caught in the trammels of political history, both are *pretending*: Elisabeth to be magnanimous (when she is merely anxious to clap eyes on her political — and, in her own mind, sexual — rival); and Maria, to be submissive.[67] It is usually suggested that Maria loses her composure in this interview, in her magnificent riposte to Elisabeth's taunts, which ends with her sudden switch in gender when asserting the legitimacy of her claim to the English throne: 'For I am your *king*!' ('denn ich bin Euer *König*'). In reality what we are witness to is Maria's finding herself, her realization that her refusal to be intimidated in the face of (now almost certain) death marks her fitness for the role of monarch that life has thrust upon her. She is making her external role her own; her vocation is to be *king*, transcending biological and cultural contingency. Like Wallenstein's early attempts at projecting serenity, the falseness of her phoney composure in the opening act (I. 2) only masks an inner turmoil that regularly breaks out, like Ferninand's too, in unmastered vehemence, but gives way, immediately before, and during, an horrifically brutal death, to a dignified and graceful calm that impresses all who witness it (V. 2). Again, as in *Wallenstein*, the reality of violence (done both by and to the central character) elicits a response that is itself non-violent and curative: for the gentle efficacy of aesthetic self-presentation consists, like all art according to Schiller, in co-ordinating the otherwise warring poles of body and mind into the peaceful co-existence that is *expressive*, of self and world alike seen outwith the distorting violations done to them by human will-to-power and the vicissitudes of nature.

In *Die Jungfrau von Orleans* Schiller presents a similar pattern of an individual's development to personal maturity through violent loss to ultimate gain. Like Hamlet (*Hamlet*, V. 2. 230), Johanna — like Maria and Wallenstein — dies fulfilled and therefore indifferent to the hour, and manner, of her death. By means of aesthetic self-definition she has discovered her integrity, she has 'become', in Nietzsche's famous phrase, 'what she is' (V. 4 and 14). Johanna appears at the outset of the play as intimidatingly repressed (*Prolog*, 2), a repression that reaches its deepest expression in her denial of her sexual identity as a woman (II. 7). Johanna finds the reminder she sees in men's eyes that she has a desirable female body unbearable (III. 4). She is repressed in the strict psychoanalytical sense: she has internalized a cultural norm (symbolized by the Virgin Mary) that blots out her concrete humanity, making for success in battle by dint of the terror her Amazon-persona incites (I. 9). She is jolted out of this pretence by her own violent experience of sexual attraction to a body (Lionel's) that *she* desires (III. 10); and she realizes (as in Wallenstein, *Tod*, I. 4) that her greatness has hitherto been bought at too high a cost (IV. 1). Thereafter, as is the case with Schiller's other classical heroes, a remarkable change comes over Johanna: without losing her zealous sense of duty she becomes 'gentle' and 'kind' (IV. 9). She is described in a stage-direction in the final Act as 'composed and gentle', utterly altered from the 'frozen heart' that was the precipitate of her earlier attempts at subduing the destructive war within her between internalized, abstract, superego-values and her particular desire. If her breaking of her chains on stage (V. 11) is a symbolism of self-emancipation that our contemporary taste is uncomfortable with, such contingent difficulties of reception should not obscure the profound significance of what Schiller is articulating in this most operatic of his plays. He is writing about that sensuous-cum-emotional-cum-intellectual experience our culture names as 'love'. He felt justified in calling this heightened response 'aesthetic' on the same grounds that English refers to what is beautiful as '*lovely*'.[68] For Schiller, the supreme — or, which comes to the same thing, the deepest, most 'primitive' — human value is the enjoyment of such self-identity, whether in nature, art, or human relations. In a word, it is what makes us human. What Johanna, like many another Schillerian hero, finds, is not simply sexual identity, nor again is it only a socio-cultural function. What she — like Wallenstein and Maria Stuart — (*re-*)gains is that spontaneity of the Child (V. 14) that, whether or not it represents a previously experienced empirical reality, certainly represents for Schiller an ideal, the achievement of which constitutive of being fully human(e).

Violence and aesthetic experience for Schiller are, then, intimately related, and in two main ways, though with infinite variation. First, aesthetic activity is precisely the specifically human way both to find (rather than impose) order in the world and to construct a self-expressive identity. (Identity is, for him as for Kant, a 'necessary idea', one that society simply compels us to realize;[69] and, long before Foucault, he saw clearly that such ineluctable constraint essentializes the subject.[70] The problem, as he sees it, is how such unavoidable subjection is yet to be made an authentic, emancipatory expression of self.) And, second, Schiller is only too aware that aesthetic creativity in itself involves, like the establishment of all order, some degree of violation of a previously obtaining, concrete state of affairs. Language, for instance, is in its own right a form of distortion, as Schiller throughout his theoretical writings, insists. But he does not see this fact as cause for cultural despair, let alone for an escapist exclusion of politics as inimical to aesthetic education. For Schiller the whole, ultimately ethical, point of cultivating aesthetic consciousness is its power to transform potentially violent destructiveness of any kind into peaceful productivity.[71]

Schiller's doctrine, of making sense of, by giving form to, the impulse to violence is also the burden of the last play he completed, *Wilhem Tell* (1804). It is a yet more radical variation on the theme of the overcoming of political and psychological subjugation. The world we enter is, to all appearances, an idyll; but an ominously negative note is immediately sounded (I. 1) and sustained throughout, notably by the storm-imagery. This is, in fact, a systematically oppressed world, culturally and politically, breeding a mood of treachery and suspicion (I. 4. 503). The Wilhelm Tell we encounter in this play is an experienced man-of-the-world, self-confident and of considerable complexity. If the first words he utters sound initially like naïve home-spun philosophy — 'A good man thinks of himself last' ('Der brave Mann denkt an sich selbst zuletzt'; I. 1. 139) — we are soon disabused of any such superficial judgement by the direct and indirect evidence that accumulates to attest to the fact that he is one of those rare people who actually do what they say. Little wonder, then, that he is seen by his community as its 'saviour' (*Retter*). When Tell declares that the only intelligent response for the time being to Austrian tyranny in Switzerland is silent passivity — 'The only thing to do now is to be quietly patient' ('Die einzige Tat ist jetzt Geduld und Schweigen'; I. 2. 420) — the audience/reader has every reason to believe that he means what he says: passivity is a mode of action appropriate to the specific situation. Similarly, we also need to weigh his words carefully when he says that he does not like to think unduly long (I. 3. 443). For he certainly does not mean that he is averse to thinking (after all, he is presented in Act III, scene 3 as deep in thought, so much so that it is commented on by Gessler; III. 3. 1903). No; to take Tell *simply* at his word, rather than interpreting his meaning, is to make the same mistake as Gessler himself, who assumes that vulgar hearsay about 'Tell the Dreamer' is true (III. 3. 1904), and is then astonished at Tell's shooting the apple from atop his son's head (l. 2033).

Schiller presents Tell from the outset as having already attained the mature integration of body and mind, heart and mind, that Maria Stuart and Johanna achieve only at the end of their respective dramatic development. Tell's consistent concern is to maintain a dynamic balance between thinking and doing, doing and thinking: 'If you reflect too much, you'll never achieve much' ('Wer zu viel bedenkt, wird wenig leisten'; III. 1. 1532), as he puts it in his characteristically qualified, almost Mandarin-like, style.[72] Schiller's Tell, in a word, is no naïve 'beautiful soul' but rather an urbane, suave sophisticate (as is clear in his address to Gessler; III. 1. 1870ff. and 2049ff.). He is, to use a key-term of Weimar Classicism, a *Lebenskünstler* ('life-artist'), one who has synthesized personality and duty by means of mastery of his art (III. 3. 1875), symbolized by both his extraordinarily skilful archery and by his superb helmsmanship (IV. 1. 2177–80). His one act of (devastating) violence, his assassination of Gessler, he describes, with some justice, as his 'masterstroke' (*Meisterschuss*; IV. 3. 2650). For it is presented as the appropriate response to systemic violence by someone who has seen into his (and his community's) plight and grasped aright the issues involved and the action necessary. It is not a personal act of revenge; nor is it impersonal, but rather supra-personal: it engages and transcends his own interests (in much the same way as did his earlier rescue of a neighbour from drowning, IV. 1. 1528–29). His 'art', his 'skill', his 'playful game' (*Spiel*) — all these concepts are synonymized throughout the work (e.g. IV. 3. 2604–05) — are his chosen way of freely expressing his sense of his own identity. The liberation accompanying such skilful art-of-life is clear to others (IV. 2. 2362–63) and contagious in its attractiveness (IV. 2. 2366–67; V. 1. 2821 and 2857). Tell's achievement is to have understood and annihilated the evil inherent in Gessler's objective of systematic enslavement: the *will* to stamp out all freedom, all growth — in short, the very life — of the Swiss. At just the moment when he is struck down by the bolt from Tell's cross-bow, Gessler is asserting exactly the same perverted, 'inhuman', destructiveness (IV. 3. 1922), issuing from a self-repressive *will*-to-power, that Schiller presents in *Kabale und Liebe*:

> My will is to break this stubborn attitude,
> to bend the insolent spirit of freedom,
> to declare a new law in these lands.
> My will [. . .].
>
> [Ich will ihn brechen, diesen starren Sinn,
> Den kecken Geist der Freiheit will ich beugen.
> Ein neu Gesetz will ich in diesen Landen
> Verkündigen — Ich will —]

Tell's motivation is revealed as the impulse to protect for himself as for others the liberty that he knows from concrete (aesthetic) experience is the joy of being human (IV. 3. 2578–80).⁷³ To underline the integrity of Tell's reluctant recourse to violence as a last resort to maintain his hard-won, representative, identity, Schiller sets up the striking contrast with the murkily mixed motives of the political terrorist Parricida, who, unlike Tell, arouses horror and fear (IV. 3. 2817; V. 1. 2950; V. 2. 3147). The fruit of Tell's act of well-judged violence is the restoration of what the Swiss conspirators longed for at the beginning of the play but were themselves impotent to bring about (2. 2. 1282–83):

> The old state of nature returns, where human beings
> come face-to-face with human beings.
>
> [Der alte Zustand der Natur kehrt wieder,
> Wo Mensch dem Menschen gegenübersteht.]

This is the return on a higher level that the aesthetic education proposed by Schiller promises: the apparently 'natural' freedom to enjoy being human that a clear, in reality hard-won, politico-cultural identity alone can give.

The traditional dilemma raised by recognition of the 'barbarism', as Schiller calls it,⁷⁴ of the structural violence implicit in the coercion exercised by civilization — namely, that the alternative would seem to be the savagery of actual bodily abuse — is overcome by his recourse to a specifically aesthetic culture.⁷⁵ Schiller notes in his essay *Über das Erhabene* (1801) that it is just the *lack* of order that makes world history such a 'sublime' spectacle, beyond the grasp of human intellect (NA, 21, 49). If the structural violence 'exercised by way of systematic restrictions on communication' distorts and reifies for us participants, 'the interrelation of the objective, social, and subjective worlds', as Jürgen Habermas puts it,⁷⁶ then such suppressive dehumanization, according to Schiller, can, indeed must, be countered in and through the aesthetic. He could not share Fichte's doctrine, elaborated in his *Über die Bestimmung des Gelehrten* (1794), of an 'identity-drive' compelling us to undertake the endless process of self-perfecting idealization that, for Fichte and many a Romantic, constitutes *Kultur*. Convinced, like the Greeks, that 'the only serious enterprise is living', the ethical point of which is human well-being,⁷⁷ Schiller saw the whole, utterly down-to-earth, point of aesthetic culture in its bringing peace to an endemically violent world — to the individual directly, by giving self-definition to otherwise inexpressible, chaotic, felt-thought, and indirectly to any community made up of such rounded individuals.

The purpose of trying to make out continuities, and discontinuities, between our contemporary cultural theorizing and Schiller's version is to throw into relief the possible relevance of both the difficult problems he so acutely analyses and the complex solutions he offers, with such vivid illustration. Certainly, because structure and genesis are, as modes of thought, mutually interdependent, the structure of our ideas is conditioned by the story we tell ourselves about their genesis, and vice versa. A prime example of the conceptual obfuscation caused by historical confusion is afforded by the early English (and, in some degree, German) reception of Schiller's ideas: the conflation of what was taken to be Humboldt's untrammelled individualism and subjectivism with Schiller's utterly different views on the relation of the State and the Individual. It has clearly led to still-persistent 200-year-old prejudices, on demonstrably false grounds, against Schiller.[78] Equally problematic is the undifferentiated application to Schiller of terms like 'harmony' and 'totality' at a time of called-for 'resistance' to dominant ideologies and the repudiation of all 'grand narratives'. Greater discrimination, both theoretical and historical, is needed, if we are not to be debarred from making potentially liberating use of our inheritance from Schiller. For the totality at which he aimed in his *Aesthetic Letters* (Letter VI, 15), bears simply no relation to the over-theoretical totality rightly (but so routinely) attacked in much contemporary cultural theory. Wholeness for Schiller is neither Platonic perfection nor the universality promoted by the German Romantics and systematically codified by Hegel. Whatever term may be used, for Schiller totality/harmony simply means the imperfect, unique integrity of a concrete *particular* — the fundamental value of all cultural theorizing.

Notes

[1] A. N. Whitehead, *Science and the Modern World* (London: Cambridge University Press, 1926, p. 73).

[2] Andrew Milner and Jeff Browitt, *Contemporary Cultural Theory: An Introduction* (London: Routledge, 2002 [1991]), p. 22.

[3] In particular, as mediated by Ernst Cassirer. Cf. R. H. Stephenson, 'What's Wrong with Cultural Studies? A Modest Proposal', *the minnesota review*, 58–60 (2003), 197–206.

[4] See for instance Robert R. Wilson, 'Play, Transgression and Carnival: Bakhtin and Derrida on *Scriptor Ludens*', *Mosaic*, 19 (1986), 73–89 (p. 85); and Juliet Sychrava, *Schiller to Derrida: Idealism in Aesthetics* (New York: Cambridge University Press, 1989).

[5] For a fuller account, see Paul Bishop and R. H. Stephenson, *Friedrich Nietzsche and Weimar Classicism* (Rochester, New York: Camden House 2005), pp. 151–95 (henceforth referred to as *Friedrich Nietzsche and Weimar Classicism*). For a more restricted focus, see R. H. Stephenson, 'The Aesthetics of Weimar Classicism, Ernst Cassirer, and the German Tradition of Thought', *Publications of the English Goethe Society*, NS 54 (2005), 67–82.

[6] For surveys of the reception history, see René Wellek, *History of Modern Criticism: 1750–1950*, 8 vols (New Haven: Yale UP, 1955–1992), vol. 1, 254–55; Friedrich Schiller, *Werke: Nationalausgabe*, ed. by Julius Peterson and Gerhard Fricke, 43 vols (Weimar: Hermann Böhlaus Nachfolger, 1943–), vol. 27, 232–40 (henceforth referred to as NA, plus volume and page number); Elizabeth M. Wilkinson and L. A. Willoughby, 'Introduction', to Schiller, *On the Aesthetic Education of Man*, pp. cxxxiii–cxcvi (henceforth referred to as *Aesthetic Letters*).

[7] Friedrich Nietzsche, *Sämtliche Werke: Kritische Studienausgabe*, ed. by Giorgio Colli and Mazzini Montinari, 15 vols (Berlin and New York/Munich: de Gruyter,/Deutscher Taschenbuchverlag, 1967–77 and 1988), vol. 6, 111.

[8] *Briefe von und an Hegel* [Hegel, *Sämtliche Werke*, vols 27–30], ed. by Johannes Hoffmeister, 4 vols (Hamburg: Felix Meiner, 1952–1960), vol. 1, 25.

⁹ First edited and published by Franz Rosenzweig (1886–1929) in *Sitzungsberichte der Heidelberger Akademie der Wissenschaften: Philosophisch-historische Klasse*, 5 (1917), 5–7; the text and detailed commentary on it are available in *Mythologie der Vernunft: Hegels 'ältestes Systemprogramm des deutschen Idealismus'*, ed. by Christoph Jamme and Helmut Schneider (Frankfurt am Main: Suhrkamp, 1984); it is translated in H. S. Harris, *Hegel's Development: Toward the Sunlight, 1770–1801* (Oxford: Clarendon Press, 1972), pp. 510–12.

¹⁰ Compare Wellek, *History of Modern Criticism*, vol. 2, 367–69. For an account of the divergence between Schelling's aesthetics and those of Weimar Classicism, see R. H. Stephenson, *Goethe's Conception of Knowledge and Science* (Edinburgh: Edinburgh University Press, 1995), pp. 27–31.

¹¹ Georg Wilhelm Friedrich Hegel, *Vorlesungen über die Philosophie der Geschichte* (Stuttgart: Reclam, 1997), p. 550.

¹² See R. H. Stephenson, 'The Cultural Theory of Weimar Classicism in the Light of Coleridge's Doctrine of Aesthetic Knowledge', in *Goethe 2000: Intercultural Readings of his Work* (Leeds: Northern UP, 2000), ed. by Paul Bishop and R. H. Stephenson, pp. 149–69 (especially pp. 161–62), where the raising by all three poet-thinkers of the traditional 'lower' faculty of sense and imagination to the top of the hierarchy of faculties is discussed.

¹³ Karl Marx, *Grundrisse der Kritik der politischen Ökonomie* (Berlin: Akademie Verlag, 1953), pp. 21–22.

¹⁴ Marx, *Grundrisse*, p. 22.

¹⁵ Marx, *Grundrisse*, p. 208.

¹⁶ See Heidi Robinson, 'The Growth of a Myth: An Examination of English Responses to Schiller's Theory of Culture', unpublished PhD thesis, University of London, 1981, chapter 3, pp. 67–93 (henceforth referred to as 'Growth of a Myth').

¹⁷ See David Simpson's Introduction to his edition, *German Aestheic and Literary Criticism: Kant, Fichte, Schelling, Schopenhauer, Hegel* (Cambridge: Cambridge University Press, 1984), p. 20.

¹⁸ See Heidi Robinson, 'Der gesellschaftsfeindliche "innere" bzw. "ganze Mensch": Mißdeutungen in der englischen Rezeption und Überlieferung von Schillers Kulturtheorie', *Arcadia*, 15 (1980), 129–48 (p. 145).

¹⁹ See 'The Growth of a Myth', pp. 126–83; compare L. A. Willoughby, 'Oscar Wilde and Goethe. The Life of Art and the Art of Life', *Publications of the English Goethe Society*, NS 35 (1965), 1–37; republished in Elizabeth M. Wilkinson and L. A. Willoughby, *Models of Wholeness: Some Attitudes to Language, Art and Life in the Age of Goethe*, ed. by Jeremy Adler, Martin Swales, and Ann Weaver, British and Irish Studies in German Language and Literature, 30 (Oxford: Peter Lang, 2002), 195–226 (especially pp. 220–22). Compare, too, *Friedrich Nietzsche and Weimar Classicism*, pp. 164–66.

²⁰ See *Aesthetic Letters*, pp. clxvi–clxvii, clxviii, clxx–clxxii.

²¹ Thomas De Quincey, *Confessions of an English Opium-Eater*, ed. by Malcolm Elwin (London: Macdonald, 1956), p. 466; compare Stephenson, *Goethe's Conception of Knowledge and Science*, pp. 55 and 66.

²² Lucien Price, *The Dialogues of Alfred North Whitehead* (Boston: Little, Brown and Company, 1954), p. 125.

²³ A. N. Whitehead, *Process and Reality: An Essay on Cosmology*, corrected edition by David Ray Griffin and Donald W. Sherburne (New York: The Free Press, 1978), p. 280; cf. Stephenson, *Goethe's Conception of Knowledge and Science*, pp. 26–27; and *Aesthetic Letters*, xx, 4 (and pp. 303–04). For the parallel closeness between Whitehead on this point and Goethe, see R. H. Stephenson, 'The Proper Object of Cultural Study: Ernst Cassirer and the Aesthetic Theory of Weimar Classicism', *Cultural Studies and the Symbolic*, 1 (2003), 82–114 (pp. 85–87).

²⁴ Whitehead, *Process and Reality*, p. 170.

²⁵ Compare with Ralph Waldo Emerson's statement that 'Beauty is the normal state' (*The Conduct of Life* (London: George Routledge and Sons, 1913), p. 283). This is exactly Schiller's

position. Besides the Great Victorians, one of the formative influences on Whitehead's high estimation of aesthetics may have been Samuel Alexander, a philosopher Whitehead held in the highest esteem, who, especially in his *Beauty and Other Forms of Value*, gave vivid and precise expression to many of the central doctrines of Weimar Classicism. Compare the following with Schiller's view of art as a sensuous-mental object: 'The work of art is a particular concrete thing, and everything that it means is embodied in this particular material' ([London: Macmillan, 1933], p. 51).

[26] See Susanne K. Langer, *Philosophy in a New Key: A Study in the Symbolism of Reason, Rite, and Art* (New York: Mentor Books, 1951 [1942]); *Feeling and Form: A Theory of Art Developed from Philosophy in a New Key* (London: Scribner's, 1953); and *Mind: An Essay on Human Feeling*, 3 vols (Baltimore: The Johns Hopkins University Press, 1967–1970).

[27] Georg Wilhelm Friedrich Hegel, *Sämtliche Werke*, ed. by Hermann Glockner, 26 vols (Stuttgart: Frommann, 1927–1930), vol. 14, 396.

[28] Alfred North Whitehead, *Adventures of Ideas* (New York: The Free Press, 1961 [1933]), p. 285.

[29] Theodor W. Adorno, *Negative Dialektik* (Frankfurt on Main: Suhrkamp, 1966).

[30] Theodor W. Adorno, *Ästhetische Theorie* (Frankfurt on Main: Suhrkamp, 1970).

[31] Adorno, *Ästhetische Theorie*, p. 205.

[32] Adorno, *Ästhetische Theorie*, p. 190.

[33] Jürgen Habermas, *Theorie des kommunikativen Handelns*, 2 vols (Frankfurt am Main: Suhrkamp, 1988 [1981]), vol. 1, 512.

[34] Martin Jay, *The Dialectical Imagination: A History of the Frankfurt School and the Institute of Social Research, 1923–1950* (Boston: Little, Brown and Company, 1973), p. 63.

[35] See Jay, *The Dialectical Imagination*, p. 82.

[36] See Jay, *The Dialectical Imagination*, pp. 256 and 179.

[37] See Jay, *The Dialectical Imagination*, p. 270. In *Dialektik der Aufklärung* Adorno and Horkheimer speak of '[das] Eingedenken der Natur im Subjekt' ['remembrance of Nature in the subject'] (*Dialektik der Aufklärung: Philosophische Fragmente* (Frankfurt on Main: Fischer, 1988[1944]), p. 47); in his *Theorie des kommunikativen Handelns*, Habermas focuses on this phrase (vol. 1, 516).

[38] Adorno, *Ästhetische Theorie*, pp. 125–27; *Aesthetic Letters*, pp. 316–17.

[39] *Aesthetic Letters*, p. clvi.

[40] Habermas, *Theorie des kommunikativen Handelns*, vol. 1, 42 and 251.

[41] Jürgen Habermas, *Der philosophische Diskurs der Moderne* (Frankfurt on Main: Suhrkamp, 1984), pp. 59–63.

[42] For further discussion, see Frances Birrell, '"Abenteuerlich mißverstanden"? Habermas's Reception and Interpretation of Schiller', *German Life and Letters*, 49 (1996), 297–310; and 'An Investigation of the Theoretical Insights of Jürgen Habermas in Relation to the Aesthetic Writings of Friedrich Schiller', unpublished PhD thesis, University of Strathclyde, 1997 (especially pp. 185, 189, 196 and 232, on the differences between Schiller's and Weber's 'aesthetic state').

[43] Jürgen Habermas, 'Bewußtmachende oder rettende Kritik — Die Aktualität Walter Benjamins' [1972], in *Kultur und Kritik* (Frankfurt on Main: Suhrkamp, 1973), pp. 302–51; *Legitimationsprobleme im Spätkapitalismus* (Frankfurt am Main: Suhrkamp, 1973), p. 120.

[44] Habermas, *Theorie des kommunikativen Handelns*, vol. 1, 41–42. Habermas's phrase 'authentischer Ausdruck einer exemplarischen Erfahrung' ['authentic expression of an exemplary experience'] seems to take aesthetics back to the presentation of the typical associated with the didacticism of a Boileau or a Gottsched.

[45] See Habermas, *Theorie des kommunikativen Handelns*, vol. 1, 128, 135 and 140.

[46] See John M. Krois, *Cassirer: Symbolic Forms and History* (New Haven: Yale University Press, 1987), pp. 176–81.

⁴⁷ Quoted — and translated — from an as yet unpublished text by John M. Krois in his 'Cassirer's "Prototype and Model" of Symbolism: Its Sources and Significance', *Science in Context*, 12 (1991), 531–47 (p. 535).
⁴⁸ Cassirer, *Freiheit und Form: Studien zur deutschen Geistesgeschichte* (Berlin: Bruno Cassirer, 1916), p. 256.
⁴⁹ See J. E. Cirlot, *A Dictionary of Symbols*, trans. by Jack Sage (London: Routledge and Kegan Paul, 1967), pp. 26, 145–47; for further discussion of this mode of argumentation, see *Aesthetic Letters*, pp. lxxxv-lxxxix, and 348–50.
⁵⁰ William James, *The Varieties of Religious Experience: A Study in Human Nature* (Glasgow: Collins, 1960 [1903]), p. 374. Although James wrote that this 'dark saying' was 'something like what the Hegelian philosophy means', and ultimately assigned such synthesis a mystical status ('to me the living sense of its reality only comes in the artificial mystic state of mind'), his description applies more accurately to Schillerian, 'binary' synthesis, and is not necessarily mystical.
⁵¹ For examples of binary synthesis at work in Goethe and Nietzsche, see *Friedrich Nietzsche and Weimar Classicism*, pp. 2, 10, 33–34, 38 and 85.
⁵² As in the case of the subject of the poem 'Gingo Biloba' in the *West-östlicher Divan*, described as 'eins und doppelt' ('one and doubled'), Faust is apostrophized with the phrase 'geeinte Zwienatur' ('unified double nature'; *Faust*, l. 11962) — variant formulations of the idea of binary synthesis. For further discussion, see Ilse Graham, 'Geeinte Zwienatur: On the Structure of Goethe's *Urfaust*,' in *Tradition and Creation*, ed. by C. P. Magill, Brian Rowley and Christopher J. Smith (Leeds: Maney, 1978), pp. 131–45.
⁵³ See R. H. Stephenson, 'Weimar Classicism's Debt to the Scottish Enlightenment', in *Goethe and the English-Speaking World*, ed. by Nicholas Boyle and John Guthrie (Rochester, New York: Camden House, 2002), pp. 61–70.
⁵⁴ See Manfred Kuehn, *Scottish Common Sense in Germany, 1768–1800: A Contribution to the History of Critical Philosophy* (Kingston: McGill-Queen's University Press, 1987), p. 200.
⁵⁵ Compare Susanne K. Langer, *Philosophy in a New Key*, pp. 92 and 202.
⁵⁶ *Lichtenberg: Gesammelte Werke*, ed. by W. Grenzmann, 1 (Stuttgart: Cotta, 1882), 296.
⁵⁷ *The Yale Edition of the Works of Samuel Johnson*, ed. by R. MacAdam et al. (New Haven: Yale University Press, 1958), pp. 14–15.
⁵⁸ *Tabulae Votivae*, 44; NA, 1, 302.
⁵⁹ See *Friedrich Nietzsche and Weimar Classicism*, pp. 113–18.
⁶⁰ *Schiller: Selected Poems*, ed. by Frank M. Fowler (London: Macmillan, 1969), p. xv.
⁶¹ See, for example, Ilse Graham, *Schiller's Drama: Talent and Integrity* (London: Methuen, 1974).
⁶² *Aesthetic Letters*, xx, 5 and pp. 156–57 and 317–18; compare the editors' comment on the 'habitual aggressiveness of [Schiller's] language' (p. xxxi). For a fuller treatment of this theme with regard to Schiller (and Goethe), see R. H. Stephenson, 'Violence and Aesthetic Identity in Weimar Classicism', in *Violence, Culture and Identity in Germany and Austria*, ed. by Helen Chambers (Berne: Peter Lang, forthcoming).
⁶³ *Aesthetic Letters*, xviii, 4.
⁶⁴ *Aesthetic Letters*, p. 305.
⁶⁵ Paul de Man, 'The Rhetoric of Temporality', in *Interpretation: Theory and Practice*, ed. by Charles S. Singleton (Baltimore: John Hopkins University Press, 1969), pp. 173–209 (p. 177).
⁶⁶ *Aesthetic Letters*, xx, 4 (footnote).
⁶⁷ See Ilse Graham, *Schiller's Drama*, pp. 186, 188, and 190–91. For a recent overview of the critical discussion of Schiller's drama, one which does not neglect the realism of his treatment of violence, even in such highly stylized plays as *Don Carlos* (1787) and *Die Braut von Messina* (1803), see Dieter Borchmeyer, *Weimarer Klassik: Portrait einer Epoche* (Weinheim: Beltz Athenäum, 1994), especially pp. 398–99, 430–31, and 442–43; see, too, Arthur Henkel, 'Wie Schiller Königinnen reden lässt. Zur Szene III/4 in der *Maria Stuart*', in *Schiller und die höfische Welt*, ed. by Achim Aurnhammer (Tübingen: Niemeyer, 1990), pp. 398–406; Nikola

Rossbach, *Das Geweb ist erstaunlich frei: Friedrich Schillers Kabale und Liebe als Text der Gewalt* (Würzburg: Königshausen und Neumann, 2001); and Robert E. Norton, *The Beautiful Soul: Aesthetic Morality in the Eighteenth Century* (Ithaca and London: Cornell University Press, 1995), especially pp. ix, 217–21, and 236–44.

[68] The burden of Schiller's youthful *Philosophische Briefe* is that the essence of Beauty is Love; compare Cassirer, *Freiheit und Form*, pp. 292–96.

[69] *Aesthetic Letters*, XI. For the analogous case of 'identity' in Goethe, see Elisabeth von Thadden, *Erzählen als Naturerzählen — 'Die Wahlverwandtschaften'* (Munich: Fink, 1993); and R. H. Stephenson, '"Man nimmt in der Welt jeden, wofür er sich gibt": The Presentation of Self in Goethe's *Die Wahlverwandtschaften*', *German Life and Letters*, 7 (1994), 400–06.

[70] Michel Foucault, *The History of Sexuality, vol. I: An Introduction*, trans. by Robert Hurley (New York: Pantheon, 1980), pp. 59–60.

[71] *Aesthetic Letters*, pp. cvii–ix; for Goethe's very similar views, see Stephenson, *Goethe's Conception of Knowledge and Science*, pp. 65–81.

[72] The inadequacy of the traditional conception of the Beautiful Soul is mercilessly pilloried in Schiller's prose narrative, *Der Geisterseher* of 1787–89. Schiller's hallucinatory German prince, locked into his own fantasy-world and alienated from reality, is a disturbing embodiment of the desire for irrational, hocus-pocus, integration with 'higher', sublime, powers that became an epidemic in Europe after the French revolution — a pathology that Schiller diagnosed as the symptom of a fundamentally philistine, anti-aesthetic, culture.

[73] Cf. Borchmeyer, pp. 442ff.; and Wilhelm Amann, *'Die stille Arbeit des Geschmacks': Die Kategorie des Geschmacks in der Ästhetik Schillers und in den Debatten der Aufklärung* (Würzburg: Königshausen und Neumann, 1999).

[74] *Aesthetic Letters*, IV.

[75] For an analysis of Goethe's analogous distinction between (mere, coercive) rhetoric and the free, *aesthetic*, deployment of language, see R. H. Stephenson, 'Goethe's Prose Style', *Publications of the English Goethe Society*, 46 (1997), 33–42; for an account of Goethe's overcoming the discursive constraints of what Foucault calls the *épistème*, see R. H. Stephenson, 'Goethe's Achievement as Aphorist', in *Configurazione dell'Aforisma*, I, ed. by Giulia Cantarutti (Bologna: Clueb, 2000), 84–105, especially pp. 100–05. Compare Beatrice Hanssen, *Critique of Violence: Between Poststructuralism and Critical Theory* (London and New York: Routledge, 2000), especially pp. 158–78.

[76] Jürgen Habermas, *Theorie des kommunikativen Handelns*, vol. 2, 278.

[77] Bernard Williams, *Ethics and the Limits of Philosophy* (London: Collins, 1985), p. 111; *Morality: An Introduction to Ethics* (Harmondsworth: Penguin, 1973), p. 88.

[78] See Robinson, 'Der gesellschaftsfeindliche "innere" bzw. "ganze Mensch"', pp. 136–38 and 195; and Richard Sheppard, 'Two Liberals: A Comparison of the Humanism of Matthew Arnold and Wilhelm von Humboldt', *German Life and Letters*, 24 (1971), 219–33.

INDEX

Abraham, Karl 51
absolute being, nature of 16
'absolute spirit' (Hegel) 16
abstract thinking 3–5, 8–11, 83, 85, 99, 102, 105
Adorno, Theodor W. 34, 47, 96–97
American civilization 47
anthropology 30
Aristotelianism 30
Arnold, Matthew 94
art
   aim and function of 78, 97
   and myth 45
   and symbolism 18, 70–71
art-of-life 111
'as if' in speech 11
Assyrian civilization and religion 22
astrology 22
Avesta religion 24

Babylonian religion and mythology 22–23
Bachofen, Johann Jakob 56–62
Baeumler, Alfred 56–58
Bakunin, Michael 74
Baudelaire, Charles 6
Beethoven, Ludwig van 71–77, 87
   Ninth Symphony 105
Begründung 15
being, concept of 17
Benjamin, Walter 1, 6–11, 29, 98
   theory of translation 7–9
Berlin, Isaiah 42
Bernoulli, Carl Albreht 56
Biblical texts 25; *see also* New Testament; Old Testament
'binary synthesis' (Schiller) 99–100
Bultmann, Rudolf 51
Burckhardt, Jacob 35, 37
Burkert, Walter 55

Campbell, Joseph 52
Cartesianism 100
Cassirer, Ernst
   academic reputation of 28–29
   on art 98–99
   and Bachofen 58–61
   and Benjamin 8–11
   death of 36–37
   experience in First World War 33
   and Goethe 35, 59–60
   linguistic theory of 1–6, 9
   and Spengler 28–37
   study of culture 30–32, 43
   on technology 34
   theory of myth 15, 19–26, 42, 45–46, 52–55, 61–62
   theory of symbolic forms 5–6, 10–12, 16, 29–30, 35, 43–45, 71
   and Warburg 42–47
   Works:
   'The Concept of Symbolic Form in the Construction of the *Geisteswissenschaften*' 19
   Goethe und die mathematische Physik 43
   'Language and Myth' 20, 52
   On the Logic of Cultural Sciences 4
   The Myth of the State 46–49
   The Phenomenology of Symbolic Forms 6
   The Philosophy of Symbolic Forms 49, 53, 58–59, 63
   'The Problem of the Symbol as the Fundamental Problem of Philosophical Anthropology' 15, 18, 58–59
Cassirer, Toni 42
caste system 20
Chamberlain, H. S. 33
children's language 4
Chirico, Giorgio de 70
chorus, theory and use of 77–80, 87
Christensen, Inger: 'I see the light clouds' 2, 6, 11–12
Christianity 21, 25
cognition, concept of 5
Cohen, Hermann 24–25
Coleridge, Samuel Taylor 94
communicative action 98
Comte, Auguste 49
consciousness, theory of 17
Corbin, Henry 52
cosmology 25
Counter-Reformation 73, 75
creation of the world 7
Creuzer, Friedrich 56
critical philosophy 16
critical theory 97
cultural theory 102
culture, philosophy of 34–37
cultures, rise and fall of 28, 30
Curtius, Wolfgang 55

Dasein 15
de Man, Paul 106
de Quincey, Thomas 95
decadence in art 73–74
deconstructionism 92
Democritus 53

Dilthey, Wilhelm 16, 31
Dionysian art 76–77, 80–84, 87
Duméry, Henri 25

Eliade, Mircea 21, 51–52
Empedocles 53
empiricism 100
entelechy, principle of 30
epistemological gap 100
epistemology 16
ethical pregnancy (*prägnant-ethische Bedeutung*) 34–35

fascism 45–47
Fichte, Johann Gottlieb 17–18, 33, 112
First World War 33, 58
Foucault, Michel 110
Fowler, Frank M. 105
Frankfurt School 96–98
Frazer, Sir James 51
Freud, Sigmund 46, 51

George, Stefan 55
German culture and the German spirit 75, 81, 87
German history 93
Gestalt psychology 99
Geworfenheit 36
Gnosticism 51
God, attributes of 19
Goethe, Johann Wolfgang von 11–12, 16, 18, 30–37, 43–45, 59–60, 73–77, 88, 92–96, 99–102
Goffman, Ernest 98
Greek drama 21, 58, 70, 73, 79–82, 85–88
Gundolf, Friedrich 55

Habermas, Jürgen 96–98, 112
Haskala, the 7
Hegel, Georg Wilhelm Friedrich 16, 32, 36–37, 58, 63, 93–96, 102, 113
Heidegger, Martin 15, 36, 46, 55–56
Heraclitus 53
Herder, Johann Gottfried 53
Herf, Geoffrey 33
hermeneutics 51
Hillman, James 52
historical determinism 36
historicity 8
history
    and music 57–58
    read as a set of symbols 29
Hölderlin, Friedrich 55, 93
holy places 22
Horkheimer, Max 34, 47, 96–97
human nature 31
Humboldt, Wilhelm von 5, 32, 94, 113
Huntington, Samuel 37

idealism 18–19, 33, 53
idylls 84–87

imagination 16
instrumentalism 48–49
Ionian philosophers 19
'iron cage' metaphor 97
irrationalism 29, 46
Islam 25
Italian opera 75–76

Jaeger, Werner 55
James, William 100
Jay, Martin 97
Johnson, Samuel 103
Jonas, Hans 51
Journal de Psychologie Normale et Pathologique 35
Judaism 7, 21, 24–25
judgement, principles of 16
Jung, Carl Gustav 20, 51, 92
Jungfrau von Orleans, Die (Schiller) 109–11

Kandinsky, Wassily 70
Kant, Immanuel 4–5, 16, 18, 56, 72, 86, 99–101
Kierkegaard, Søren 58
Klages, Ludwig 46, 56
Kleist, Heinrich von 105–06
knowledge, theory of 16; *see also* epistemology

Langer, Susanne K. 96
language
    Benjamin's concept of 7–10
    as a form of cognition 8
    function of 18
    fundamental theory of 6–7
    origin of 7
    plurality of 11
    symbolic potential of 11
    as a system of symbolic references 5
Leavis, F. R. 94
Leibniz, Gottfried Wilhelm 30–31
Lessing, Gotthold Ephraim 73–74
Levi-Strauss, Claude 20, 24
Lichtenberg, G. C. 102–03
'lifeworld' concept 98
Lukács, Georg 33–34
Luther, Martin 72, 74, 76

Malinowski, Bronislaw 24, 51
Maria Stuart (Schiller) 108–11
Marx, Karl (and Marxism) 20, 93–94, 97, 102
mass media 96–97
meaning, theory of 7
metabasis (*eis allo genos*) 3–6, 12
metaphysics 17–18, 80, 87–88
Mill, John Stuart 94
mimetic moments 4
Morris, William 94
Müller, Max 20
music 70–88
    and myth 83
    and tragedy 81–82

mythical space 22
'mythistory' (Duméry) 25
mythology 18–26, 32, 44–45
  alternative approaches to 51
  break-up of 23
  Cassirer's theorisation of 52–55, 61–62
  creation of 23–24
  as distinct from religion 18–19, 22–26
  fourfold function of 20
  and history 46, 57–58
  and music 83
  source of 19–20
  structural form of 19–20
  and symbolism 56–58

naming of things 4–8
national identity 72–73
Natorp, Paul 17–18
naturalism and the cult of nature 85, 88
neo-Kantianism 15, 48
New Testament 51
Newton, Isaac 43
Nicolas of Cusa 18, 31–32
Nietzsche, Friedrich 37, 56, 58, 70–72, 75–77, 80–88, 92–93, 104, 109
noumenal world 72
Novalis 92

objectivity 16
Old Testament 25
ontology 16
opera 75–76, 84–87
Orth, Ernst W. 16, 18
Otto, Walter F. 55

paganism 47
Parmenides 53
Pater, Walter 94–95
phenomenology 55
philology 55
philosophy, goal of 35–36, 45
Plato and Platonism 10, 21, 52–53, 93–96
poetry 11, 16, 44, 86–88, 99, 102–05
Pollock, Jackson 70
Pope, Alexander 102
positivism 48–49
postage stamps 46
postmodernism 92, 100
Presocratics, the 17
primordial music 84–85
primordial time and primordial events 20–21
profane reality 24
prophets of Israel 24–25
psychoanalytic theory 51–52
Puebo Indian culture and mythology 47
pure language 9
pure meaning 3

Rank, Otto 51
rationalism 45, 96, 100–01
referentiality in symbolic forms 11
Reid, Thomas 100
Reik, Theodor 52
religion 29, 45
  as distinct from myth 18–19, 22–26
  symbolism of 22
Renaissance art 44, 83
Renaissance ideas 31–32
revolutionary spirit 74
Ricœur, Paul 20
ritual 21
Romanticism 92–96, 112–13
Rossini, Gioacchino 87
Rothko, Marc 70

sacredness 24, 26
Saxl, Fritz 42, 45, 47, 52
Schadewaldt, Wolfgang 55
Schelling, Friedrich Wilhelm Joseph 19–20, 26, 53–56, 59, 93
Schiller, Friedrich 16, 18, 71–80, 83–88, 92–113
  Aesthetic Letters 107, 113
  Ode to Joy (*An die Freude*) 76, 102–05
  plays 106–12
Schmitt, Carl 28–29, 33
Scholem, Gershom 52
Schopenhauer, Arthur 71–73, 77, 80, 87–88
Schröter, Manfred 56, 58
Schweitzer, Albert 35
Scottish school of philosophy 100
semiotic theory 10
semioticity 8
serpent ritual 47
Shakespeare, William 73, 85
Siegfried Idyll 86
signification, process of 10
Simmel, Georg 33–34
sincerity 98
Snell, Bruno 55
social order 20
Socratism 83
Sorbin, T. R. 98
Spengler, Oswald 28–37
  The Decline of the West 29, 37, 47
spirit (*Geist*) (Cassirer) 16
subjectivity 88
symbolic forms
  in art 70
  Benjamin's theory of 9–10
  Cassirer's theory of 5–6, 10–12, 16, 29–30, 35, 43–45, 71
  definition of 60
  meaning of 29–30, 99
  in myth 56–58

number and nature of 18
for understanding the world 1–4, 6–8, 12, 71, 85, 88
'symbolic pregnance' 5–7, 10–12, 99

taboo 24
Taine, Hippolyte 36
technology 19, 33–34
theogony 25, 55
Tillich, Paul 23
time, *ordinary* and *primordial* 20–21
totalitarianism 49
Toynbee, Arnold 28
tragedy
  and music 81–82
  see also Greek drama
transcendence 24
transcendental unity of perception (Kant) 18
transformation, symbolic processes of 3, 6
transition between genres 3
translation (in linguistic theory) 1–3, 6–12
Tristan und Isolde 30, 80, 84
Tucholsky, Kurt 29
Tylor, Sir Edward 51
'type of intending' (Benjamin) 9

ursymbols 30–31
Usener, Hermann 52, 70

Vedic myths 20, 23
Vergeistigung 59
Verstehen 31
Villa Pamphili 61
Vischer, Friedrich Theodor 43–44, 47

Wagner, Richard 30, 70–77, 80–88
Wagner, Siegfried 33
Wallenstein (Schiller) 107–09
Warburg, Aby 42–49, 71
Warburg Library 18, 42–43, 49
Wasserstrom, Steven M. 52
Weber, Max 33–34, 45, 96–97
Weimar classicism 94–97, 100, 111
Weimar Republic 28, 33
Whitehead, Alfred North 95–96
Wilde, Oscar 95
Wilhelm Tell (Schiller) 110–12
Winckelmann, Johann Joachim 58
Wind, Edgar 44–45

Yom Kippur liturgy 21

Zeitwende 36